Transnational Professionals and their Cosmopolitan Universes

D1809045

Magdalena Nowicka is research assistant in the Institute of Sociology at the Ludwig Maximilian University in Munich.

Magdalena Nowicka

Transnational Professionals and their Cosmopolitan Universes

Foreword by Ulrich Beck

Campus Verlag
Frankfurt/New York

Bibliographic Information published by the Deutsche Nationalbibliothek.
Die Deutsche Nationalbibliothek lists this publication in the Deutsche Nationalbibliografie;
detailed bibliographic data are available in the Internet at http://dnd.d-nb.de.
ISBN 978-3-593-38155-8

For further information: www.campus.de

Contents

Foreword

I was delighted to be asked to write the foreword to this outstanding book. It is an innovative treatise on a very important and difficult subject that has, so far, been insufficiently researched. It fills a serious gap in the literature, and provides the reader with fascinating insights into the mobile life-styles of a group of transnational professionals in an international organization that has never been the subject of sociological investigation.

Nowicka diagnoses a change in society, which by no means discards the idea of the nation-state, but does not require it for its spatial organization. She makes clear that the relationship between social transformation, mobility and time-space can be observed only as praxis, and must be described as such.

At the beginning of the twenty-first century, we are witnessing a global transformation of modernity. The transition from modern to second-modern society should be reconceived as a transition (with many permutations) between different sets of basic ontological categories, and centrally those of time and space. New realities are arising: a new mapping of space and time, and new co-ordinates for the social and the political, are emerging; and these have to be theoretically and empirically researched and elaborated.

Yet contemporary discussions are repeatedly based on the identification of social space with geographical space, a view that is imprisoned within methodological nationalism. Methodological nationalism understands borders mostly as nation-state borders, and in consequence equates mobility with migration between container societies. Nowicka reformulates the theoretical positions that have been applied thus far, and sees social space as an external factor determining social coherences. The merit of »Transnational professionals and their cosmopolitan universes« is to present the relationship between space and mobility as a relationship that not only does not require this spatial determinism, but also explicitly abstracts from it. Thus, at both the theoretical and the empirical level Nowicka's spatio-sociological observations provide an important contribution to the globalization debate.

The first modernity was made possible by, and reinforced, the vision of space as divided into nation-state territories, dominated by territorial societies and societies of the present. The historical metaphysics of such a society rests on the homology of space and time and the identity of space and people. All these identities are called into question by the dynamics of second-modern society. It suddenly becomes obvious that it is neither possible to distinguish clearly between the national and the international, nor, correspondingly, to make a convincing contrast between homogeneous units. Nowicka makes this problem her central concern. "Transnational professionals and their cosmopolitan universes" is a brilliantly conceptualized study, which develops a quite novel account of the vital and socially tense processes that are occurring at all levels, from the location of an individual home to the setting of borders between cultures.

To grasp these new realities emerging in front of our eyes, we need a new, cosmopolitan sociology that imposes fundamental questions of redefinition, reinvention and reorganization. »Transnational professionals and their cosmopolitan universes« is an important contribution to this new social science, which deals consciously with its own premises. Nowicka masters this challenge and makes an important contribution to the development of cosmopolitan sociology.

At the same time, Nowicka opens new theoretical and empirical perspectives in sociological mobility research. She presents in a discrete way a new theoretical approach to the understanding and sociological role of mobility, and shows, in an exemplary fashion, the directions that mobility research should take in the future. The clear structure and the clear formulations of this book are also impressive, and it gives me great pleasure to recommend this most original work.

Ulrich Beck
Munich 2006

List of figures

List of tables

PART 1
MOBILITY AND SPACE IN MODERNITY

1. Introduction

Migration and mobility are as old as humankind. Movement was a facet of tribal life long before the invention of territories as politically marked geographic units of space (Pries 2001). Organization in units guaranteed the people of tribal nations political and economic security, but this territorial demarcation also represented and reproduced mental maps in the form of religious, ethnic, and cultural belonging. The culmination of these processes was reached with the full development of nation-states (Brubaker 1994). Since then, the movement of people has been conceptualized primarily as migration within or between nation-states. As such, mobility can be seen as a flow that can be regulated and restricted. This has tremendous consequences for the migrating individuals, for nation-states as the political actors primarily responsible for regulating these flows, and for the social sciences.

The recent voluminous literature on migration and diasporas has considerably enhanced our awareness and understanding of the phenomenon of movement between the container spaces of nation-states (Glick Schiller et al. 1992; Basch et al. 1994; Chan 1997; Cohen 1997; Vertovec/Cohen 1999; Faist 2000; Kennedy 2002; 2004; Favell 2003). The recognition that people are increasingly mobile is associated with the placing of boundaries and borderlands at the center of the analytic framework. However, the concern with boundaries and their transgression often reflects a broad concern with the cultural displacement of people. What Edward Said (1979), for instance, calls a »generalized condition of homelessness« is seen as characterizing contemporary life everywhere. This points to the deeply territorializing concepts of identity and culture, which dominate in the literature and see mobile people as uprooted and displaced (Malkki 1997).

The degree of power that these associations of territory, culture, and identity have becomes apparent when one changes country of residence.

Migrants are frequently asked where they come from, what their reasons for leaving »their« country were, whether they plan to go back to their home country »one day«, and whether they miss their »home«. In fact, these polite and innocently meant questions, arising from people's curiosity, relate to deeply rooted assumptions about the territorial boundaries of culture and identity. Being a migrant, one may ask, what difference does living in another country make? How much do these couple of hundred kilometers matter? Would such a distance matter if the move had been between two towns within one country? And if not, does movement in geographical space actually matter, or is it rather the change between two political systems that makes the difference? Is social space more important than geographical space? What is the difference between geographical and social space? And if there is no difference in moving between the countries, is the concept of nation-states as containers just fiction? If a citizen of the European Union can cross a bordering member state at any time, is this border at all relevant? And if not, what difference does being on one side or the other make? If nation-states are becoming increasingly irrelevant, and if they lose their functionality, where, if at all, do the boundaries between »us« and »them« exist?

Behind such questions and discussions hide particular imaginations of space. When we conceive space as a surface, we can travel across it. If we consider space as divided into units, we can make an effort to reconnect it. When we imagine that space has the same qualities everywhere, we can also imagine that people are the same everywhere. When we think of space as consisting of many places, we can think of people as attached to places and moving freely in space. The opposite is also true: our practices have an impact on how we conceive of space.

These questions are central to the topic of this present work. My interest in mobility and spatial relations is twofold: first, it has its source in my own experience of migration, international marriage, and family, of being embedded in two countries, and in international social networks. Second, my interest also arose from reading the substantial literature on transnational mobility and globalization. The literature review reveals that the everyday questions that migrants must confront are also extremely relevant in the professional debate, and that the vast majority of the conceptualizations based on »spatial determinism« are ambivalent from the point of view of a migrant, and should also be so from the point of view of a researcher.

The (new) global experience

Various commentators point to the overwhelming impression that we are living through extraordinary times that involve massive changes to the very fabric of economic, political, and social life. The sources (and the outcomes) of these changes are conceptualized as processes of globalization, which is currently one of the most frequently used and most powerful terms. Across disciplines, various authors draw attention to the global interdependency resulting from the increased mobility of people, images, information, commodities, and risks. These flows are said to increase the permeability of borders, especially those of nation-states, and to contribute to the vision of a single, united, and »borderless world« (Ohmae 1992). Globalization calls up a vision of totally unfettered mobility, of free unbounded space. In the scientific and public discourse, the world is now imagined as a world of flows, as relational through connections (Massey 2005: 81).

These global connections are becoming increasingly varied and pervasive. People move about across national boundary lines; the technologies of mobility have changed, and a growing range of media reaching across borders seems to make claims on our senses (Hannerz 1996). Boundaries, and distances, are not what they used to be. The social science of globalization declares a shift from two-dimensional (Euclidian) space, with its centers, peripheries, and sharp boundaries, to a multidimensional global space with unbounded and often discontinuous and interpenetrating sub-spaces (Kearney 1995). Within this global system, localities, regions, nation-states, environments, and cultures are transformed in a way in which social is no longer imaginable as merely society (durable structure), but as mobility (structure-in-becoming) (Urry 2000a; 2003). The consequence of diverse mobilities is to produce what Beck terms the growth of »inner mobility«, for which coming and going, being both here and there at the same time, has become much more normal globally (Beck 1999: 75f).

Mobilities thus seem to challenge »spatial securities« and the social theory that is based on them. They seem to be disconnected from space. Together with flow, the most powerful metaphors used in relation to modernity in recent years include those of disembeddedness and distanciation from space. These contrast with the long-term focus of sociology on societies, which were conceptualized as spatially bounded, and often looked like nation-states (Urry 2000a). Virtual and physical mobility and territoriality are placed in opposition to each other, and it is often suggested that one excludes the other. Embeddedness in space has been associated with territorial fixation, and mobility with a lack of such fixation.

The death of distance (Cairncross 1998), time-space compression (Harvey), time-space annihilation (Virilio), and time-space distanciation (Giddens) are among the notions commonly used to describe the new, global reality. They all suggest that something has changed in the spatial organization of society. New technological and organizational innovations have »compressed« the time taken to communicate and travel across large distances. Some authors suggest that time and space are dematerializing as people, machines, images, power, money, and risks travel at bewildering speed and in unexpected directions from place to place.

On the other hand, spatial imaginations have always involved mobility. The stories of spatial expansion, geographical discoveries, conquistadores and conquered cultures, exchange, and globalization all relate to various forms of movement (Massey 2005). It is not surprising that mobility is often evoked as a preferred indicator to explain our current experience of time-space (Bauman 1997). These three interrelated dimensions – mobility, space-time-relations, and change in social structuration – are presented in the following sections. They are central to current discussions of globalization, and also to this book.

Mobile professionals

Although the vast majority of globalization studies have focused primarily on the new technologies of communication, and the flows of information and capital, as the means of, and reasons for, globalization, it has also been recognized that people belong to the global flows. However, from the point of view of globalization studies, mobile people have usually been considered as anonymous moving masses (Sassen 1998; Hyndman 2000). Rarely has any kind of human face been given to the macro-level transactions and data-sets that describe the flows of people between locations (Sassen 1994; Castells 2000), except when researchers focus on the role of highly-skilled professionals in the global economy and elite transnational professional networks (Salt 1997; Castells 2000; Doyle/Nathan 2001; Beaverstock 2005). Although there is knowledge of how such groups conduct their life in international financial centers, and how their social networks spread around the globe, the decline of the nation-state, signaled by the globalists, is almost never considered against the basic everyday durability of nationally specific practices and identities in organizing the behavior of people (Favell 2003: 10). With some significant exceptions (Dezalay 1990; King 1990; O'Rian 2000; Colic-Peisker 2002; Hannerz 2003), there has been rather less interest in the more informal and smaller-scale yet expanding transnational networks that consist of the interpersonal connections established by mobile individuals (Kennedy 2002; 2004). Rather, in this respect the interest has primarily concentrated on diasporas: communities of migrants who settle in a host society.

In contrast to these groups, mobile individuals do not constitute a community – a unit of belonging with clear boundaries that provide a source of common identity (Kennedy 2004: 161). Unlike cross-border migrants, they are not bounded by ties of family and kinship, land, ethnicity, race, nationality, and language. Therefore, the problems and life situations of migrants and mobiles are different, despite certain similarities. The migrants are told to integrate with the host society and to »find their second home« in the host country, whereas mobile people, who re-settle every couple of years or spend half the year in hotel rooms in various countries, are often considered as uprooted, or they develop multiple roots (Rushdie 1983). It is very likely that migrants maintain extensive connections with their home countries. They may belong to both the country of origin and the host country, and be well anchored socially in both locations. Such connections may induce the creation of international migration networks, and increase the flows of people between the two locations (Chaney 1985; Boyd 1989; Fawcett 1989; Grasmuck/Pessar 1991; Durand/Massey 1992; Wilpert 1992; Portes/Sensenbrenner 1993; Espinosa/Massey 1997). The migration systems (Zolberg/Smith 1996; Faist 2000) or transnational social space may be based on them (Glick Schiller et al. 1992; Basch et al. 1997; Pries 2000). It has not yet been investigated how chronically mobile people, disembedded from the context of nation-states, maintain their relationships with diverse localities.

Studies in transnationalism analyze the flows and lives of people beyond one locality: even so, they regard nation-states as the primary factor structuring these flows (Pries 2001: 50). In contrast, the present study concentrates on mobile individuals who are disembedded from nation-states, and are »globally ubiquitous«. It focuses on »chronically mobile« individuals and »follows this flow«. The sample for the empirical research was chosen from the employees of an international organization that is part of the United Nations system. The special feature of this organization is that it has the power to separate its employees from national ties: people employed by it do not participate in their national health or pension systems, and they do not pay taxes in their country of residence or origin. All the informants are characterized by extensive mobility. They stay abroad over one hundred days a year. Many of them have changed countries of residence more than twice in their life course, and often four, or even nine times. Their lives are thus characterized by geographical promiscuity. This situation makes it possible to investigate how boundaries and belongings are constructed in a de-nationalized context. The sample is described in detail in Chapter Four, and Chapter Five describes the specific context of the research.

The questions driving this study can be best answered by focusing on the everyday experience of the mobile individuals. Whitehead, a British philosopher at the turn of the nineteenth and twentieth centuries, first stressed the need to include the human experience of space in philosophical reflection. This idea was taken up by Heidegger and Hägerstrand, who re-combined society and space as two sides of the same process. Later, the same approach was used in human geography, and also in sociology, thanks to Anthony Giddens (1984). These approaches define space as socially constructed in daily actions. Social geography speaks, for example, of action spaces: spatial units within which human actions will, by and large, take place. Such action spaces based on human activities can be demarcated. Every individual has different action spaces for each act (van der Velde 2000). However, these single individual spaces are not the subject of the present work, which, despite employing the idea of space-in-construction, does not aim at a simple description of mundane individual activities, and their spatial distribution. Rather, the focus on individuals and their activities serves to discover the significance of place, which, as Entrikin (1999: 269) puts it, becomes evident when place is conceived not as a location in space, but instead as related to an individual subject.

The primary focus of the study is not on individual strategies for dealing with extensive mobility. Rather, the understanding of individual strategies and actions serves to determine the concrete spatial relations that are developed in the context of extensive mobility. The spotlight on everyday activities in relation to mobility requires an understanding of mobility as a complex system, in which practices are mediated between structural opportunities and constraints. This in turn makes it possible to include in the analysis the immobilities, such as infrastructure, that shape mobility practices. Moreover, the concept of mediation also makes it possible to examine the relation to space as a process that depends, to a certain extent, on individuals. The concept of mediation draws on Giddens' theory of structuration, which is introduced in Chapter Three, which also sets out in detail the methodological design of the empirical study.

Space-time

The focus of social sciences on globalization and global flows reveals the important, though ambivalent, role that space has in social relations and personal identities. When people, information, commodities, capital, and risks flow seemingly freely around the globe, the divisions into local, regional, and national spatial units, and the territorial bond of social structures and processes, become more ambivalent and crucial, both for the individuals involved and for the scientists comprehending them. A »spatial turn« can be seen in social sciences in the last two decades. Within globalization studies, »local« is mostly associated with place, with particularities, with identity construction, and the essential qualities of human dwelling, while the »global« is linked to the unlimited scope of possibilities and unrestrained flows, primarily of capital (Daniels/Lever 1996; Cox 1997; Herod et al. 1998).

The seemingly new dualism of »local« and »global« reflects, in fact, the historical dichotomy of place and space. A single, indisputable concept of space has never existed. Reflection on space, first philosophical and later also sociological, has always been occupied with certain dualisms: for example, whether or not space is relative or absolute (Earman 1970; 1989). At the end of the eighteenth century, absolute empty space was to the infinity of God, and a century later with the unlimited possibilities of free movement. Yet an absolute empty space, which is beyond human

Women - connected with place
men - somehow above place.

experience, contradicts individuals' everyday practices, which happen in places. This contradiction enhanced the dualism of space-place, in which the latter was coupled with particularity and concrete social relationships. This dualism achieved its peak in modernity, when it correlated with other dualisms. In the period of technical developments in the media of transportation and communication, and the increase of speed of movement in space, the problem of relative or absolute, and, to an extent, the issue of space or place, gave way to the related dichotomies resulting from them: the dualisms of presence-absence, near-far, here-there, us-them, and inclusion-exclusion, which were especially important in the works of the first sociologists and commentators of modernity, and particularly in Georg Simmel's theory of space. Certainly these dichotomies remain relevant, perhaps increasingly so, as suggested by various globalization studies that examined the mutual relations between global flows and local processes.

Various researchers have tried to tackle this dialectic of global-local by proposing the term »glocalization« (Robertson 1998; Tomlinson 1999; Helvacioglu 2000; Salamandra 2002; Knorr-Cetina 2003; Roudometof 2003). However, they do not move beyond understanding the processes of globalization as the interaction between two different units of space. Although the concept of glocalization is barely successful when used in this sense, it does point to the epistemological shift in the perception of spatial units, and the scales of social processes. A break with the territorial orthodoxy and a reconsideration of the reference system of human action and social sciences has been explicitly postulated (Beck 1997a: 26). It requires the re-definition of boundaries, and reflection on the order that appears when we abandon the categories and scales of local-regional-national-global. It is, however, an open question whether the fading away of the order of discreteness of cultural boundaries will turn the world into »a gradual spectrum of mixed-up differences« (Geertz 1988: 147). It is imaginable that the old units of perceiving and analyzing socio-spatial order may be replaced by new ones, that the boundaries transform but not disappear, and that new principles of ordering take over the old distinctions (Beck/Bonß 2001; Beck 2004a; b). However, re-nationalization appears more likely than the »cosmopolitanization« of spatial order.

These considerations can be conceptualized as a shift from methodological nationalism to cosmopolitan methodology. The state-political fixation and control of space is a condition of the amalgamation of society and the (nation) state. The territorial unit of a state is a container for societies, individual identities, and lifestyles. Beck (1997: 116; 2004a: 21; 2004b) calls the conceptualization of societies within such containers methodological nationalism (see also Martins 1974: 276; Smith 1983: 26; Wimmer/Glick Schiller 2002). Globalization brings to light the inadequacy of this approach. Methodological nationalism involves and intensifies a territorial misunderstanding of culture and cultural plurality. If culture is seen as territorially defined, the question of plurality leads to the impasse of the false alternative: either universal sameness or non-comparable perspectives (Beck 2004a: 142). Inherent in the methodological perspective is also the dichotomy of national-international, as well as local-global and national-global. For the social sciences, this means that it is necessary to adopt a different, cosmopolitan perspective, in order to be able to comprehend the new, global, and cosmopolized reality. The cosmopolitan perspective makes it possible to go beyond the vision of space fragmented into nation-states, and the (national) territorial fixation of cultures and people.

However, the application of the cosmopolitan perspective should not be mistaken for the emergence of the no-border single global space. The shift from the domination of the nation-state perspective and the cosmopolitanization of reality (Beck 2004a) is a non-linear transformation (Lash 2003). Friedman (1994: 205) notices that cosmopolitanism cannot exist without boundaries. There is no reason to suspect that global social processes remain in opposition to the principles of human territoriality, and that globalization equals de-territorialization (Berking 1998). Space, and control over an area, remain means of control over people and material resources (Sack 1986). It should rather be assumed that, due to globalization, particular spatial relations are transformed. It is an open question whether and how new boundaries will replace all territorially marked borders (Beck/Bonß 2001: 39, Beck 2004b).

Transition

It seems impossible to talk about mobility and spatial relations without relating to transition, in two dimensions. First, several authors explicitly bring together the issues of mobility and spatial relations, and change in social structuration; second, each of these aspects is separately discussed as undergoing a transformation. The concepts of space have been evolving, and have resulted in a virtual consensus that space is a social construct and, as such, is subject to change. Space-in-time, space-in-becoming, means also that it depends on various social processes, for example, as is also claimed by many authors on mobility, which is also changing.

Analogies have been drawn from a century ago, when a somewhat similar restructuring of the dimensions of time and space took place, due to the rapid development of new means of transportation and communication, and thus an increase in mobility (Kern 1983). Observers at the turn of the nineteenth and twentieth centuries focused on disjunctions, dislocation, and disorientations: they directed their research towards the social environments of cities, where all these processes cumulated (Frisby 1984; 1986). They related the change and the exceptionality of the modern experience to new modes of capital accumulation (Marx), to the permeability of contemporary daily life and societal structures (Nietzsche), to transitory character (Baudelaire), to processes of (economic) rationalization (Krakauer), and to the discontinuous experience of time-space and, increasingly, to the qualitatively new mobility of people (Simmel).

Various present-day authors regard mobility as a typical modern phenomenon that is undergoing radical change. The modern notion of mobility is strongly entangled with the idea that physical movement is a major dynamic factor of modernization (Zorn 1977; Zapf 1993; 1998; Kesselring/Vogt 2004), especially as the opposition to the stable order defined by class and nation-state societies. Physical mobility is thus believed to have the power of liquefying social structures, as mobile individuals free themselves from the ties of social class; thus it brings about a social change (Bauman 2000a). Physical mobility in this model is associated with social mobility. However, recent studies show that these developments are non-directional, and that physical mobility does not necessarily result in social mobility. Diagnosing social change directly from physical mobility and the increasing ease and speed of transportation is thus highly problematic (Kaufmann 2002). Various authors too easily associate mobility (flow) with liquidity (fluidity), and permanent changes of location with the supposedly ever-transitory character of modernity. Though flow may be a useful metaphor for certain social processes, it should not be mistaken for them.

Many authors indirectly relate social change to mobility (Bauman 2000a). They claim that mobility has changed the perception and experience of space and time, and that this, in turn, has led to the transformation of social structures. The obvious example is that of nation-states: due to mobility and border crossing, the container-spaces of nation-states are being questioned. In addition, the concept of locality must be reviewed, given the increased mobility that brings together very distant places: for example, those of the origin and residence of diasporic communities (Appadurai 1988; 1990; 1998; Clifford 1988; Gupta/Ferguson 1992; Hannerz 1996).

The changes within modernity have also been conceptualized in the theory of reflexive modernization (Beck 1994; Beck/Giddens/Lash 1995; Beck/Bonß 2001; Beck 2004a; b). This presumes the existence of two phases of modernity. At the empirical level, the methodological shift from nationalism to cosmopolitanism, discussed earlier in this chapter, corresponds to the transition from the first modernity to the second modernity. It is a shift from programmatic mobilization, individualization, and inclusion (within), and exclusion (from) the nation-state container, with its clearly defined territorial borders. The first modernity aimed at clear definitions, whereas the second modernity accepts the ambiguity of such distinctions. The processes of modernization that first made them possible have finally rendered them obsolete (for the controversy, see Latour 2003). This second modernity is (by its own definition) still being negotiated, as are, within it, its premises. It means, however, that, in one or another form, the old distinctions prevail.

This is the starting point of the present work: it assumes that contemporary spatial relations are not necessarily radically different from those at the turn of the nineteenth and twentieth centuries. In this respect, it diverges from the post-modern conceptualizations. It presupposes a non-linear development, and thus assumes that concrete spatial relations can be comprehended only by means of empirical inquiry. It focuses, in particular, on the first modern dualism of inclusion-exclusion, place-space, local-global, embedded-disembedded; but it does not close off the possibility of any new dualism, issues, or problems that may be identified in the course of the research.

The organization of the book

The present work sheds more light on the very ambiguous relationship between mobility, spatial relations, and social change. The opening two chapters sketch a theoretical framework for the study. Chapter Two analyzes the various concepts of mobility, and their development in the last decades. It illuminates the relationship between mobility and social structuration, and provides details of the concepts that are brought together by the liquefaction of social structures: time-space compression, acceleration, and abstraction. It then discusses in detail the so-called liquid models of analysis, and their comprehension of space-time, from the changes in which they derive the shift towards a new stage in modernity. Finally, the chapter points to the deficiencies of these models' conceptualizations of time-space.

Chapter Three undertakes this critique and conceptualizes the deficiencies, employing the theory of reflexive modernization. First, the chapter discusses the periodization that the liquid models include, and briefly describes the alternative models. However, in various ways all these models relate space-time to change in social structuration. At this point, particular attention is paid to the model of periodization that is included in the theory of reflexive modernization. This theory focuses on dissonances between three perspectives: those of actors and their self-reflectivity, of scientific observers, and of the public. When this is applied to the question of spatial relations, three levels emerge: the theory of space, the spatial discourse, and the level of individual and collective practices that make use of and reproduce space.

Each of these points is considered in the following sections. Chapter Three continues to explore the development of the modern concepts of space. It shows, for example, how the dualisms of space-place, absolute-relative matured in philosophical thought, and found their reflection in the modern and post-modern programmatic. This chapter also considers how each understanding of space is related to particular discourses on space. Finally, a separate section is dedicated to the possibility of researching space and spatial relations, as produced and reproduced in the daily practices of individual actors. This is the basis of the empirical study.

The second part of the book begins with an exploration of the mobility practices of the individuals (Chapter Four). It describes the methods that the individuals develop to sustain their extensive mobility. They move within transnational social and infrastructural networks that ensure standardized conditions and practices all around the globe. When such networks are insufficient, the individuals themselves constitute similarity, which reduces the stress of frequent travel. This chapter therefore dedicates special attention to their routines. The chapter also proposes to examine individual mobility as the result of active mediation between various elements of the material and social networks (exogenous factors), and personal motivations and life plans (endogenous factors). It discusses both in detail, in relation, separately, to short-term mobility and resettlement. The last section of the chapter considers the problems for individuals that result from extensive mobility, and how they deal with them. Mobility interferes with private commitments, and leads to a situation in which the individuals become part-time family members. Their social networks, although transnational, are restricted to people similar to themselves, and their ties to old friends and wider family members weaken with the time spent abroad. Moreover, they live under constant pressure of time, and their main concern is coordination. In turn, their individual life-projects and daily activities are individualized, and their temporal perspective is shortened. Instead of planning for life, the individuals grab the chances that are open to them.

The following chapters investigate the (re)production of space in mundane practices at all scales. Chapter Five introduces the institutional context of the empirical study, and focuses on the process of mobilization through networks and disembedding mechanisms. The chapter proceeds with a description of the organizational networks that support the individual decision of mobility, and make resettlement and frequent travel possible and unproblematic. Finally, the chapter discusses the principle of spatial positioning. The central question concerns the kind of forms of fixation individuals choose when they are not subject to the territorial principle of fixation. The analysis shows that individuals position themselves primarily in socio-technical structures, and constitute their spatial relations indirectly through work, family, and friends. The attachment to places of work and residence seem to have a subordinate role. Also, the organized forms that parties or associations play points to the specific profile of a »highly mobile« personality.

Chapter Six is organized around two main themes: location of home, and relationship to hosting places. In the first section of the chapter, under the condition of disembeddedness from territorial national structures, the question of the location of an individual's home is of key interest. Further, the chapter asks about an individual's relationship to places of residence and of origin, and travel destinations. The individuals develop a range of strategies to regulate their exposure to localities, and to deal with the otherness of their inhabitants. The chapter concludes by reconsidering the definition of a place. It argues that under the conditions of mobility, places are dynamic constituents: their aspects dissolve, and they no longer act as clearly territorially-defined units that encompass a single population within defined borders.

Chapter Seven focuses on the territorial delimitation of communities and their cultures. It asks how individuals construct the delineation between the similar and the different, between what is inside and outside, and who belongs and does not belong. The chapter examines which differences between people and places are important to the mobile individuals, and how they are coded. The analysis focuses on the construction of borders and their territorial binding. It is explicitly asked whether the changing role of nation-state borders leads to the creation of a borderless cosmopolitan space, and how such a space could be structured. It argues that complementary topologies exist, in which different logics play a key role: the regional, which aims at clear-cut bordering in and bordering out of differences; the network, interconnecting similar elements; and the fluid, where variations do not have boundaries and transformations are continuous. Additionally, the study reveals a new topology type.

The last chapter summarizes the results, and asks what the spatial relations at the turn of the millennium are. In so doing, it relates to the exit questions and critiques expressed in Chapter Two. It proves that the thesis of a radical change of spatialization is highly problematic. The chapter also suggests the perspective for further research on space and mobility.

2. Mobility in the age of globalization

In sociology there has been extensive discussion of the diverse mobilities that characterize modern contemporary societies. At the beginning of the twentieth century, sociology drew attention to the numerous consequences of the geographical mobility of people for the relationships in social groups (Simmel 1983 [1903]: 236).[1] Simmel distinguished between situations in which the entire group, or a part of it, or only some elements of it are mobile. The first type, nomad mobility, is the basis of social integration and the development of specific relations of power in the group. For example, nomadic tribes are less differentiated and more consolidated than spatially fixed groupings (Simmel 1983 [1903]: 238). When only some elements of a group are mobile, the group needs to develop a complex system of methods to bind their looser elements, despite the physical distance between the mobile peripheral and the immobile core parts. Any institution, for example, a state, the church, or an association, possesses administrative tools to integrate mobile elements (Simmel 1983 [1903]: 240). The mobility of a part of a group may become an instrument of centralization, especially in the political sense, when a governing entity enlarges the area of influence. However, when the functional tools that bind distant elements together lose their efficiency, mobility may lead to separation. In any situation, the mobility of a part influences the whole group and its socialization.[2]

---

1 Karl Marx showed in his works unusual (for the time) awareness of the importance of space and spatial mobility for social structures. However, he hardly developed this thesis. Paradoxically, his influence on his successors is much larger than that of Simmel (comp. Marx 1973: 238f; Harvey 1982; Martins 1982: 162; Urry 1987: 436).

2 Arguably, Simmel was the first sociologist of mobility. His treatment of the symptoms of modernity focused upon inner experience and the dissolution of stable forms of experiencing time, space, and causality. Modern reality is experienced in permanent flux (comp. Frisby 1986: 46; 1992: 65).

Nowadays, a qualitatively different mobility is at the core of sociological interest.[3] Various authors focus increasingly on non-human mobilities: capital, labor, commodities, information, and images that circulate around the globe (Lash/Urry 1994: 12; Urry 2000a: 49ff). Mobility implies the production of instability in a world, and this instability disagrees with the old focus of sociology on such stable structures as societies and nation-states. John Urry therefore postulates »mobile sociology«, which should research these diverse mobilities, including imaginative travel, movement of images and information, virtual, object, and corporeal travel, as they reconstruct national societies, and their power to structure the social (Urry 2000b: 186). They undermine societal borders and increase their permeability, and – what was already Simmel's interest – they influence relations of power and the forms of togetherness of social groups.

Despite the growing interest in mobility, there exists as yet no consistent theory of mobility. Much classical sociological literature considers social mobility, defined primarily as the movement – usually of individuals but sometimes of whole groups – between different positions in the system of social stratification in any society (Marshall 1998: 422). Most sociological attention has focused on intergenerational mobility, in particular the role of educational achievement as compared to that of social background, or of such ascriptive characteristics as race, in explaining patters of occupational attainment (comp. Beteille 1965; Blau/Duncan 1967; Giddens/Stanworth 1974; Kaeble 1977; Heath 1981). The second spectrum of researchers concentrated on geographical movement – that is, on migration – and focused on the more or less permanent movement of individuals or groups across symbolic or political boundaries into new residential areas and communities. Usually sociological studies of migration

---

3 Some authors claim that the importance of mobility results from its increase. However, it is not certain whether spatial mobility in general has increased in the past hundred years (Castles/Miller 1997). Although the average distance covered during a trip has increased due to new technological developments, for example, the number of journeys per person per day has remained stable and pedestrian mobility is in constant decline. International tourism is increasing but at the cost of the resorts in several countries. In the same way, local mobility is losing ground to new forms of mobility like long-distance commuting. Likewise, although we are witnessing a growth of transmitted information in terms of volume, one may question whether this growth is accompanied by a growth in the reception of this information. It seems rather that we are dealing with substitution phenomena between forms of mobility (Kaufmann 2002: 12).

formed a part of a larger research into kinship, social networks, or economic development (comp. Arensberg/Kimball 1940; Castle/Kosack 1973; Miles 1982; Grieco 1987). These regarded society as a uniform surface, and failed to register the geographical intersections of region, city, and place, with the social categories of class, gender, and ethnicity (Urry 2000a: 3).

The main difference from the orthodox theories and studies is that the term »mobility«, as it is used currently, relates to different phenomena. As already mentioned, it encompasses not only people but also movement of information, images, and objects. Second, mobility is seen as a permanent movement. It is not a movement from-to but rather from-to-and-back or within circles (Chaney 1985; Grasmund/Pessar 1991; Zolberg/Smith 1996; Papastergiadis 2000: 91). Third, mobility is taken for granted: it is seen as a normal state of affairs. No mobility is an unrealistic situation. Fourth, mobility not only crosses diverse boundaries, but also sets new ones. Mobilities at the end of the twentieth century and the beginning of the twenty-first century are said to be much more complex, and not to take place within simple geographical entities and clearly defined social structures. They cannot be exclusively analyzed within and between the old distinct units, for example, nation-states, and their analysis requires the employment of new methodologies. Comprehending such mobilities involves the employment of various kinds of metaphor of movement, which involve especially networks and flows, liquids, fluids, flux, nomad, waves, pilgrim, and motel (Urry 2000a: 2). They criss-cross the metaphors of the global, globalization, and globality (network, interconnectedness, and simultaneity, and generate new theories and terminologies, in which mobilities attain a global and unrestricted character.

Recently, attempts have been made to involve mobility in studies of the changing social order (in relation to globalization or micro-structures), and to sharpen the term itself. Studies of mobility touch on many other problems: for example, the role of nation-states, individual and collective identities, social equality and exclusion, and technology studies. The last topic, in particular, has in recent years developed tremendously in relation to automobility, mobile technologies (for example, mobile phones), transportation systems, etc. The discussion splits into the following main areas:

– Defining mobility itself and its relation to other terms, especially in relation to immobility;

- Implications of geographical mobility for individuals; and
- Implications of geographical mobility for social structuration, especially in relation to a changed spatio-temporal experience.

Within these areas, it is possible to distinguish two mainstreams. The first involves those studies that concentrate on the level of a subject. They have their origin in migration studies, family studies, anthropology, and the sociology of social inequalities and organizations. It is typical for them to research the influence of mobility on individuals, their lifestyles, family, social networks, and careers. The second group of studies focuses on macro-structures, and it is less cohesive. These mobility studies were clearly inspired by the Actor-Network-Theory, and these globalization studies focus on its geographical aspects (John Urry can be mentioned as a main author of this approach). In parallel, mobility is seen as a basis of social structuration (Bauman, Kaufmann). However, some authors escape this classification. For example, Bonß and Kesselring (2001) focus primarily on a mobile subject and state flexibilization, and the liquefaction of social structure at the macro-sociological level.

2.1. From physical movement to mobility potential

Mobility as a term remains highly problematic. Recently, the trend has been toward the breakdown of the traditional distinction between social and geographical mobility.[4] There is also a tendency to broaden the term to include the phenomena of change, and thus, at the same time, spatial, temporal, social, cultural, and/or generational patterns of movement. In this approach, physical and social mobility are related to each other. Mobility so defined is a »cross-sectional phenomenon of considerable importance for creating structures« (Bonß/Kesselring 2001: 177). The authors presenting this approach claim that all parts of society are shaped by growing mobility requirements, and that, at the same time, mobility increasingly turns out to be a process of social structures becoming more

---

4 It is claimed that this distinction originates in the ontological division between nature (physical and material space) and society (social space). Social geography, for example, makes this distinction its central topic (comp. Werlen 1995). The most recent studies question, however, the (single) border between society and nature (Strathern 1992; Franklin et al. 2000; Viehöver et al. 2004; Inglis/Bone 2006)

fluid. Solid and sometimes rigid structures are replaced by more flexible and changing forms of integration or coordination (Bonß/Kesselring 2001: 178). This is because physical mobility used to be a desired phenomenon that was associated with freedom and positive social change: enlargement and enrichment of social interconnectedness, learning through contact with the foreign, self-realization, breaking down of boundaries, etc. Physical mobility was thus an instrument of individualization and a symbol of development (Sennett 1994; 1995: 319). It led to social mobility, no longer understood as an upward or downward movement in a social structure, but rather as a horizontal subject-centered development and enlargement of social networks. In this approach, however, the term mobility is unclear. It simultaneously involves the reason for, and the outcome of, social processes, and often it means the same as flexibility. Moreover, the outcomes of an increased physical mobility are ambivalent in their social dimensions. Some authors suspect that a mobilized social structure may lead to social anomie, and the disintegration and disorientation of individuals (Sennett). Others stress that physical mobility may be accompanied by social immobility (Kesselring 2001b).

Some authors consider the mutual relations between social and physical mobility, and assume (disregarding the shift in its definition) that mobility is an old phenomenon. They distinguish certain types or phases of mobility and mobility concepts – traditional, territorial, globalized, and virtual – as well as the types of mobile individuals – pilgrims, travelers, cosmopolitans, and net surfers – that are typical of each phase (Bonß/Kesselring 2001: 188). Understood in this way, traditional mobility relates to a physical movement that is accompanied by social change, both in relation to macro-structures and individual biographies (Kesselring 2001a: 37). An opposite type, virtual mobility, would mean social mobility and physical immobility (Bonß/Kesselring 2001: 186).

From this point of view, the distinction between mobility and immobility becomes crucial. Given the existing infrastructure for mobility in space (airports and airlines, train connection, highways and cars, etc.), the question arises why this potential is not used, or, in other words: what are the barriers to mobility, why do people stay immobile? On the other hand, when considering strong mobility pressure (global corporations and their activities), problems may arise for individuals who may attempt to follow or withstand this pressure, and organize their life accordingly. In the second case, there can be observed the phenomenon of people remaining socially immobile, although they move in space (Kesselring 2001b). This observation leads directly to a problem: whether, in such situations, we should still talk about mobility, or rather about the flexibility of the individuals who fit into an institutional requirement of mobility (Kesselring 2003). In this case, mobility as a term approximates a notion of free will and human agency.

The opponents therefore stress that various barriers to mobility and fluidity should be more strongly embedded in the analysis, to make it impossible to ignore the complexity of the phenomenon (Ritzer/Murphy 2002: 52). Their thesis is that fluidity cannot exist without solid structures that shape, direct, or even block flows. Four types of such structures exist: barrier, hurdle, sieve, and blockade (Ritzer/Murphy 2002: 53), all of which regulate, steer, and direct flows. The difference between them lies in their durability and permeability. The importance of all these types of barriers is that they allow some structures to survive, despite the increased pressure to liquefaction. They are also themselves durable structures. Although a blockade can, under the pressure of mobility, change into a sieve, mobility is never unrestricted, because some immobile assemblies always exist. The task for empirical research is to investigate the interaction of both mobility and stable structures.

Similarly, Urry postulates that we should not underestimate the importance of diverse material bases for global flows and connections.[5] No matter how mobile humans are, they are intricately networked with machines, software, texts, objects, databases, and so on. The interdependent systems of immobile material worlds and, in particular, some exceptionally immobile platforms (transmitters, roads, garages, stations, airports, docks), structure the nature of the global experience. The complex character of such systems stems from the multiple fixities or moorings, often on a substantial physical scale, that enable the fluidities of liquid modernity to be realized. There is no linear increase in fluidity without extensive systems of immobility (Urry 2004: 123). Sassen also points out that cities include multiple functions without which mobility would not be possible: for example, labor, cultural diversity, and technical systems, which themselves are often immobile (Sassen 1994: 72).

---

5 Similarly, Harvey (2001a; 2003) focuses on the dynamics between mobility and fixity, but in relation to capitalism (and its internal contradictions, for example airport-aircraft, commodity centers-commodity flows).

In this context, confusion arises between movement and potentiality of movement. Kaufmann (2002; Kaufmann et al. 2004) therefore claims that, at the level of social structuration, the term mobility should be enlarged to the term »motility«. Motility can be defined as the capacity of a person to be mobile or, more precisely, as the way in which an individual appropriates what is possible in the domain of mobility, and puts this potential to use for his or her activities (Kaufmann 2002: 37; Kaufmann et al. 2004). Motility is comprised of all the factors that define a person's capacity to be mobile: elements of access (available choice in a broad sense), skills (competence), and appropriation (evaluation of the available access). In this framework, mobility refers to migration, residential mobility, travel, and daily mobility (Kaufmann 2002: 40).[6] The acquisition of motility and its transformation into mobility is built through the compromises made between aspirations, projects, and lifestyle, and is linked to multiple logics of action (Kaufmann 2002: 45). In this perspective, mobility remains restricted to physical movement, and the social component or context of it is defined as mobility potential.

2.2. Geographical mobility and its consequences for individuals

It is recognized that individuals live under constant pressure to be mobile. Shove (2002) speaks about the mobility burden, and Urry about the compulsion to proximity, which necessitates movement in space (Urry 2002; also Boden/Molotch 1994). Travel is essential for those who want to operate effectively in business, to sustain social networks, or to enjoy entertainment and leisure. Systems of mobility not only permit people to fulfill necessary practices: they have the further consequence of modifying what those practices are, and how they are »normally« configured and structured (Shove 2002: 2). Mobility means a permanent or temporary absence in some places and »social worlds«. This in turn may have several consequences: physical absence can be substituted by means of distance communication (Berger 1999); there may arise issues of coordination and time management; daily life practices and social networks may be

---

6 There is no really good reason why motility should be related exclusively to mobility; its definition applies to other phenomena as well, which in turn weakens the concept.

influenced; a readiness to be mobile can be a handicap in family but an aid in career life; mobility may decide on social inclusion or exclusion.

Different authors have undertaken research in one or more of the fields in this set of possible issues. All these studies start from the assumption that mobility has become a requirement: that is, as a feature of structure, it is demanded of every organization, and, as a feature of personality, it is more and more expected of human beings. The idol of the modern times is the mobile man – flexible, independent, and highly efficient (Sennett). This development is visible in many domains of life, especially working life (Paulu 2001).

Occupational mobility, in particular, and its impact on and compatibility with conventional family life, have drawn the attention of researchers. According to some studies (Schneider et al. 2002), mobility delays and prevents the development of families. On the one hand, decisions about being mobile are influenced by family, occupational, and personal circumstances. Family considerations are the most important, especially maintenance of the partner's employment and consideration for the children, who should not be expected to put up with mobility. On the other hand, the researched individuals reported several burdens of mobility, of which the most significant are the psychological state, loss of social contacts, lack of time, alienation from the partner, and family and financial burdens. Many mobile individuals report mainly negative consequences for the quality of their relationship, and partner interaction. Mobility is also connected with several advantages, the most significant of these being higher individual autonomy, improved quality of the partnership, development of personality, and the attractiveness of the work place. Two-thirds of the partners of mobile persons feel the same amount of mobility-caused burdens as the mobile persons themselves, or even more. The situations of persons with mobile jobs and those with long-distance relationships are ambivalent: positive consequences for the job and negative consequences for family and partnership stand directly opposed to each other.

There has also been investigation into the kinds of strategies individuals apply to deal with the mobility demand, in order to balance occupational and private life (Pelizäus-Hoffmeister 2001). For example, private and occupational lives are both modified so as to find an optimum: daily life is structured in a way in which both the requirements of family members and the demands of a job can be fulfilled. This strategy requires great flexibility and coordination skills. Another possibility is the limitation of mobility in the case of a potential conflict between private and occupational life. If this strategy cannot be realized, many individuals modify the criteria for social interaction: primarily, they make extensive use of distance communication tools. As the study discussed earlier proved, another option used by mobile individuals is a shift from a long-term stable partnership to a different form of relationship, or the substitution of a partnership with other forms of social interaction. The application of these strategies can change the character and shape of the social networks of mobile individuals.

Urry (2002) presents another thesis: he views private obligations as a reason for geographical mobility. In turn, movement in space serves rather to uphold and stabilize social networks. Axhausen (2001) argues that people in major European countries have increasingly larger social networks, but they are not able to maintain contact with all network members. This is because increased time and effort are needed, and the networks are more spatially spread (less likelihood of casual meetings), on the one hand; and because people lack time in general, on the other hand. The influence of mobility on individuals' social networks and social involvement is ambivalent. Mobility may cause the breakup of social networks (permanent migration), but it may also increase the number of interactions. The problem lies rather in sustaining these enlarged networks. In this case, mobility is, next to the media of distance communication, a tool to maintain social networks. However, many other factors play a role, among them family situation, working time, leisure, and lifestyle.

Mobile individuals have to face the problems of coordination and time management. Shove notes the socio-temporal fragmentation that results from increased mobility. The mobilization of society is of significance for the collective socio-temporal order. Travel is a practice through which people move between other discrete activities and events. These moments of co-presence must somehow be distributed and structured. Multiple systems in the infrastructure of mobility speed up things, offer increased flexibility and, at the same time, permit the fragmentation of episodes into smaller »units«, thereby increasing the challenge of coordinating what become separate events. Individuals have to adopt strategies that enhance their ability to follow space-time trajectories of their own choosing. Organizing co-presence becomes more demanding. In this context, the problem is not to get to a place but to get there on time. Time schedules must be negotiated. In the long term, it is possible that new solutions will be needed. In turn, social convention, obligation, and participation may need to be redefined (Shove 2002: 5-8).

2.3. Mobility and social structuration

Spatial mobility is at the centre of the debate on social structuration (Bauman 2000a; 2000b; Bonß/Kesselring 2001; Kesselring 2001, 2004; Kaufmann 2002; Urry 2003; Kaufmann et al. 2004). What, at the level of individual, is described as flexibilization is, at the level of macro structures, conceptualized as fluidification. All these theories and approaches can be called liquid models of analysis They represent the view that mobility belongs to the melting powers (Gane 2001: 269; Bauman 2002: 6). These theories assign a paradigmatic role to mobility's acceleration and increase, and investigate the extent to which mobility can be considered as a generator of a social change, especially the liquefaction of nation-state divisions. The diagnosis is that social order becomes contingent and unusual as the result of a variety of mobile processes (Urry 2003: 118). The thesis is that the speed of circulation brings about the progressive weakening of the social structure and its categories, in favor of a world organized around mobility (Urry 2004). At first, the melting powers affect the extant institutions that constitute the frames of possible action-choices. The liquidizing powers have moved from the »system« to »society«, from politics to life-policies, or have descended from the macro to the micro level of social cohabitation (Bauman 2000a: 7).

Various networks and fluids that roam the globe possess the power of rapid movement across, over, and under many societal clusters, primarily those of nation-states. Thanks to these networks, the national societies and nationalisms that were previously seen and celebrated as separate have become familiar to each society within the wider global order. Each such »banal« nationalism (Billig 1995) is increasingly consumed by others, compared, and evaluated. Each national society can incorporate any other nationalism in its structures. The first consequence of these processes is that nation-states, as political organizations that seek to striate the space they occupy, are no longer able to govern a community (and culture) that can no longer be defined as a fixed, territorially bound, and clearly separate population (Urry 2003: 109). States can thus be said to act increasingly as legal, economic, and social regulators of practices and mobilities that are predominantly provided by and generated through the often unpredictable consequences of many other entities (from individuals to international organizations). Paradoxically, we can observe a growing diversity of states, which are organized around the promotion and prohibition of various mobilities. The second great consequence of global mobilities is new inequalities of access. What becomes significant is the relative, as opposed to the absolute, location of a particular social group or town or society, in relationship to multiple systems. Flows can pass by some areas while connecting others along information-rich and transportation-rich tunnels. These can compress the distance of time and space between some places and enlarge those between others (Urry 2003: 5). Inclusion or exclusion is defined by access to the flows and the infrastructure generating them.

Many of these authors claim that mobility itself is not a direct cause of liquefaction. Rather, the new ways of interacting in space and time, related to the mobility of people and information, melt the old social structures. At present, the patterns of communication and co-ordination, between individually conducted life policies and the political actions of human collectiveness, change and affect the structures, thus interlocking individual choices in collective projects and actions.

The liquid models thus increasingly consider space as a source of change in contemporary sociation patterns.[7] They assume that mobility influences the existing spatial relations. They claim that if the otherwise separate »container«-like societies are incorporated into the global flows, their boundaries will become fluid, and the frontiers between societies and their cultures will have to be negotiated anew. In turn, the complete spatial »order of things« (Foucault 1994) changes.

However, these models, as I will argue later, do not sufficiently reflect on space-time, and therefore they do not keep their promise to explain the current patterns of sociation. In the next section, I discuss the mechanisms of liquefaction. I show that the liquid models frequently support their judgments on the understanding of space and geographical mobility as separate from the social realm, and treat social mobility as individual

---

7 This approach has become common in the contemporary social sciences since the 1980s: one speaks of »spatial turn«. Either explicitly, as in the liquid models, or implicitly, as in complexity approaches (Thrift 1999; Urry 2003; 2004), they refer to a supposedly new, relational, fleeting, and transitory spatial order that undermines the current sociation.

structure positioning. Consequently, they draw conclusions on social change without working out the exact relationship between socialization and spatialization, and they fail to explain the latter. They are inclined to employ an understanding of space-time as the interplay of proximity and distance. They also retain the container view of space.

The deficiencies of the liquid models can be best conceptualized using the theory of reflexive modernization, which I introduce in Chapter Four. When applied to the liquid models of analysis, this theory shows that they rely on the first-modern understanding of space in their diagnosis of post-modern, light-modern, or second-modern socialization. The dual incongruence of social realm and geographical space, in addition to first-modern spatialization and second-modern socialization, should thus be the exit thesis of the empirical inquiry presented in Chapters Five, Six and Seven.

2.3.1. Instruments of liquefaction

This time-space experience has been identified as novel, and conceptualized as compression (Jameson 1984; Harvey 1990; 1994; Virilio 1991; 1993; 1995) and distanciation (Giddens 1990; 1991). This epochal story dates back to the eighteenth century when, in most countries in Europe, people began to comment on the gathering speed of travel and communication, and the simple fact that places were therefore starting to come closer together in time. According to these authors, the process of time-space compression affects the complete spatialities of traditional societies. Their limited incorporations are gradually replaced by a new world full of intermediary machines, which enable bodies to travel and communicate more swiftly, thus rewriting the horizons of experience, including notions of space (Harvey 1994: 61). In turn, space becomes a playground for new modes of organization, most especially that of the state, which, through the powers granted to it by these intermediaries (and the »facts« that they make possible), is able to parcel out and govern territory in ways heretofore undreamt of. As this process continues, it reaches a new millennial phase. The process of speed-up, boosted especially by new electronic communications media, reaches a new place where travel is increasingly a by-product of all but instantaneous communication, rather than vice versa (Virilio 1993). In this concept, technologies play a very large role and dramatically influence all dimensions of life, including the experience of space and place. They accelerate flows, mainly the electronic circulation of information, money, and images. These increase mobility, and thus these models compress time-space and induce social change (Cwerner 2000). The new demands can only be fulfilled by increased mobility and new technological developments, and this leads to an endless loop. This may produce only a restless »space of flows« (Castells), or something akin to a total dissolution of space: space as an isochronic plane, space degree zero, or space as the »lost dimension« (Virilio). »Spaces from diverse worlds seem to fall one into another« – therefore locality is a collage of images of different spaces, which each individual can choose for himself (Harvey 1994: 71). Space is fragmented and connected anew, as in a kaleidoscope.[8]

The concepts of time-space compression assign complexity and heterogeneity exclusively to space, and refuse it to time (Jessop 2004: 6). Harvey and Giddens understand time as standardized metric time, which they consider a key feature of modernity. In pre-modern settings, time and space were connected through the situatedness of place.[9] Larger pre-modern societies developed formal methods for the calculation of time and the ordering of space: calendars and maps. These were the prerequisites of »distancing« across time and space. The separation of time from space involved, above all, the development of the empty dimension of time, the main lever that pulled space away from place (Giddens 1991: 16). Such measurable standard time »distanciates« space, and provides the

---

8 Harvey focused primarily on new modes of circulation and the accelerated flow of money. Again, it can be seen as a typical modern issue, the analysis of which we owe to Simmel. In his essay »Money and Modern Culture«, for instance, Simmel showed how money can be considered as the medium through which cultural relationships are formed. He pointed to an acceleration of the rhythm of modern life and he believed that with it our experience of space and time changed. Harvey is also concerned with the process of capital's annihilation of space through time. However, Harvey's and Virilio's diagnosis of annihilation is debatable. Rather, as Simmel puts it, these developments have the effect of re-working our sense of what is near and what is far. In his more recent writings, Harvey focuses strongly on the relationship of power and two logics: capitalist and territorial. In this way he rather stresses the dualism of mobility and fixity, the tension within the internal structure or logic of capitalism, referring to Marx in this concept (comp. Harvey 2001a, b, 2003).

9 Oakes (1993), based on his own empirical research in China, questions the supposed past unity of place and space. He argues that locality was a contingent component of a »space of flows« rather than its antithesis.

very basis for their recombination in ways that coordinate social activity without any necessary reference to the particularities of place (Giddens 1990; 1991: 16). People, events, organizations, and whole societies are no longer simply tied to single places or particular times.[10] Instead, local times and people are tied to global agendas, standardized time horizons, and constantly shifting spatial arrangements. This process is crucial for the disembedding of social institutions, and means a »lifting out« of social relations from local context, and their rearticulation across indefinite tracts of time-space. [11]

---

10 The disembeddedness of social systems from space and time has also been considered by other authors. For example, Appadurai (1998: 11) diagnoses the end of fixation of groups and their identities to particular territories and spaces. De-territorialization results in multiple processes; in order to research them, Appadurai proposes a new term, the suffix »scape« which combines with five dimensions of global flows – ethnicity, media, technology, finance, and ideology. This points to multi-perspectival constructs, sets of relations inflected by the historical, linguistic, and political situatedness of different sorts of actors: nation-states, multinationals, diasporic communities, religious, political, or economic movements, and face-to-face social groupings (Appadurai 1990: 296). Albrow points out that, traditionally, place was connected to local culture and community. At the same time, actions undertaken at a far distance may have consequences in this particular locality; the social networks of an individual from this locality may stretch globally (at this point, Albrow re-calls the term time-space compression, which enables global expansion of social networks); and the resources of a locality enable a connection between the local and the global (Albrow 1997: 308). In relation to community, Albrow (1997: 311) speaks of a structure that is independent (distanciated) from a particular time-space, networks that stretch in space globally; thus, locality can stretch spatially.

11 Robertson (1998: 194) notices that, due to the development of terms like time-space distanciation, the discussion has been brought to such an abstract level that the particular problems can be considered only relatively. Using Giddens' argument that globalization is about a play of absence and presence, and the interconnectedness of social relationships in the distance, he proposes rather to speak about glocalization – as a process in which the global is being included and transformed in the local, and vice versa. Similarly, Kirby (1998: 172) argues against placelessness and de-territorialization of the social in the course of globalization. All kinds of social interconnectedness meets in the local – from face-to-face relationships in a village to globally organized mass-media. Therefore human actions and institutions need to be researched in local contexts (Kirby 1998: 174). Tickamyer (2000) points to the fact that all relations of power, inclusion, and exclusion are supported by the spatial extension of institutions such as political parties, community government, and nation-states. As Immerfall (1998: 173) argues, globalization as a process should not be mistaken for globalization as perception. The first inevitably involves local and territorial involvement; the second may mean an impression of an annihilated compressed space.

The understanding of space and time in these concepts reminds one of the analyses of the first modernists like Benjamin or Simmel. As the following chapter shows in detail, their central concern was the discontinuous experience of time, space, and causality as transitory, fleeting, and fortuitous or arbitrary (Frisby 1986: 4). The pre-form of the concept of distanciation can be also found in Simmel's considerations on abstractive thinking, which makes it possible to span larger spatial distances (Simmel 1958: 494; Kuhn 1994: 43). The echoes of Bergson's primacy of time over space also come to mind (Massey 2005: 21).

On the other hand, the dominating idea in both concepts is the interplay of presence and absence (temporal dimension) and proximity and distance (spatial dimension). This arose around the problem of how system integration[12] is possible beyond the condition of direct (non-mediated) co-presence. Giddens argues that the continuity of everyday life depends, in large measure, on routinized interactions between people who are co-present in time and space (social integration). This is also what »society« meant before the eighteenth century: the company of others (Gregory 1989: 188). Measurable time-space (abstraction) and thus de-localized, standardized, and empty time-space bind diverse localities and local actions within one scheme, and enable sociation beyond co-presence. Harvey observes a change of relation between a unit of distance and the unit of time required to overcome this distance. The consequence of the acceleration of mobility – the falling together of diverse worlds – is however unsure, a fact to which Simmel drew attention. It is a peculiar modern dilemma that, due to mobility, the relation of what is far and strange to what is close and familiar is ambivalent (Allen 2000: 55). What is far does not necessarily have to be strange – this recognition questions the sanctity of presence (Shields 1992: 189). This dilemma is discussed by Simmel in his essay on the Stranger, of 1908: the person who disturbs the status quo of a given locality, breaching its walls, and bringing the places of everyday life into contact with indefinable, seemingly limitless spaces beyond (Simmel 1908: 510). The relations of far and close conceptualized as the »falling of spaces into another« (Harvey 1994: 71), and as the existence of multiple spaces, each of them characterized by different social formations, as well as the resulting possibility of change of perspectives, were described at the turn of the nineteenth and twentieth centuries. Some

---

12 For the detailed positioning of the concept of time-space distanciation in Giddens' theory of structuration see Gregory (1989).

authors, for example, Nietzsche and Jose Ortega y Gasset, went even further and developed the philosophy of »perspectivism«, based on the novel spatial experience of relativity (Kern 1983: 132, 150f). Henri Picare identified visual, tactile, and motor spaces, each of them having different characteristics. The proliferation of perspectives and the breakup of a homogeneous three-dimensional space found its expression in the art of the modern age, most profoundly in Cubism. Simultaneously, the dynamics of spatial construction and the process of becoming in time and space were undertaken in literature, for example, by Proust and Joyce. These most innovative novelists of the period transformed the stage of modern literature from a series of fixed settings in a homogenous space into a multitude of qualitatively different spaces that varied with the shifting moods and perspectives of human consciousness (Kern 1983: 149).

The concepts of time-space compression and distanciation can thus be seen as useful conceptualizations that encompass the observations of the changing pattern of social-spatial experience initiated by the modernists, and bring them into a broader framework of social change. Their virtues should not be neglected. However, it is questionable whether these concepts, and the changed spatialization of presence and absence announced by them, can alone fulfill the claim, made by the liquid models, of a radical change in social structuration at the turn of the twentieth and twenty-first centuries (Shields 1992: 181).

More important, the liquid models have been criticized for connecting two orders of reality – the spatial and the social – that do not necessarily go together. According to these critiques, spatial mobility may not be a good indicator of social fluidity. Movement in geographical space can be seen as a constraint on, not a widening of, the possibilities of moving in social space (Kaufmann 2002: 13; Kaufmann et al. 2004: 747). The alternative thesis argues that the normative value of mobility influences social positioning at the level of individuals (Sennett 1998). In this sense, Castells argues that increased mobility leads to the distinction of a global mobile elite, and the rise of a new social order in which a global well-connected leader-elite rules over a mass of locally bounded, altogether disconnected people (Castells 2001: 471). This elite owes its power to the possibility of interconnectedness and of overcoming spatial distance. The attributes of these elites are a homogenizing lifestyle and unlimited access to certain spaces, for example, VIP Lounges at airports. Thus, the new social order is about shifting patterns of exclusion and inclusion that are based on the possibilities of access.

Further, the liquid models understand modernity as characterized by qualitatively new spatio-temporal settings. Yet, at the same time, according to such authors as Harvey, Virilio, and Bauman, space becomes increasingly irrelevant. It no longer sets limits to action and its effects, and it counts for little, or not at all, as a structuring factor (Bauman 2000a: 117). Assuming that space no longer counts, the liquid models care little about explaining its exact role in social relations and its effects on social order, even though they explicitly relate it to the supposedly new space-time relations.

To disregard space as a factor structuring the social realm is possible, in my judgment, as long as a clear-cut distinction between geographical and social space is assumed. Such a methodological assumption is common to many mobility studies.[13] Their implicit assumption is twofold: that space is a material matrix of movement, and that each place is a unit of space from which movement starts, or in which it ends. Second, space is divided into units, for example, nation-states, between which movements occur and can be observed and measured. Therefore it is possible for these approaches to suspect that movement from Country A to Country B should be accompanied by social change, first at the level of individuals and their life-projects, and in consequence at the level of institutions reacting to the new life-politics. Though implicit, such an assumption runs alongside spatial determinism: movement between spatial units is assumed to be a reason for movement in social space. On the other hand, this line of argumentation leads to the paradox that space becomes unimportant: nation-states, between which movement takes place, are particular political and organizational systems, and to stay consistent with this approach they should, as such, be qualified rather as a social space. Any movement between them is thus a movement between differently structured social spaces, and this may induce change in the social spaces of moving individuals. The diagnosis of change is thus a mere shift of scale, and

---

13 Some authors have noticed that such assumptions are misleading, and have proposed to speak of motility (Kaufmann 2002, Kaufmann et al. 2004). This has, in turn, implications for their understanding of time-space. However, in my opinion, the idea of time-space, as constructed in social practices and therefore undividable from the social realm, results rather from coping with the understanding of mobility on time-space. Consequently, these studies focus on motility, and not on exact spatial relations and their construction in the practices of individuals.

geographical space is merely a material matrix, a scene on which processes take place. This geographical space is thus an empty, container-like space and as such is ignored by those studies, which focus predominantly on mobile individuals and their life-projects.[14]

Such an insufficient reflection on space, which leads to the blind employment of the container understanding of space, is typical of methodological nationalism (Wimmer/Glick Schiller 2002). Paradoxically, it can also be found in those approaches that explicitly try to tackle it. The key example can be found in the concept of transnational social spaces (Pries 1997: 17; 2001a: 49; 2001b: 55). This substitutes the nationally limited concept of society with the idea of a space (Bommes 2003: 103) that contains exactly the same kind of relationships as those typical of a nation-state, but over which a single nation-state has less control powers.

To sum up, social structuration at the turn of the millennium is conceptualized as liquefaction. It is argued that time-space compression and distanciation are the instruments of this process. However, the analysis shows several problems and incongruities: first, the liquid models are based on the distinction between physical or geographic space and social space, which is highly problematic, because it also supports methodological nationalism. Second, the concepts of time-space compression and distanciation, on which these models support their arguments, make sense only within the modernist terms of absolute container-like space. Such a comprehension of space, however, was questioned almost a century ago, and deliberated on in both the science and the art of the period. The merits of both concepts in understanding modernity should not be neglected. It is, however, questionable whether they are suitable tools to explain the recent processes taking place under the conditions of extensive mobility (Beck/Lau 2004: 20). These cannot be explained solely by reference to a debatable, quantitative increase in the speed and volume of mobility.

---

14 The difference in interest dedicated by these studies to space originates in their background. Those studies that include space in the analysis originate either in the studies on geographical aspects of globalization, or in anthropology. Geography was the first discipline to use the terms »space« and »place« as descriptive concepts of globalization (comp. Soja 1989; Harvey 1990; Thrift 1996). Anthropology questioned the concepts of territorially bound homogenous cultural units (comp. Hannerz 1996; Appadurai 1996; Gupta/Ferguson 1997). Berking notices that the generalization of this perspective led to the amalgamation of the geographical and anthropological analyses, and the inclusion of spatiality in social analysis of politics, culture, space, gender, race, and ethnicity (Berking 1998: 383).

3. Towards the modern universes

3.1. Periodization

The liquid models explicitly introduce a certain periodization, which the concepts of time-space compression and of time-space distanciation also contain. They all try to explain changing patterns of social structuration by relating them to distinct time-space relations. Giddens distinguishes between pre-modern and modern settings, each with its own dominant concept of space. Harvey speaks of time-space compression as a process initiated by the technical revolution, and now achieving its new millennial stage. Bauman distinguishes two stages within modernity. The first »heavy« period was characterized by the conquest of territory (compression), in contrast to the current stage of »light« modernity, which started when space and time were separated from each other, and from living practices (distanciation). »Light« modernity is characterized by exterritorialization of power, and the revenge of nomadism over the principle of territoriality and settlement (Bauman 2000a: 13).

Similarly, Lefebvre relates particular modes of social structuration with space. He goes beyond human geography, which considers people and things merely in space, and presents a coherent theory of the development of different systems of spatiality in different historical periods. These »spatializations« are not only physical arrangements of things but also spatial patterns of social action and routine (Shields 1999: 146). Lefebvre uses the historical types of spatialization to explain why capitalistic accumulation, for example, occurred at that particular point in time and not earlier: it was a secular space, itself commodified and quantified, that made this particular type of production possible. Space is thus a medium: the way we understand, practice, and live.[15] Lefebvre's space appears at

---

15 Lefebvre's understanding of space cannot be separated from his discourse with Marxism, as Martins (1982) showed. Structuralist Marxism postulated a calendar for the

various levels: the physical, the mental, and the cultural. Having established the notion of social space as produced, Lefebvre historicizes it as absolute-nature, sacred-historical, abstract-capitalist, and differential-contradictory (Lefebvre 1970 [2003]; 1991; 1996).[16] All these spaces are interrelated, and together they make up space, they are the aspects of space.[17] Foucault (1991: 66) also claims that space and place are historical entities, subject to temporal change. Specific modalities in the social organization of space are the expression of a specific distribution of power, which is scattered and concentrated in different ways in different historical periods.

The weak point of these periodization models is, however, that they suggest that time is the ultimate ordering system of space. History therefore becomes a series of epochs, to each of which is assigned an essentialized spatialization of production modes. In each period, the previous patterns of spatialization persist, slowly become transformed, and finally give way to a new doctrine (Shields 1999: 170-177).

Other authors explain the change of social structuration by making a parallel between publicly shared and scientific notions of space, and a variety of processes and concepts. Thus, instead of investigating the precise spatial relations, they sought a change at the level of the common understanding of space, connecting mutually fruitful laical and scientific imaginations. The way we imagine space has social and political effects, so they claim (Massey 2005: 4), but, in addition, the imagination of space results from development in our general understanding of the world around us. For example, in the Middle Ages, conceptualizations of space

---

evolution of societies; this led to the introduction of a steering force that must itself be free of any substantial interference: economic production. The reproduction of the relations of production then became a precondition for the maintenance and extension of the capital relation. For Lefebvre, however, the question concerned how they were reproduced, and his answer was that they are maintained by and within space as a whole. Space, thus, was the medium that ordered the production relations.

16 For a detailed discussion of Lefebvre's understanding of space, and the shortcomings of the periodization he applied to space, see Martins 1982.

17 This trialectics of space has been undertaken by Soja (1996: 70-82), who based his three epistemologies on it: firstspace, secondspace, and thirdspace. Firstspace epistemologies focus primarily on physical and material spatiality, i.e., empirically measurable configurations: locations of things and activities, patterns of distribution, movements of people and goods, etc. Secondspace epistemologies concentrate on conceived space, on projections, imaginations and »thought things«, cognitive maps and mental images of space. Thirdspace epistemologies derive from the deconstruction of the firstspace-secondspace duality; they are based on a radical skepticism towards all established epistemologies.

were directly linked with theology. Space was considered infinite, as God is infinite: it exists without relation to anything outside of it; it is absolute and cannot be comprehended by humans (Ariew 1985; Casey 1998: 106). Parallel to the theological debate, philosophers pondered the ontological status of space (its substance, reality, or objectivity) and its structure (dimension, continuity, divisibility). Philosophy tried to answer questions as to whether space can be perceived or penetrated, whether it can change or be a condition of a change, and whether it can be effective. In the following era, which saw the dominance of physics over alchemy, philosophy over theology, and politics over religion, Newton combined the idea of infinite space with the concept of relative space, in which motion can be measured, and which exists independently of matter (Rynasiewicz 1995). Such space could be assessed, and objects that are in this space could be related to each other, and positioned in a particular order. Measurable space of this type contradicts God's absoluteness, and thus at that time both concepts had to co-exist (Sturm 2000).

The seventeenth century witnessed the creation of metrically precise maps of the earth, constructed as a global scene for the site of discovery and exploitation. These developments relate to the birth of the comprehension of space as »site« or »striated space«, as Deleuze names them (Deleuze/Guattari 1976; Doel 1996; Casey unpublished). This means the leveled-down, emptied-out, planiform residuum. Such space is powerless: it does not retain any of the inherent properties of encompassing, holding, sustaining, or gathering. It may be a location of a function (for example as a territory of a state), or of knowledge, as shown by Foucault (1973, 1977), and serve the particular needs of an institution that demands a certain specific form of a building, which is its location, its residence. Such space can also be conquered, occupied, and divided into units. Societies and cultures can be mapped on such space, can be placed and made immobile, as though awaiting discovery by (mobile) conquerors (Massey 2005: 4).

At the same time, the dominant royalist and aristocratic politics of the period, which had much to do with »knowing one's place« in society (Casey 1998: 183), went hand in hand with the focus of the philosophers on positioning in space. Leibniz (1646-1716), among others, stressed that space is the ordering principle of position relations. As a consequence, one should not say that an object is located in this place, but that the object is in this location when seen there by another object. The description of space thus depends on the perspective of an observer.

Furthermore, secularization and diminishing anthropocentrism can be related to the comprehension of space as heterogeneous, depending on the observer and location. This change was brought about by natural scientists (such as Elie de Cyon and Jacob von Uexküll) who investigated the spatial orientation of living organisms. As early as 1903, when Emil Durkheim and Marcel Mauss published »Primitive Classification«, the heterogeneity of spaces and spatial experience was also assigned to humans: space varies from society to society and within societies, and it has different properties in different regions.

The greatest changes to the concept of space were brought about in the twentieth century, by the discoveries in physics. Einstein introduced the idea of field, which made it possible to combine space and matter anew. In this way, physical space can be thought of as the order of things, or as a positioning quality of material objects. The theory of relativity disproves the concepts of absolute space and time. Space and time, according to Einstein, are relative to the reference system of an observer. Speed cannot be related to absolute, motionless space, but only to objects in motion, including the system of reference itself. Thus, on the basis of the theory of relativity, the idea of space as a fixed three-dimensional container cannot be upheld. First of all, however, Einstein's theory questioned the idea of measuring time and space with fixed units, which made us associate time and space with their units of measurement, which are absolute and the same to all subjects. The inclusion of speed in the problematic of space shifts the focus towards motion. Einstein's space was constituted by bodies, which were constantly in motion. Motion is always spatial and temporal. This means that space is being constituted in time (Ritter 1982: 104).

The periodization of social structuration, as it relates to changing spatial relations, was also popularized by the American sociology of the twentieth century, which claimed that the modern world was the product of transition from a place-based community to a placeless or national society. When the modernizing forces of society overpower the traditional forces of community, place too is overpowered, and continues to exist only as the location of nationally defined social activities (Agnew 1989: 12). This idea dates from Tönnies' dichotomy of *Gemeinschaft/Gesellschaft* (1887) and

Weber's perspective on community, as based on subjective feeling, in contrast to the rationality of national social relationships.

However, detailed review of the concepts of space in philosophy and sociology argues against these models of periodization. It leads to the recognition that particular understandings of space serve particular needs in society, and that more than one concept can exist simultaneously. The different imaginations necessarily coexist, although not without tensions. The most prominent example relates to the discussion as to whether space is relative or absolute, and to the dichotomy of space and place. Both have troubled philosophers from ancient times to the present day. The three main approaches to space meet in modernity.[18] It is primarily the idea of space as absolute and infinite and container-like (Newtonian space). It is a necessary space that enables our experience, yet itself escapes our experience, as defined by Kant (Casey 1998: 202; Warren 1998; Grier 2004). It is an ordering principle of things that are in it – we are able to describe it with the categories of distance (Leibniz); however, this positioning opens up the possibility of relational order. Since Einstein, we have been aware that units of measurement are also relative, and that a different spatial order could exist.

The dichotomy of place-space first appeared in the thought of Plato (Casey 1998: 54; Konstan 2005), and confused thinkers in the medieval period and the Renaissance. Thus, for example, Gianfranceso Pico said that place was space, and Campanella (1568-1639) claimed that space was place. A century later, Gassendi (1592-1633) stated that place was nothing other than empty space, and thus empty space encompassed and eclipsed place, and therefore place as a category was no longer useful (Trusted 1991; Schuhmann 2004; Zalta 2004). By the end of the eighteenth century, place had vanished altogether from serious theoretical discourse in physics

---

18 The commentators do not agree on the exact division between pre-modern and modern understanding of space. Casey identified it with the birth of infinite space in the late 13th century, exactly contemporary with the publication, by Etienne Tempier in 1288, of 219 condemnations of doctrines that denied or limited the power of God (Casey 1998: 106). He therefore opposes Foucault, who claims that the medieval conception of space was restricted to the space of emplacement, to a hierarchical ensemble of places, without any significant sense of infinite space. He also opposes Koyré (1957), who believes that only in the seventeenth century do we find a substitution for the conception of the world as a finite and well-ordered whole, in which spatial structure embodied a hierarchy of perfection and value: that of an indefinite or even infinite universe no longer united by natural subordination, but unified only by the identity of its ultimate and basic components and laws.

and philosophy (Casey 1998: 133). Interestingly, Descartes ascribed position to place and volume to space, and Leibniz reduced place to a position, a spot in space vis-à-vis another spot or sets of spots. These ideas are still present in modernity: they have reappeared in the vivid discussions of globalization, in which place has been related to locality, encompassing cosiness, the development of individual identity and well-being, community and emotional binding; and space has been associated with free movement, endless possibilities, and the playground for impersonal modes of production and capital transfers.

These concepts co-exist but give rise to tensions, because each comprehension of space corresponds to certain experiences and ideologies. Conceiving space as absolute served the secular idea of modernization and development well. Relative space enabled measurement and order positioning. The nineteenth century was a period of immense social change and perceived disorder in social relations; it was also a time of economic discontent and political revolt. In this framework, it was understood that the concept of unlimited space, especially in relation to movement, offered a fertile ground for considering the modern developments of speed. Freed from the limiting relativity of a place, a body could move in infinite space. Empty space matched the experience of acceleration, and the apparently unrestrained possibilities of moving from place to place. Such uniform space enabled discoveries and the conquest of new territories, but also imagined the world as one, and explained any differences between cultures as a difference in the level of development; thus placing them on a time scale, rather than accepting the heterogeneity of space (Massey 2005: 5, 81ff). Comprehending space as abstract made it possible to abstract space from what it is not – for example, social – and units of space one from another. This is a basis of modernity, the development of modern sciences and nation-states.

However, such empty, abstract, and infinite space was inconsistent with the experience of being in a particular community of a small village, and so, towards the twentieth century, the relative versus absolute controversy became more heated, rather than dissolving. Such disorientations, disjunctions, and dislocation were taken up in a variety of ways by the literary, artistic, and scientific movements of the late nineteenth century (Frisby 1986: 4), although their origins can be traced back to the eighteenth century. The dominant royalist and aristocratic politics of that period also had much to do with »knowing one's place« in society (Casey 1998: 183), and in postmodern rhetoric they continue to do so.

The adaptation of the periodization of the liquid models, and the alternatives offered by such authors as Lefebvre, to explain contemporary social structuration, lead to at least two dilemmas: at the methodological level, we need to ask what is new in the spatial experience of the twenty-first century, if the dualisms of near-far, absent-present, relative-absolute, and place-space were already vividly present at least a century ago. At the analytical and empirical level, we need to ask how we can move research beyond these dualisms, and beyond the public discourse of space-time, to describe actual spatial relations and their role in structuring the social realm. Shields (1992) drew attention to this problem, and noted that the concepts of time-space compression and distanciation focus exclusively on relations of proximity and distance, which were inherent at the turn of the nineteenth and twentieth century. He concluded that we cannot state a radical change in social structuration that would result in the shift from modernity to post-modernity. However, he overlooked the actual problems of these models and their periodization, which does not go beyond the search for a meta-change, either at the level of individual time-space experience, or at the level of scientific or public discourse on space. Therefore, these models repeat the dualism of relative-absolute, space-society, place-space, etc., instead of analyzing the dynamics of socio-spatial structuration as a whole, and integrating scientific and public reflection with the practices of individuals and institutions. Other authors suggested instead that there is no meta-change, no change of the system (König 1979: 360), no great transformation (Polanyi 1973) observable. Only certain moments of discontinuity can be described, but there is no consensus about how radical such discontinuities must be for them to be conceptualized properly as meta-changes (Latour 1995; Smelser 2003). Concerning space, the question is, thus, whether spatial relations have been transformed to an extent that justifies the thesis of a shift to a new epoch of spatial relations, and the thesis of radical changes to social structuration induced by these new spatial relations.

3.2. Dissonances

These deficiencies and concerns can be better conceptualized in the framework of the theory of reflexive modernization (Beck/Bonß 2001; Beck/Bonß/Lau 2003; Beck/Lau 2004). It offers an alternative periodization that distinguishes between two periods within modernity: the first (simple) modernity, and the second (reflexive) modernity. In the course of modernization, the very coordinates, categories, and conception of change itself have undergone transformation (Beck/Giddens/Lash 1994; Beck/Bonß 2001; Beck/Bonß/Lau 2003; 2004; Beck/Lau 2005). Thus, discontinuity results from continuity (Adam 2003: 60). This meta-change takes place within modernity: it means that modernity has not vanished but it is becoming extremely problematic. Although social change has always been a (desired) part of modernity, the transition from the first to the second modernity revolutionizes its premises and basic institutions. By premises of modernity, the theory of reflexive modernization understands the foundations of its self-description: the explicit or implicit assumptions expressed in the actions and self-understanding of citizens, the goals of politics, and the routines of social institutions. The first modern premises were nation-state, individualization, gainful employment societies, the concept of nature and its exploitation, rationality, and the principle of functional differentiation (Beck/Bonß/Lau 2003). These premises were a basis for the development of social institutions like nation-states, the nuclear family, and the class structure.

Can space be understood as the premise of modernity, the premise which undergoes a change? At first glance, it cannot, as we tend to understand space as a matrix. Under these circumstances, only a particular notion of space could constitute a premise of any particular epoch. Consequently, the notion of premise would need to be limited to a meta-ideology, but this is certainly not the intention of the authors of the theory of reflexive modernization. However, Lefebvre's (1991) definition of space (or spatialization) as constituted by three inseparable components – lived, perceived, and conceived space – corresponds to the notion of the premises in the sense of the theory of reflexive modernization. This premise is a basis of institutions: nation-state, nuclear family, and capitalism. Assuming that the first modern principle was an abstract space, it corresponds to a particular mode of production, in which capital is disembedded from the particularities of a place and freely located. A distinction between spatial units is consistent with the territorial exclusiveness of nation-states, and a principal division between geographical and social space underlies the territorial embeddedness of a nuclear family, as a unit assigned to a particular place.

As change occurs within modernity, the processes of dissolution of the old structure are accompanied by the reassertion of some of its institutions, although in a changed role, or by some prevailing concepts. The tensions associated with these transformations can be termed boundary management. Thus, the problem of dating the social change precisely becomes less relevant: change is an irregular process that stretches over large spans of time, its velocity varying at each level (individuals, institutions, and observers). The theory of reflexive modernization sets the following general time framework: the first modernity started at the turn of the nineteenth and twentieth centuries and finished around 1960; the second, reflexive modernity started when modernization had dealt with its problems, unintended consequences, and contradictions.

However, the theory of reflexive modernization claims that a structural change is located not in the transition of basic premises, understood as a common, agreed notion (for example, space), but in the categorial dissonance between three perspectives: those of actors and their self-reflexivity, scientific observers, and the public (Beck/Bonß/Lau 2004: 57). Applying this to the question of spatial relations, three levels emerge: the theory of space (its scientific and philosophical notions), the spatial discourse (the role and meaning assigned to space by groups and single actors), and the level of individual and collective practices that make use of space and produce it.

Accordingly, the first modernity was characterized by categorial consonance between actors', scientists', and the public's perspectives, despite all textual differences. Categorial consonance often means latent, and unproblematic, presumed principles, within which programmatic-textual conflicts are articulated. This categorial consonance shatters in the transition to the second modernity. The theory points to the fragmentation of actors' self-reflection and the scientific observers' perspective (which relativized all perspectives) as the triggering factor. In other words, it influences the premises, as a consequence of which the basic social institutions undergo a change (Beck/Bonß 2001; Beck/Bonß/Lau 2004: 21). Searching for a radical change in any of these dimensions taken separately is problematic and erroneous.

At this point, there appears the first incongruity in the liquid models discussed, which see current radical change in social structuration happening in the changed spatio-temporal relations. According to the theory of reflexive modernization, the deficiencies of the liquid models can be conceptualized as the application of the first modern concepts of time-space to diagnose the second modern social structuration.[19]

The claim made by the theory of reflexive modernization has thus significant methodological consequences: any analysis and empirical research should not be restrained to a single dimension, but should investigate at all three levels. Second, it needs to break with methodological nationalism, which unifies the three dimensions in a single interpretation. These consequences will be discussed in the following sections of this chapter.

Strangely enough, the theory of reflexive modernization has not applied its own model to the problematic of space. Instead, it goes in two directions: at the theoretical level, it sees the transition from the first to the second modernity, as it relates to space, in the end of the homogenization between space and time, space and population, and past and future (Beck/Bonß 2001: 30). It describes first modernity as based on nation-state societies, where social relations, networks, and communities are essentially understood in a territorial sense (Beck/Lau 2005: 526). It thus reduces the space-time dimension to the problem of methodological nationalism (Wimmer/Glick Schiller 2002), within which space was understood as divided into nation-state territories, and ordered according to a certain temporal national principle. In this respect, it undertakes the periodization of the liquid models. However, both space and time are relevant in this concept only in relation to a population (nation-state population or a society), to support the thesis of binding national societies to a particular, nationally structured, territory and a particular, nationally »written«, history. Society, time, and space are seen as containers. The break with the homogeneity of society and nation-state territory is also a break with methodological nationalism, but it does not lead to the abandonment of the notion of space as container-like. The role of a nation-state in modern spatialization should definitely not be underestimated, but modern spatialization cannot be reduced to this aspect.

---

19 The division between social structuration and spatial relations needs to be treated with caution. As the following sections explain, such a division is in fact incorrect and leads to various mis-assumptions in social sciences.

At the empirical level, it supports the theses of the liquid models of analysis, by introducing the triad mobility-space-social structuration. Like these models, it focuses on the relationship between geographical and social mobility (Bonß/Kesselring 2001), but it seeks the transition in the transformation of mobility, rather than of time-space relations. It argues that the change in mobility, as a basic principle of modernity, lies in the separation of geographical and social mobility, and the disembedding of the latter from space-time (Bonß/Kesselring 2001: 189; Bonß/Kesselring/Weiß 2004: 261). Further, it links the transition to the breaking out of the equivalent of movement (in space) and movability, and the consequent dramatic reduction in spatial power's ability to structure the social (Bonß/Kesselring/Weiß 2004: 278). It thus draws attention to the following dualisms: geographical-social movement, geographical-social space, mobility-immobility, physical-virtual, and their spatial and temporal equivalents: near-far, here-there, absent-present, now-then. The thesis of the dissolution of such dualisms is the core of postmodern reflection (Shields 1992). Focusing exclusively on a transformation of mobility, however, does not sufficiently support the thesis of the dissolution of these dualisms: paradoxically, it supports their understanding as dichotomies, rather than two sides of a coin.

In line with this theory, the change from the first to the second modernity should be accompanied by dissonances between individual practices in space, public use and discourse on space, and scientific interpretation. The dissonance may be driven by processes within any of these dimensions, or in all three simultaneously. This is an important point, especially in relation to space: the impulse of the shift towards reflexive modernization cannot be conceptualized as the »reflective« reaction of social science, in the form of the deconstruction of a dominant logic of spatialization, as Adam claims in relation to time (Adam 2003: 60). Methodological »isms« of social sciences (nationalism, territorialism, and temporalism, which analyze societies only within the container categories of nation, territory, and history), and their recent deconstruction, are (only) part of this broader change. According to the theory of reflexive modernization, the dissonances between the categories lead to de-naturalization of the first modern space, as a result of which space, as a premise of the first modernity, is altered and takes its new, second modern form. This involves both an institutional and an individual response. It is to be expected that this change will be accompanied by conflicts, attempts to restore the old notions, or smooth adaptation to new conditions. Institutional and individual responses may differ. The emerging patterns of social structuration can only be recognized by empirical research.

3.2. Cosmopolitan sociology of spatial relations

The theory of reflexive modernization postulates methodological change. Empirical research should break with the territorial social ontology of national perspective (Beck 2004b: 41). In this perspective, individuals are ascribed to particular territorially defined units, for example, nation-states. In this approach, the mobility of individuals is thus an unwished for disruption of the »either-or« principle (Beck 1997b), and is treated as a pathology (comp. Malkki 1997). Methodological nationalism presumes that societies are territorially bound, and closes them within state-constructed and state-controlled borders. This supposition leads to such dualisms as local-global, local-national, national-global, national-international. It also leads to (mis)understanding of culture and cultural plurality. When culture is implicitly mapped on to a territory, cultural plurality may suggest incorrect alternatives: universal uniformity or incommensurability of perspectives (Beck 2004b: 47). A national perspective is also an essentialist perspective: it projects nation-state borders on to culture, society, history, and space, and enforces the »either-or« alternative. This perspective cannot cope with the requirements of times of flows and mobility (Urry 2000a; 2003; Beck 2004b: 45).

A cosmopolitan perspective has been postulated as an alternative starting point for researching contemporary societies (Beck 2002a; 2004a; 2004b: 117). This perspective presumes the necessary openness. It emerges from the assumption that territorial mapping of societies and their spatial exclusion is a construct. Temporal and spatial dimensions are necessary elements of the analysis of contemporary societies, and their mutual relations depend on contemporary forms of social relationships (Beck 2004b: 120). However, most of the theoretical and empirical studies fail to conceptualize these new forms of relationships, because they habitually fall into the old schemes, either by applying the old »container« terms, or by focusing on nation-state societies (Urry 2003: 39ff).

Urry argues that the container-categories of societies, understood as nation-state societies, must be abandoned. They have lost their relevance, and are no longer appropriate tools to research contemporary processes of sociation: »those diverse mobilities are materially reconstructing the »social as society« into the »social as mobility« (Urry 2000a: 2). Mobility and various other flows should be at the center of the new sociology (Beck 2004b: 118, 124), because »they criss-cross societal borders in strikingly new temporal-spatial patterns« (Urry 2000a: 2). A sociology that focuses on mobility is able to separate itself from the old categories, and to realize the postulate of methodological cosmopolitanism.

A sociology that goes beyond methodological nationalism should focus also on the networks (patterned relationships of heterogeneous bits) that span the world. Focus on mobility should thus not exclude material objects: micro and macro structures are constituted of the same materials and relations, and the constructed reality is thus constantly changing. For this point, Urry draws on Actor-Network Theory (ANT). The ANT (based on its own empirical research) differentiates between society and scientific or technical contents (Latour 1991: 106). It argues that the »stuff of the social« is not only human: it is always composed of people, machines, animals, texts, money, architectures, and any other materials (Law 1992: 381). Urry employs this approach, says that »there is nothing like society« (Urry 2000a), and also introduces the notion of complexity, which »can illuminate inhuman, mobile intersecting hybrids« (Urry 2000b). Urry's mobile sociology also assumes that the macro-structure of society consists of the same stuff as the micro-structure (Latour 1991: 118). This means that the socio-technical world does not have a fixed, unchanging scale. The focus on mobilities, often used by the ANT (comp. Law 1986, 2000b) also frees the observer (sociologist) from the unnecessary fixed dimensions of macro or micro structures. Taking mobility as the starting point of analysis, it is possible to document change at the level of both an individual and a nation-state, and thus abandon the container approach of methodological nationalism.

In this approach, it is possible to prove how a single individual's movement in space can lead to a change in the policy of a nation-state, and thus to integrate the studies on mobility that focus on individuals and macro structures. As Urry notes, there occur billions of individuals' local actions. However, these local actions do not remain merely local, because they are captured, represented, marketed, circulated, and generalized elsewhere. »They are carried along the scapes and flows of the emerging global world, transporting ideas, people, images, monies and technologies to potentially everywhere« (Urry 2000b: 197).[20] This means that what happens locally matters globally. However, this is not a planned action but rather an uncontrolled side effect. »Mobile sociology« thus breaks with the vision of a society as a uniform and rigid surface. Structures can also be mobile. The »reality« is not a final, definite state demanding no further effort. Processes take place simultaneously and maintain and transform »reality« (Latour 1991: 118). Mobile sociology thus focuses on »local« practices to research »global« complexities.

In relation to space, this methodological shift has already taken place. The following section describes in detail the nature of this change, and how it opens up a perspective for the empirical research. In the last century, the social sciences moved away from considering space, and towards the analysis of processes of spatialization, which cannot be separated from socialization. Thus, they de facto abandoned the container perspective, and acknowledged the multiplicity of space. They also increasingly focused on mobility, and on the processes of construction of borders and boundaries. Recognition of borders, and the possibility of their renegotiation, is possible only when space is comprehended as relational. Postulated by the theory of reflexive modernization, a »future« agenda has already become everyday practice in current reflection on space.

3.2.1. From space to spatialities

In recent decades, the so-called »spatial turn« has occurred in social sciences. Space has become an explicit topic in the analysis of societies. Once again, the turn towards space and its importance for social relations reflected the tensions between the absolute and relative comprehension of space. Geography has been criticized (and self-criticized) for supporting analysis based on the container view of space, and treating it as a simple, absolute matrix, a surface on which social relations happen to constitute certain positioning. Attention was drawn to the relational understandings

---

20 The parallels to the Actor-Network-Theory should not be overlooked (comp. especially Law 2000a on the large scale consequences of the small scale explosion of an aeroengine Olympus 22R).

of space, which has origins in phenomenology, especially the work of Whitehead, Husserl, Merleau-Ponty, and Heidegger.

In his philosophical reflection, Whitehead (1861-1947) postulated to focus on human experience in space. He criticized philosophers who abstracted space from concrete experience. He noticed that seventeenth-century reflection on space denied full status to the concrete qualities of places, such as their color, texture, luminosity, etc. For Whitehead, an implaced body perceives space. The spatio-temporal world is mirrored within bodily life (Casey 1998: 213).

Husserl (1859-1938) was struck by what he termed »the privileged position« of the human body. In his first essays, Husserl used the terms place and position interchangeably, and regarded space as something strictly objective. The body is stationary in relation to itself, while everything else is in a position in relation to it. To connect the lived-body and objective space, he used terms such as visual space or tactile space, but he did not escape the dualism abstract space-concrete bodily experience.[21] In his later texts, Husserl linked movement, lived-body, and lived-space: through the experience of moving (walking), an »I« builds up a coherent core-world out of the fragmentary appearances that, taken in isolated groupings, would be merely kaleidoscopic. The core-world contains both the near-sphere of familiar and accessible appearances and the far-sphere of unfamiliar and unknown things (Casey 1998: 223-225).

Merleau-Ponty too (1908-1961) saw space as produced by movement. The lived-body is the origin of »spatializing«, and of »spatialized« space (the space of geometry). If the lived-body is the subject and source of space, then place is not somewhere I might come to, but it is rather an indefinite horizon of my possible action. In other words, place is not something experienced but something that can potentially be experienced. Such lived places are familiar settings, our anchorage in the world. They are *loci* of intimacy and particularity, settled on permeable boundaries and open orientations (Casey 1998: 233). This does not mean that wherever there is no body, there is no place. As long as we are able to imagine someone's body inhabiting it, there is a place. One needs to call on a virtual body, which is capable of inhabiting even the most remote and seemingly vacuous place. Without such a corporeal or virtual presence, there exists only a site.

---

21 For a very detailed analysis of Husserl's constitution of space, see Claesges 1963.

Heidegger comes to the issues of place from a different angle, focusing not on the body, but on time and being. Being-in is about dwelling or residing. The world emerges in Being; meaning in coming across, being familiar with, inhabiting (Michalski 1978: 63-72). These expressions bear on place, especially on home-place, and conjure up a dense and suggestive sense of implacement as in-dwelling. Existential spatiality is the distracted involvement in the affairs of the everyday world. Heidegger concentrates on the practicality of place, its familiar infrastructure as experienced by those who spend their workaday lives there. Place is thus pragmatic, the realm of worked-on-things (Casey 1998: 246). It is always something constituted by our intervention.

In *The Constitution of Society* (1984), Giddens relates it explicitly to the concepts of Heidegger and Hägerstrand, and the concepts of time geography and regionalization, thus bringing space back into social science, and returning to the tradition of Georg Simmel. Simmel was the first sociologist to examine the topic of space in modernity (Allen 2000: 55), at a time when any theory of space was suspected of promoting the political geography of expansion, and equalizing the state with territory and nation (Konau 1977: 77, 89).

The importance of the »spatial turn« does not lie, however, in considering space and its meaning for social relations. Rather, the »spatial turn« brought a shift in the understanding of space. The early twentieth century was concerned with space and the basis of social relations, as I subsequently show in discussing Simmel's sociology of space. However, it focused on one single space and its experience by individuals. The late twentieth century, in contrast, was concerned with multiple spaces, and with their becoming, in diverse social processes.

For Simmel, who understood society as the sum of social interactions (immediate or at a distance), space was clearly an integral (though relatively small) part of his work (Kuhn 1994: 33). [22] According to him, modern times are experienced largely through changing relations of proximity and

---

22 For example, Simmel made a distinction between natural, physical, infinite spaces and a space constructed through social interaction. This distinction is similar to some elements of the phenomenological perspective on space. However, when Simmel wrote his essays, the idea of space as a social construct was relatively new and innovative. The contemporary social sciences have taken the same path and moved away from a sense of space as empty container of social action towards space as a socially produced set of manifolds. It is a shift from the Kantian perspective on space as an absolute category towards space as process and in process (comp. Crang/Thrift 2000).

distance (Shields 1992; Allen 2000: 55). Therefore, the key figure in his works is played by »the Stranger«: the person who comes today and stays tomorrow, disturbs the status quo, breaches the walls of locality, and brings the places of everyday life into contact with the indefinable, seemingly limitless spaces beyond.[23] In doing so, the stranger violates the sanctity of the spatial oppositions of near and far, inside and outside, proximate and distant. In everyday life, the world is given as presence and as what is present. However, strangeness means that he, who is far, is actually near: he is known to exist but in the absence; he does not belong to the group yet imports qualities into it, and the relations to and with the stranger produce a pattern of coordination and consistent interaction (Simmel 1908: 509).[24] The stranger is a potential wanderer: he is quite free of coming and going. At the same time, he unifies two opposite conceptions: fixation and liberation from any given point (Simmel 1908: 509).

A wanderer who »constructs the way« between different spatially separated places, through movement back and forth, plays an important role in human spatiality: he connects what was separated, or disconnects what was linked. In this process, which Simmel describes as bridging, he overcomes spatial separation and gains power over space. Bridging points to how space is socially constructed: without a bridge, two river banks would only be next to each other: connecting them, with the help of a bridge, makes it apparent that without this bridge the banks would be separated, as only what is separated can be (re)connected (Simmel 1909). Similarly, the metaphor of door explains the human power to disconnect what spatially belongs together, thus to divide the continuum of space into units. The inside, the outside, the belonging, and the excluded are social constructs marked symbolically, with the help of the material door. The fact that they can open and close gives an additional feeling of power over

---

23 The stranger is more than an individual: a particular type, a non-common element (Simmel 1908: 510).

24 The special role of the stranger can be recognized in the study by Albrow (1997), which shows how a community is shaped by those who are spatially absent. Instead of passing from one presence to another in spatial proximity, its members engage in remote events. In this community, members maintain relationships to many other places and people, and therefore disturb the natural relations of temporal and spatial presence and absence. In the local community researched by Albrow, the stranger is always present. (see also Berger 1995 on the role of communication in shaping human practices over large distances)

space. It belongs to a human being to set the boundary and to re-connect with what is behind the door (Simmel 1909).

The metaphors of door, wanderer, and bridges point to the issue of boundaries between here and there. The constitution of borders and the ordering of space into territorial units was a live issue at the time of expansion by imperial states, and the emergence of new nation-states (first in South America and later in Europe, from Italy to Germany and finally Serbia, Romania, and Bulgaria). Simmel tried to show that there are no absolute borders. Rather, every boundary is in the processes of interaction and relations of power between social groups and individuals. The border is not a spatial fact of sociological consequences, but a sociological fact that has a spatial form (Simmel 1958: 467). Its territorial existence and clear known borders make it possible for a society to establish its unity, and the opposite: any functional relation of every element achieves spatial manifestation within inclusive borders (Simmel 1958: 465). Simmel emphasizes the extent to which the concept of a boundary is important in all relations between people. The social boundary signifies unique interaction, in that each element affects the other, insofar as it sets a boundary, but without wishing to extend its effects to the other element (Simmel 1983[1903]: 226).[25] Most major sets of social relationships flow within the territorial boundaries of a society (Billig 1995). The territorially marked boundary of a social group aids it: spatial difference over time changes territory into tradition, and society into unity (Bhabha 2000: 222). Nation-states, in particular, made use of territorial differentiation and the exclusion of the »other«. A strong relation to a particular territory made it durable and immutable.

Simmel's very complex theory of space relates to two main experiences of his period: increased mobility and the emergence of new nation-states,

---

25 Simmel does not restrict the relation between space and social organization to territorial exclusion. He illustrated the complicated nature of this relation with examples of a state, a town, and the Church (Simmel 1983|1903|: 223). This relation is especially clear in the example of a medieval guild. A guild as an organization of members of any single craft was strongly embedded territorially: at any one place there could exist only one single guild of any particular occupational group (for example a guild of any violin makers who live in a city). However, guild as a form of organization is not territorially bound: at any one place (for example, in a city), many guilds of different craftsmen can co-exist. This illustrates the tendency to fill out space not quantitatively, but functionally. These spatial relations, from absolute territorial embeddedness (exclusion) to absolute separation from space (disembeddedness), influence the forms of interaction of different social forms (Kuhn 1994: 35).

and the consolidation and domination of old nation-states in the political arena. In the metaphors of a stranger, a wanderer, door, and bridges, Simmel incorporated the individual, community, and group experience related to physical mobility: the possibility of spanning communities and relationships over large distances, the impossibility of setting clear-cut boundaries between »us« and »them«; but also the possibility of constructing these as an expression of power over the »other«, and thus the ability to spatially include or exclude different or unfamiliar elements. At the level of institutions, he used the concept of the general qualities of space to demonstrate how nation-states and other organizations use space for their own purposes. However, the principles governing the relationships of such organizations are more general: they do not reduce to organizations, and they can be found in every aspect of human sociation: for example, in the processes of production and exchange. Fixation of social forms in space, exclusiveness, and bordering of them in space, as well as the complexity of proximity and remoteness relationships, constitute the experience of space and spatial order as fragmented and separated (Foucault 1994): as such, celebrated yet in constant flux, due to the steady presence of the Stranger, and bridging relationships with the distant. This questions the cognitive mapping of our life-world, and suggests the erasure of a set of crucial oppositions structuring space: cultural conceptions, social constructions, and practices. Modernity appeared as a distinctive mode of experiencing social and spatial reality that involved seeing society and the social relations within it as temporally transitory and spatially filling. This implies that traditional, permanent structures were absent from human experience.

Simmel pointed to three components of importance in the modern spatial order: first, presence and absence. The complex nature of proximity and distance relations points to the problems of analyzing social relationships in categories of units of space: distance and size. Space matters, insofar as it allows matter to be in a position in a certain relation, i.e., the relation of distance. However, the social order of things goes beyond a simple spatial material determinism: emotional proximity can be achieved despite physical distance. Nonetheless, a certain social labor is necessary to overcome physical distance or proximity. There is thus a certain dualism in the relations of proximity and distance, and this dualism is relevant in each relationship. It is not the qualities of social objects that decide solely on the relationship, but rather the opposite: their relationship is mediated by space. In turn, space is mediated by relationships.[26]

The second element is the differentiation (contrast) that pervades regional oppositions, and status distinction by geographical division. The nature of a formation, an internal character of it, decides whether it can share a position with another formation of the same character at the same location. In this case, both must have no internal necessary relation to space.[27] In investigating the relation of a social formation to space, it is necessary to research its internal character and its functions. Social formations can exclude space and set borders. In this way, they cluster within these borders elements that, given their characteristics, would otherwise not belong together. Another possibility of order in space occurs when elements are connected by a particular relation and remain together, either in physical proximity, or with the help of abstract thinking, despite physical distance. This is a principle of network building.

The third element is the dualism of inclusion and exclusion (inside and outside) that characterizes the foundational notions of the individual, the community, the nation-state, and belonging. These dualisms are the fundamental themes in the modern social construction of the world.

---

26 Though space is constituted by social relationships, it cannot be reduced to them. Nor can it be reduced to the material constituents. In everyday life, we tend to separate and recombine space and substance in our thinking (Sayer 1985: 60). As Sack notes, we repeatedly abstract form from content and content from form. We cannot have an independent science of space, as space is only an abstraction. However, it is common to speak of the effects or uses of space, as if it were a thing existing independently of objects. Our language uses separate spatial, temporal, and process categories to refer to what are actually inseparable aspects. This rarely causes problems in everyday life, but it can lead to confusion in providing theoretical explanations (Sack 1980, in Sayer 1985: 52).

27 It is possible to extend by distinguishing necessary (internal) and contingent (external) relations. The nature of the relata in necessary relation depends on the relation. Asymmetric internal relations can be distinguished, in which one object in a relation can exist without the other, but not vice versa. An example is money and the banking system. In contingent relations, relata is independent of the relation. It is neither necessary nor impossible that, for example, a chair and a table stand in any particular relation. In contingent relations, it may nevertheless be possible for one object to affect the other, but the nature of each object does not necessarily depend on its standing in such a relation. There are also necessary conditions for the existence and reproduction of objects and relations. For example, it is contingent where industrial capital is located, and it can involve itself in the production of an enormous variety of commodities, but if it happens (contingently) to be involved in producing a fixed resource such as coal (conditional statement), then obviously its location is constrained (Sayer 1985: 50).

Shields notices that these spatial qualities operate together: they constitute constellations that are not unified, clear-cut, and universal orders (Shields 1992: 184). The catalogue of the modern dualisms can be completed to include abstract-relative; space-place; proximity-distance (presence-absence); inclusion-exclusion; and embedded-disembedded.

Most important, Simmel drew attention to complexity, to multiple possibilities, to how this socio-spatial order can appear at multiple layers: as excluded spatial units of territorial nation-states, networks of relationships between families and friends at a distance, or at the level of communities that must include the stranger in their self-definition. He also pointed to the possibility of overcoming these dichotomies, and their inclusion into a much more complex spatial order.

Contemporary social science undertook to examine the complexity of spatial relations. In contrast to the works of the first modernists, it focused not on a single space and its meaning for social structuring, but on how space is being (re)produced in social interaction. Thus, it combined the ideas of relational space, derived from phenomenology, and at the same time drew on the most recent achievements in other disciplines, mostly physics, to include the ideas of complexity and indeterminacy (Thrift 1999; Urry 2003, 2004; Massey 2005: 126ff).[28]

Common to current reflection on space is the conviction that place itself is not a fixed thing. Contemporary authors try to find place at work, part of something ongoing and dynamic, and an ingredient in something else. If Simmel pointed to the possibilities of multiple spatial forms of different social formations, and thus to the complexity of existing spatial relations, contemporary authors rather focus on space in construction, including the temporal dimension of spatial relations. Some track place in history, for example Foucault and Braudel; in the natural world, Berry, Snyder; in the political realm, Nancy, Lefebvre; in gender relations and sexual difference, Irigaray; in the production of poetic imagination, Bachelard, Otto; in the geographic experience of reality, Foucault, Tuan, Soja, Relph, Entrekin; in the sociology of polis and the city, Benjamin, Arendt, Walter; in nomadism, Deleuze and Guattari; in architecture, Derrida, Eisenman, Tschumi; in religion, Irigaray, Nancy (Casey 1998:

---

28 At the same time, many authors implicitly (especially those in the post-modern movement) or explicitly (globalists) do deal with the concerns so central to the works of the first modernists: the duality of proximity and distance, presence and absence, etc.

287).[29] All these different trails suggest that there is no single place, no ideal space.

With the recognition that space does not have to be absolute, fixed, and motionless, there came the idea of the multiplicity of spaces. Space can be constructed, and, if so, it can be produced and reproduced in multiple ways. For example, Castells claims that there exist different types of spaces, one of flows and the other of places, each having different characteristics, features, and consequences (Castells 2001). Such different spaces were also noted by Law, who speaks about the space of networks, the space of regions, and fluid space (Mol/Law 1994). Some authors have included mobility, in various ways, in their conceptualizations of space: as medium of simultaneity and juxtaposition, and of near and far (Foucault); as the opposite of embeddedness (Augé 1994); as a constituent part of places (Hetherington 1997); as the underlying quality of space (Thrift 2004); and as the attribute of space (Deleuze/Guattari 1976; Mol/Law 1994).

Hetherington, for example, assumes that place is constituted through an ongoing and recursive process that has three parts: the placing of materials within a network, arranging those placings, and naming those arrangements. Places are thus the effects of the processes of placing, ordering, and naming (Hetherington 1997: 192). Hetherington's departure point is the Actor–Network Theory (comp. Callon 1980; Latour 1990, Law 1992; 1997) and the belief that human agency is a product of heterogeneous material networks. He argues against treating places as constructed entirely by human intervention. He criticizes the common geographical approaches, deriving from phenomenology, that led to the belief that spaces became remembered landscapes, and that those landscapes were the substance of place (Hetherington 1997: 184). He proposed looking at places from the point of view of their materialities: »let the objects speak of places«. He does not neglect subjective experiences and memories of space, but sees them rather as folded into the material world, and imbricated in the agency of the other. Places are always unfinished, deferred, and lacking a unity or order, such as the one established by representation. They make no sense themselves; rather they establish a system of differences that requires an ordering. They become

---

29 Another distinction between authors and works can be made on the basis of their treatment of space as relative or abstract (with all the shorcomings of this division, as shown in the previous sections), as material or social, as symbolic or as a material consumer good, etc. (For further distinction and overview, see Löw 2001.)

agents themselves and generate the semiotic representations. Places are always reconfigured by networks (Hetherington 1997: 188). Referring to Foucault, Hetherington imagines place as a ship – mobile within networks of human and material agents. Place is about relationships of heterogeneous materials, about an ordering effect of agents. Such a mobile place can cross the boundaries of regions (Mol/Law 1994). Places can become detached and re-attached through mobile arrangements constituted by human and non-human agents. Places are assembled through immutable mobiles, for example, maps, photographs, paintings, televised images, textual descriptions, poems etc. They generate representation of a place, and the difference between one place and the next (Hetherington 1997: 189).

A new kind of space is arising, claims Thrift (2004). Space is represented as fluid force that has no beginning or end, and that generates new cultural conventions, techniques, forms, genres, concepts, and even senses. This space is in the background of other space(s). Production of this space is related to a massive increase in computing power, and new ways of dealing with the previously unknown and uncertain. In return, this space produces a new sense of space as folded and animate, one that assumes a moving point of view.

The world that arises from this imagination is a layered one: there are humans whose activities depend upon an imputed background, the content of which is rarely questioned. It is the surface on which life floats. This background existed in a »natural order«, by which Thrift means physical, sensual order. Yet over time, this background was filled in with artificial components, so that much of the background of life is »second nature«. This second nature is constituted through such object frames as cables, wireless signals, screens, software, and so on. This is the other structure of action, the invisible one, a new kinetic surface to the world, which demands certain kinds of engagement, which is both geophysical and phenomenological.

At the basis of the production of a new space lies not only a simple increase in the number of diverse types of technical equipment, but also developments of a qualitatively different nature. The measurability of time and space, models based on loops (a repeating set number of steps), the new sense of simultaneity, and endless calculations and recalculations are continually building a new space. They lead to shifts in understanding of the environment. Here Thrift reckons these encounters of space, which see space as relative, meaning folded, animated, and in perpetual movement, like a river (Carter 1992). The new background space is made out of fabric that is open-ended rather than enclosing, and mobile and adjustable. Yet this is not the only background space that underlines human activity. There is also a »carefully constructed absolute space that begets this relative space« (Thrift 2004: 13).

The most important point is that not only do multiple spaces exist simultaneously, but each of them influences our human experience, sensuality, and action in different ways. Thrift does not aim at describing space itself but rather at understanding the changing nature of contemporary western societies (Thrift 1996: 266). We now live in an almost/not quite world – a world of almost/not quite subjects, almost/not quite selves, and almost/not quite spaces and times. It is a predominantly mobile world in which machines and humans cannot be clearly distinguished from one another. Here Thrift does not really mean a hybrid human, but rather a hybrid agency, in the sense of Actor-Network-Theory. In such a world, what is place becomes problematic. Thrift answers that place is compromised – permanently in a state of enunciation, between addresses, always deferred (Thrift 1996: 291). Places are stages of intensity, traces of movement, speed, and circulation. In such places, there is no stability. No configuration of time-space can be seen as bounded. These are almost-places. These are not bounded places. Unfortunately, Thrift does not elaborate on this, and tends rather to adopt other authors' understanding of places.

Law also acknowledges the multiplicity of space. »The social does not exist as a single spatial type. Rather, it performs as several kinds of space in which different operations take place« (Mol/Law 1994: 643). There are regions and there are networks, and there is a third type of space, a fluid space. Three different topologies thus co-exist. The first, the one which is very familiar to social science, is the topology of regions, in which objects are clustered together and boundaries are drawn around each cluster. [30] When a region is defined, the differences inside it are suppressed, minimized, and marginalized. However, such regions could not be drawn

---

30 Shields talks about a spatial form of differentiation due to which zones are separated in order to establish the identity of one space: in this way, a mosaic is being created. Zones remain in a permanent juxtaposition. All not-belonging elements are foreign in the zone, and their sudden presence could 'pollute' the ordered differentiation of zones (Shields 1992: 185).

and differentiated without the existence of networks. There is thus also a space of networks, in which distance is a function of the relations between the elements, and difference is a matter of relational variety. A network is a series of elements with well-defined relations between them. In a network space, proximity is not metric. Proximity has, instead, to do with the identity of the pattern. Places with a similar set of elements and similar relations between them are close to one another, and those with different elements or relations are far apart. Both spaces have their limitations. Sometimes neither boundaries nor relations mark the difference between one place and another. Instead, boundaries sometimes come and go, allow leakage, or disappear, while relations transform themselves without fracture. Social space is then fluid. In such cases, place matters. Place is empowered, it has a power to influence the social. A region starts to flatten out and a network dissolves. In this fluid space, a mobile moves and is mutable (Mol/Law 1994: 655). It varies from place to place, and its elements change depending on location. Fluid spaces are defined by liquid continuity. Another type is fire space, which is constituted by discontinuity, sudden »eruptive« changes, and the interplay of presence and absence (Mol/Law 2000). All four topologies co-exist. It may happen that when one element moves to a place it alters there, and shifts from a network to a fluid space. Therefore nothing in this complex spatial order is fixed. It may be different elsewhere. The place matters much more than ever. It has the power to change elements and shift them from one topology to another, from one order to another.

3.2.2. Space in empirical inquiry

These recent conceptualizations of space as being in construction, in becoming, in (re)production, relative, multiple and multi-layered, and an ingredient in other processes, have made possible empirical research on spatial relations. Despite the »spatial turn« in social sciences, most recent authors feel obliged to explain their interest in space (e.g., Giddens 1984; 1997, Urry 2000). As Martina Löw writes, »sociology needs the term space for it helps to describe the organization of co-existence« (Löw 2001: 12, author's translation). Space, according to Löw, is, on the one hand, a tool to describe the structures of behavior and action on the micro level and, on the other hand, it is useful to comprehend relations between technical networks and urban structures and the living conditions that are shaped by them.

Much has been written on space in human geography, and a virtual consensus as to the concepts about space has emerged. [31] Traditional geography mostly reproduces the distinction between absolutist and relativist views on space (Löw 2001). Sociology adds to this distinction its own dialectic of structure and action (Kuhn 1994). Often, the newest research is said to employ a relative understanding of space. Much of social theory, however, implicitly relies on absolute concepts of space.

The absolute view is implicit in common sense, but is incoherent because what is empty is nothing, and what is nothing cannot be (Sayer 1985, after Blaut 1961); and because it is implied that nothingness is capable of having an effect – as when one speaks of the »friction of distance« or the »effect of space«. Therefore social research, which assumes an absolute view on space, does not in fact research either the space or the spatial relations of the social actors. Empty, infinite space cannot be researched at all, and thus absolute space cannot be a subject of social research. [32] As we proved by tracing philosophical reflection, the discussion on the nature of space was closely related to theology or cosmology: infinite space arose from discussion of the infinity of the Creator. It operates at a level beyond the borders of sociological inquiry.

On the other hand, the advocates of the relative concept fail to see that while objects constitute space, it is not reducible to them. A simple example (Sayer 1985, after Harré 1970) demonstrates this point: if we take a set of letters R O W D, then the spatial relations between W and O and R and D are exactly equivalent. We can swap O and W, and this would not change this spatial relation of »between-ness« or distance. However, depending on what kind of things the letters represent, the move might

---

31 The newer works added to it a distinction between real and imagined space (comp. Duncan (ed.) 1996). For the discussion in geography, compare Hard 1970; Bartles 1974; Bartels/Hard 1975; Eisel 1980; Sack 1980; Smith 1984; Agnew/Duncan 1989; Entrikin 1991; Pohl 1993; Weichhart 1993; Werlen 1993; Klüter 1994; Blotevogel 1995; for the new »relative« concepts of space (space in construction) in human geography compare Soja 1989; 1995; Harvey 1990; 1996; Lefebvre 1991; Gregory 1994; Thrift 1996; Massey et al. 1999; for an overview compare Gregory/Johnston (eds.) 2000, especially pp. 767-772.

32 This recognition is however not generally accepted. For example, Läpple claims that absolute container space is »a thing for its own«, and as a substantive object can be researched similarly to the material objects that it contains (Läpple 1991: 36). Werlen (1993: 245f) presents similar views. Compare also Pott (2002: 73f).

activate or block certain casual mechanisms possessed by these objects. Depending on the nature of the constituents, their spatial relations may make a crucial difference. For example, in the case of the spatial relations between the four walls that define a room, significant differences exist temporally as to whether the four walls create a room in a home, or enclose a cell in a prison. Space makes a difference, in terms of the particular causal powers and liabilities constituting it (Sayer 1985: 52). Space can thus exist only in and through objects. However, space is also independent of the particular types of objects present.[33]

The question whether space can be interesting to social science can be reversed: Is »a spatial social science« possible? The answer depends on the kind of research involved – in particular whether it is abstract or concrete (Sayer 1985: 53). Abstract research is concerned with structures – sets of internally or necessarily related objects or practices – and with the causal powers and liabilities necessarily possessed by objects in virtue of their nature. As this is contingent upon whether and how these are exercised, concrete empirical research is needed to determine the actual effects of the causal powers.

Abstract social theory need only consider space insofar as the necessary properties of objects are involved. It must be acknowledged that all matter possesses a spatial extension, and that processes do not take place on the head of a pin, and that no two objects may occupy the same place at the same time.[34] This says little about actual spatial forms. Even where objects necessarily have certain spatial forms – as in the linearity of many types of communication media – this still leaves room for enormous contingent variety, and the spatial form of the conditions in which such objects exist. For example, settlement patterns are also contingent. Hence, while it is important for abstract theory to be aware of the existence of space, the

---

33 Indeed, when we talk about »spatial relations« we abstract and objectify space, spatial relations, and matter at the same time. We abstract form from content. Abstractions involve concepts designed to refer to particular one-sided aspects of objects (Sayer 1984: 80). Yet objects are many-sided, and constitutive elements isolated by abstractions need to be synthesized. Thus space is often isolated from matter and relations and is therefore considered to be abstract itself, existing independently of matter, as a container of social relations. Making abstractions is, however helpful in distinguishing relations of different types. Abstractions should identify the incidental and essential characteristics of concrete objects, but not lump together divisible and heterogeneous ones.

34 The perfect example of such an acknowledgement of space and time can be found in Giddens' The Constitution of Societies (1984) – especially Chapter 3: Time, Space and Regionalization.

claims that can be made about it are inevitably rather indifferent ones. Abstract theory, if used to try and explain events directly, without any need for empirical research (thus being a pseudo-concrete research), often makes the mistake of reducing the concrete to the abstract (Sayer 1984: 217). Such research cannot make any statements on space and spatial forms. Some concepts, for example, distanciation (Giddens), have a useful theoretical role, but cannot be expected to say much about concrete spatial forms.

The actual nature of the difference that space makes can be specified only by empirical research on concrete instances. Empirical sociology cannot ignore space. It needs it as a basic term to describe the organization or order of co-existence. For example, micro-sociology requires »space« to name any construction that arises from the connectedness of diverse goods and people, and actions: macro-sociology can use the term »space« to describe relational linkages resulting from technology and other structures that determine living conditions (Löw 2001: 12).

However, empirical research on contemporary concrete spatial relations must fulfill certain requirements. It should not reproduce the dualisms absolute-relative, place-space, empty-essential, and social-geographical. It should not treat space as a simple physical matrix of movement, nor reproduce the scale division of local-regional-national-global, which is not a spatial but a socio-political, if not a methodological, division. It should not amalgamate the socio-organizational and political units of communities (villages, cities, nation-states) with their territorial location. It should look at borders as social constructs and not physical reality. It should abandon the container-view on space, which assumes that movement takes place only between defined units of space (comp. Mackensen 1975).

3.2.3. Space in construction – from mobility to spatial relations

Understanding space as a dynamic construction opens up the possibility of researching how the precise concrete spatial relations are being constituted. This involves changing the combinations and recombinations of the »social«, »cultural«, »economic«, and »political« in the research, to the same extent as the »spatial«. Indeed, all these categories can be distinguished only as analytical categories, and every »spatial« or »social« relationship is always socio-spatial. In this approach, space cannot be understood as a simple matrix, a surface, or a structure for practices. Elsewhere, social science has already offered a conceptualization to address exactly this problem.

With his theory of structuration, Giddens attempted to overcome the dualistic opposition between practice and structure. According to him, practice (agency) and structure are two moments of the same phenomenon (Giddens 1984: 25). He points to the mistake made by those theories and studies that consider structure as something external, objective, and material. Such a perspective means that structure is seen as a unity.[35] The same problem affects these social theories and studies, in how they relate to space: space and practices are treated as separate and contradictory categories (Löw 2001: 130). They imply that practices take place in space, understood as a material structure (usually as a constraint) for human agency.

The theorem of the duality of structure is crucial to the idea of structuration. The term structure can be understood only within the concept of social structuration (Giddens 1977: 118). Structure is virtual: it has no »objective« existence. It comes into being in practices; it is a set of rules and resources. Structure is not »external« to individuals and cannot be equated with constraint. It is always both constraining and enabling. The structural properties of social systems are both the medium and the outcome of the practices they recursively organize.

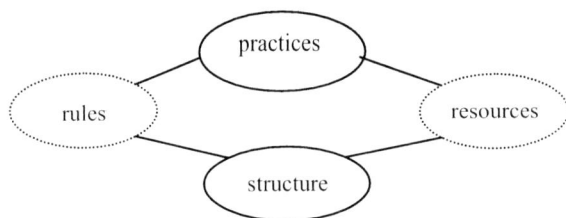

Figure 1. The theorem of the duality of structure

This does not prevent the structured properties of social systems from stretching far beyond the control of any individual actors. Nor does it exclude the possibility that an actor's own theories concerning the social system may reify those systems. The duality of structure is always the main

---

35 Giddens does not objectify structure as a »social fact« in the Durkheim tradition; rather, he situates the objectivity of structure in the unrecognized conditions and unintended consequences of human agency (Neuberger 1995: 300).

grounding of continuities in social reproduction (Giddens 1984: 26). Giddens understands social systems as reproduced practices in interaction settings (Giddens 1984: 27). Thus, structure refers to the structuring properties that make it possible for discernibly similar social practices to exist across varying spans of time and space. Structure as »virtual order« means that social systems (the orders of social relations, reproduced practices), as reproduced by social practices, do not have »structures«, but exhibit »structural properties«; it also means that structure exists only in its instantiations in such practices.

Structure (or social structure) is a set of rules and resources (Giddens 1984: 17). Rules are regarded as techniques or generalizable procedures applied in the enactment/reproduction of social practices (Giddens 1984: 21). Some rules are formulated, which means that they are codified interpretations of rules: they are given verbal expressions as canons of law, bureaucratic rules, rules of games, and so on. The discursive formulation of a rule is already an interpretation of it (Giddens 1984: 23). The awareness of social rules, expressed in practical consciousness, is the very core of the »knowledgability« of human agents – their knowledge and ability to perform actions. In the course of their daily activities, actors employ rules to negotiate routinely the situations of social life. Such knowledge provides a generalized capacity to respond and influence an indeterminate range of social circumstances.

Resources are brought together by Giddens in relation to power (Giddens 1997: 86f). Resources are of two kinds: authoritative resources, which derive from the ability of human agents to generate a change (power) in relation to other actors, and allocative resources, which stem from control of material products or of aspects of the material world (raw materials, ground, etc.).[36]

Routines play an important role in the (re)production of structure (Giddens 1997: 111). Routinization is implicated strongly in sustaining ontological security. The maintaining of habits and routines is a crucial bulwark against anxieties. Routine activities are never just carried out in an automatic way: they involve vigilance (Giddens 1991: 39). Giddens (1991: 126) argues that the familiar, the »normal«, is reassuring, and that time-space routines are of vital importance in sustaining a stable psychological existence. Time-space routines are also integral to the institutions of

---

36 For a critical assessment of Giddens' account of structure as a set of rules and resources see Thompson (1989: 62f).

society, and exist as such only through their continued reproduction. Giddens treats time-space routines as the material grounding of the recursiveness of social life (Gregory 1989: 197). Further, Giddens distinguishes between structure and structures. The latter relate to the institutional aspects of societies. Structures are sets of rules and resources that participate in the institutional networking of social systems (Giddens 1997: 240). The analysis of structures encompasses the isolation of different clusterings of transformation-mediation relations, which participate in the formation of principles regarding the organization of social totalities. An example of such a structure is private ownership: it encompasses the relations between money, capital, and profit, and labor contract. These relations characterize the change in the course of development of capitalism, and at the same time importantly influence the restructuring of the social system of capitalism (for details, see Giddens 1997: 241f).

Through the concepts of social integration (reciprocity of practices between actors in a situation of co-presence, and their continuity in, and their disjunction between, encounters – presence in time and space); and system integration (reciprocity between actors or collectives over larger spans of time and space beyond situations of co-presence – absence in time and space), Giddens paid considerable attention to questions of temporality. However, he paid little or no attention to the problem of spatiality. Structuration theory is virtually silent about the production of space (Gregory 1989: 187). Giddens (1997: 168f) argues that the continuity of everyday practices depends in large part upon routinized interactions between people who are co-present in time and space. Space in the theory of structuration is reduced to a matrix for interaction and routine behavior.

Nevertheless, the theory of structuration offers an interesting perspective on the production of space, as Martina Löw shows. She proposes to see space as constituted in the processes of spacing and synthesizing. »Space is created in the interaction between practices and structures« (Löw 2001: 158, author's translation). This means that space is constituted through the positioning of things in relation to one another, and in the process of the »confirmation« of this positioning. Both processes take place in daily routines that reproduce the spatial structure. Löw, after Giddens, makes a distinction between the structure, understood as a general set of rules and resources, and the structures, understood as functionally differentiated systems organized through institutions.

However, unlike Giddens, who treats space as an external matrix for social structures, Löw (2001: 166) understands space as one of the structures, alongside the legal, political, and economic ones. She speaks of spatial and temporal structures. Thus, as for Giddens, space for Löw is a »third dimension« which co-constitutes the »whole« social structure. Spatial and temporal structures are »external« to other social structures, and it is possible that these structures are incongruent (Löw 2001: 178).

I propose to see space as the structure. It means that space is constituted in practices. For such an understanding of space, it is superfluous to distinguish between rules and resources, and to define the latter, as Giddens does. Rather, space enables and constrains social relationships and is constituted in and through practices, including daily routines. Unlike Löw, I do not distinguish between spatial, temporal, political, and economic or legal structures, and thus spatial and social. Space is in this understanding not external to social practices but is their constitutive element. As Gregory and Urry (1985: 3) write,

»Spatial structure is now seen not merely as an arena in which social life unfolds, but rather as a medium through which social relations are produced and reproduced.«

This approach is reflected in many contemporary studies that understand space as in construction. It separates itself from the dichotomies space-matter and spatial-social relation. The research based on this approach does not reduce space to the relative positioning of elements in relation to one another.

The research must not be based on the spatial aspects of social conditions *per se*, but on those activities that constitute the socio-spatial relations. Space has to be thought of as an aspect of action, not as a container of actors and actions. The starting point should not be space or spatiality, but practices (Werlen 2004: 153).

However, the greatest challenge is to research the diversity of socio-spatial relations. »Without a multi-perspective analysis any sociological investigation of social positions and social function remains one-dimensional« (Elias 1993, quoted in Löw 2001: 218). Different perspectives can be achieved: for example, by focusing on more than one particular investigated group (Löw 2001: 219). Several authors have »searched« for space in diverse processes and practices: religion, sexual and gender relations, history, architecture, etc. However, the problem of incomparability of perspectives arises. How to compare those spaces produced by women and those spaces produced by men, in their daily practices?[37] How to compare the spaces of handicapped blind men with those of young sportsman, or those of Muslims and those of Christians, or that of a child and that of a prisoner? Considering space as structure helps to avoid spatial particularism and subjectivity: in this understanding, space is a rule and resource accessible to, and shared by, all actors, and as such is institutionalized in practices. Space as structure presumes the institutionalization of practices.

Although any practices could potentially give an account of spatial relation, mobility seems especially suitable, for several reasons. Mobility, understood as a set of practices that involves physical movement, routine behavior in different locations, adjustment to diverse conditions, and interaction with various people, offers the required multi-dimensional perspective on spatial relations.

Various other motives underlie the decision to research contemporary spatial relations on the basis of mobility practices. First, it has already been argued that mobility has the power to liquefy social structures and re-shape contemporary societies. Further, contemporary mobility practices are said to differ significantly from those in modernity, and therefore promise to escape the (first) modern concepts of space. Second, focusing on mobile individuals and their practices has other comparative advantages: when considering a certain dwelling and researching its inhabitants and their practices, only a fraction of spatial relations in this particular location may be investigated. In considering architecture or urban planning as a process of construction of space, there is a danger of reducing spatial relations to the positioning of material elements. Third, mobile individuals maintain very special relationships with diverse groups and locations: they change locations, transgress the already existing boundaries, and are steadily confronted with diverse groups constituting space. Their mobility challenges the concepts of space as container, and makes the limitations of some concepts of space apparent. Moreover, mobility means an inevitable combination of presence and absence in time-space, and thus directs attention to the forms of social structuration beyond co-presence.

These ideas dictated the choice of a sample for the empirical study. The researched individuals are characterized by extensive physical mobility.

---

37 Compare Löw 1995, Ecarius/Löw 1997 (eds).

Their practices stretch over large distances. All of the interviewees are employees of the same international organization, which made it possible to assure the unity of the context while providing a broad scope of practices in diverse places. Moreover, the choice of the sample made it possible to undertake the research within a de-nationalized context. A full description of the sample and the context can be found in the following chapter.

PART 2
MOBILITY BEYOND THE NATIONS

4. Mobile professionals and their life-projects

4.1. Structure, content and course of the empirical study

Given the general outline of the theoretical question of the research – how space is constructed in the practices of mobile individuals – and the methodological concept of it, the empirical question of the study can be narrowed only by a process of gradual investigation of mobile practices. Grounded Theory makes it possible to conduct such an investigation.

Grounded Theory offers a set of useful methods for empirically based theory building, in which the theoretical concepts are inductively derived from the investigation of a phenomenon. It can be applied effectively when not all the concepts that relate to the investigated phenomenon have already been identified and conceptually developed, and when the research question is new and open, with variables that are relevant (Strauss/Corbin 1996: 22). Our research problem is such that this research method enables us to find answers to currently unknown problems. For these reasons, Grounded Theory is the appropriate method for researching contemporary spatial relations in a way that should lead to the development of new concepts of space within methodological cosmopolitanism (Beck). The research question is in this case open, and limited to the determination of the research phenomenon; it can be narrowed down only in the course of the investigation. Depending on the primary research question, the researcher can limit and focus the area of research, and steer it in different directions, or focus on different problems. Moreover, Grounded Theory is orientated towards practices and processes (Strauss/Corbin 1996: 23).

Grounded Theory as a method requires from the researcher openness towards the empirical phenomenon, sensibility, and creativity. In its identification of the research question, and in the analysis of the empirical material, the theory should be open enough to ensure the lack of restrictions necessary for the in-depth investigation of the phenomenon.

The resulting theory is based on a systematic collection and analysis of data related to the researched phenomenon. In the course of this work, interim concepts are developed. Through constant comparison with the empirical material, they are confirmed or rejected, so that at the end of the study only those concepts that remain constitute a theory, one that fully reflects and represents the empirical object of the study. The course of the study reveals which concepts are relevant. The method forces the researcher to part from his or her presumptions, and to allow new concepts to develop (Strauss/Corbin 1996: 12). Creativity manifests itself in the researcher's ability to assess categories, ramble on with thoughts, build free connotations, ask interesting questions, and make comparisons that lead to new discoveries. The aim of research that applies Grounded Theory is thus neither a description of the phenomenon, nor the verification of a theory, but the development of a theory.

The first step of the study was to determine the general research interest in mobility and spatial relations. This interest, as mentioned in the Introduction, was primarily induced by personal experiences and through interaction with highly mobile individuals. Following Grounded Theory, the theoretical framework of the research was determined only in the course of the research (Strauss/Corbin 1996: 32). The review of the professional literature served, first, to increase the level of theoretical sensibility. The applied principle of openness required suspending the theoretical knowledge gained prior to the research (Hoffmann-Riem 1980: 343). Partly structured, problem-centered, in-depth interviews (Witzel 1982: 66f; 1985: 230f; 2000; Hopf 1995: 177f; Bohnsack 2000: 107f), and an accompanying short questionnaire, were used as the tools of data collection.

The problem-centered interview (PCI) is a theory-generating method that tries to neutralize the alleged contradiction between being directed by theory and being open-minded, to enable the interplay of inductive and deductive thinking to contribute to increasing knowledge. The aim is to gather objective evidence on human behavior, as well as on subjective perceptions and ways of processing social reality (Witzel 2000: 1). Methodologically, the concept of a PCI borrows from the theory-generating procedure of Grounded Theory, and helps to avoid the naïve inductive position of »sociological naturalism« (Witzel 2000: 2). Knowledge is generated by PCI during the course of the interview, and in the analysis phase. Knowledge that is already given is integrated into the PCI, in the general design of the questions, and in any dialog there may be between interviewee and interviewer. At the same time, the principle of openness is realized through flexible design, and questions that prompt the interviewees' narration. Theoretical knowledge is generated in the analysis, and subsequently confirmed or rejected on the basis of the subsequent interviews.

PCIs constituted the main part of the collection of data. Complementary methods included the short standardized questionnaire and the analysis of documents. The questionnaire consisted of 25 questions organized in four parts: general data (age, sex, citizenship, place of birth); education and job (occupation, qualifications, position in the job, education level of the interviewee, and his/her parents), household (place, type, and changes of residence, marital status, spouse's educational level and occupation and employment, children – age, child care), travel, and technology (use of technical items at home, office, and while traveling).

The complementary analysis, mainly of publicly accessible documents from the IO, was intended to obtain better understanding of the International Organization and its networks. The analysis of web resources concerning organizations and individuals, from the destination countries of the IO's operations, provided information on the judgment of the IO's activities, and its attitudes towards its employees. In a few cases, additional literature on the destination countries facilitated better understanding of the problems related to traveling, which the interviewees had outlined during the interviews.

The first interview was conducted in December 2002. All other interviews were conducted between February 2003 and September 2004. This relatively large time span was dictated by the periods of data analysis, reflection, and literature review. The second »interview period« encompassed two months (four interviews), and was followed by a three-months review of the literature. The third »interview period« was from June to October 2003, and was followed by a three-months reflection phase. The next two interviews (Numbers 10 and 11) took place in January 2004. Thereafter, until September 2004, the results were compiled. The last two interviews were used to answer the last remaining, very detailed, and specific questions. They were conducted at a time when most of the results had already been compiled.

The first version of the interview focused primarily on the practices of the individuals. It was intended to collect as much general information on the context of their mobility as possible. The interview questions were divided into six sections:

– Organization of work and business mobility
– Mobility in private life
– Communication and social networks in private life
– Communication and social networks at work place
– Organization of private/family life
– Technology use at home and at work place

It provided understanding of the situation in which the mobile individuals function. It gathered information on travel practices – destination, frequency, and duration – and provided the first outline of the specific context of their mobility. It also gave the first overview of the motivation to mobility, and the individuals' positive and negative experiences of it. Additional information on the interviewee's family, education, mobility, and technology use was gathered, with the help of the accompanying short questionnaire (the interview structure and the questionnaire can be found in the Annex).

The first interview showed which issues would be most relevant to the study. For example, the role of the IO and its networks were first identified. The following interviews focused on these issues. New questions addressed support by the IO in settling in a new place of residence, and during travel. In addition, these interviews were conducted more openly: individuals were asked fewer questions from the list, and the interview followed the inner logic of their story more. Questions on their most interesting trip, for example, encouraged the interviewees to talk about unexpected experiences and problems, and the gratifications related to mobility.

After analysis of the first four interviews, the interview design was modified slightly, by adding some more specific questions. At the same time, certain questions were no longer relevant, or had already been fully explored. For example, most of the questions related to the use of technology in the office and home were dropped.

The next five interviews thus focused more on the relationship to the destinations of mobility, and the construction of private spaces. The additional questions focused on where the individuals feel at home, what are their favorite places, where they like to spend their leisure time, where they would like to live when retired, where they shop, etc. In this phase, the interviews also encompassed the temporal dimension of mobility practices: for example, they included individuals' plans for the future, and their retrospection.

The last four interviews were again more limited, and focused upon the experiences of individuals in different locations, regarding, in particular, different and familiar elements. This focus was derived from the analysis of the previous interviews, which showed the high relevance of such experiences for the construction of space. The interviewees were asked to describe in detail their daily routines in two different places, for example the current and previous place of residence, or place of residence and destination of a business trip. They were also encouraged to talk about the most interesting and the most boring sides of traveling.

This gradual redesign of the interviews allowed greater flexibility. When certain practices and experiences turned out to be common to the four interviewees, the topic was either reduced or dropped in the following interviews. In this way, the interviews were able to focus on the most relevant issues. This also had the advantage of limiting the duration of the interviews, to an average of two hours.

All interviews were tape-recorded and entirely transcribed. Additionally, each interview was accompanied by a short protocol on the interview course.

The analysis of the interviews occurred in several stages (so-called open coding – compare Strauss/Corbin 1996: 44f). First, the phenomena were identified and labeled. For example, the interviewees described in detail their practices before and after the flight: which documents they prepare, whom they contact, what they pack into their suitcases, etc. Each of these actions was labeled for example, phone calls and exchange of emails with counterparts and team colleagues, and with their family, were given the name »coordination«. Next, all these activities were classified as »travel«. This concept encompasses not only the hours in a plane (transportation from one place to another), but the complete set of practices that precede this physical movement, and are more important for the individuals than the fact of changing locations. Some of the names of the concepts were »suggested« by the interviewees themselves: a word or phrase used by the interviewee served as the name of a concept (so-called in-vivo-codes – comp. Glaser 1978: 70; Strauss 1987: 33). An example is the concept »regulated exposure«, which stands for a strategy individuals use in relation to the local culture and inhabitants.

Later the concepts were grouped into categories. In this way, concepts (descriptive character) were ordered into categories (abstract character). Subsequently, the categories were compared, for the first time, with the existing literature. Those concepts and categories that turned out to be new or especially interesting, in some aspects, were included in the next interviews: they were operationalized into interview questions. This procedure was repeated in each reflection phase. After nine interviews, all the categories were compared with each other and with the literature (axial coding – compare Strauss/Corbin 1996: 76f). This enabled a detailed matching of the practices with their context, analysis of the conditions and consequences of individual practices, and greater emphasis on the temporal dimension of the processes. In the last step of the analysis, new relationships between the already-identified categories were developed, and the data was assembled anew (Strauss/Corbin 1996: 188f).

Alongside the development of concepts and categories, the analysis encompassed free associations, which were compiled in the form of memos (a form of written notes and analysis protocols that serve to work out a theory – comp. Strauss/Corbin 1996: 169f). These notes were not necessarily immediately related to the empirical material, but they helped to develop theoretical categories and overall concepts. Moreover, several tools were applied to increase the theoretical sensibility. In addition to the methods recommended by Strauss and Corbin (1996: 56f), some of the instruments of objective hermeneutic were applied: for example, experimental context variations, and sequential analysis (Oevermann 1983; Bohnsack 2000: 87f). The aim of this analysis was to reconstruct the context of a particular behavior in which this behavior makes sense. In this way, the social unconscious – the latent social structures – becomes visible.

In this procedure, a statement is first »tested« for possible contexts: the researcher imagines all possible contexts in which this statement is logical. These imagined contexts rest upon culturally rehearsed normality patterns, which are reflected in institutions-relations, milieu-relations, age-relations, gender-relations, etc. Next, the possible imaginary contexts are compared with the available facts on the person who made the statement. This in turn makes it possible to judge whether the statement is in accordance with the external contextual conditions.

If the statement cannot be explained by relating it to the context, sequential analysis is used. It can reconstruct the internal logic of the context – the case-specific structure. In this procedure, the researcher interprets a sequence of bits of a statement by imagining (simulating) a possible following bit, as a logical reaction to a preceding bit (what could A say after saying a; or: what would B answer when A said a), as in the following example (I2: 88):

Reiner: »Yea, the trip ... starts usually ... «

[possible continuation: when you enter the plane; earlier at home when you have to pack; when you check in at the airport; when you land at the destination]

Reiner: »Yea, let me not overdo it...«

[perhaps when you say goodbye to your wife; it is not so important ...]

Reiner: »a week or ... two before you enter the plane.«

The analysis revealed that for the mobile individuals a practice of travel involves much more than the simple physical movement in space, as the following chapters will show.

4.2. General description of the sample

In the course of the study, thirteen individuals were interviewed, six women and seven men. At the time of interview, the youngest person was in her early thirties, and the oldest was over sixty. The average age in the sample was circa forty-four years. Some individuals left the questionnaire field »age« blank, and therefore their age was estimated on the basis of the interview. Nine people were married, two of them for the second time. There was one widow and one single person in the sample. One interviewee indicated having a steady life partner and another having a girlfriend. Ten people had children; five of them had (also) adult children who no longer lived with them. These statistics are displayed in Table 1.38

All interviewees have higher education, and most of them completed their studies with an M.A. degree. The majority of occupations are related

---

38 All names of people and geographical locations have been changed to ensure anonymity.

to economics, though small variations are possible: for example, occupations related primarily to project, team, or office management, or to macroeconomic analysis and modeling.

Table 1. Basic demographic data regarding the research sample

interviewee	sex	age	marital status	# children	age of children	care of children
Samir	M	37*	girlfriend	none	-	-
Reiner	M	62*	married	3	35, 27, 25	self-sufficient
Martin	M	36*	married	1**	3*	n.a.
Steven	M	48	life partner	none	-	-
Tolga	F	41	married	2	5, 4	full day kindergarden and mother
Lenka	F	34*	married	none	-	-
Ludmila	F	31	single	none	-	-
Sabah	F	46	married	2	14, 18	self-sufficient, husband
Cecile	F	54	widow	2	24, 23	self-sufficient
Diego	M	46	married (2nd)	5	23, 21, 9, 7, 7	2 adult self-sufficient, 3 school full day
Ann	F	58	married (2nd)	2	35, 33	self-sufficient
Atanas	M	55	married	3	25, 15, 10	self-sufficient, school
Rodrigo	M	43	married	2	9, 7	school, mother

M – male, F – female
*estimated age; **wife is pregnant with 2nd child; n.a. no data from questionnaire

The next table provides an overview of the informants' education level and the occupation learnt, and the highest level of education achieved by their parents. The category »job title« relates to the job performed at the time of the interview. A month after the interview, Lenka changed her assignment, job title, and the scope of her duties, from project management to macroeconomic analysis. Steven changed his job within the IO some two or three months after the interview, and, at the time of the interview, he was not sure what his next assignment would be. Tolga was in the last two months of a three-year-long maternity leave and, as far as I know, she then returned to her previous job as an economist.

Table 2. Education and occupation – interviewees and their parents

interviewee	education	education (mother, father)	occupation	current tasks
Samir	M.B.A., Ph.D.	primary, post-secondary	engineering and finance/business administration	team manager
Reiner	n.a	n.a.	economist	team manager
Martin	n.a.	n.a.	economist	team manager
Steven	M.A.	M.A., M.A.	economist	office manager
Tolga	M.A.	compulsory, compulsory	economist	economist
Lenka	M.A.	n.a.	economist	project manager
Ludmila	M.A.	n.a.	economist	project manager
Sabah	M.A.	primary, M.A.	political science	office manager
Cecile	M.A.	post-secondary, post-secondary	economist	office manager
Diego	M.Sc.	M.A., post-secondary	engineer	office manager
Ann	Ph.D.	n.a.	social scientist	project manager
Atanas	M.Sc.	M.A., Ph.D.	engineer	project manager
Rodrigo	Ph.D.	M.A., M.A.	economist	project maanger

In terms of mobility, in addition to family structure (marital status and number of children), it is important to know whether a spouse or steady partner is occupied outside, or at home. Table 3 shows the situations of the interviewees and their families.

The selected group is characterized by extensive mobility. All the interviewees have changed their place of residence at least once. Most of them moved as an adult person. Only three people moved as children or as teenagers. Two of them moved from their home town to boarding school.

Table 3. Education and occupation – spouse

interviewee	spouse's education	spouse's occupation	spouse's current job situation
Samir	n.a.	n.a.	active full-time employed*
Reiner	n.a.	n.a.	n.a.
Martin	n.a.	n.a.	active, soon on maternity leave*
Steven	post-secondary	consultant	active, working from home
Tolga	Ph.D.	economist	active full-time employed*
Lenka	n.a.	economist*	active full-time employed*
Ludmila	-	-	-
Sabah	post-secondary	businessman	works from home
Cecile	-	-	-
Diego	post-secondary		inactive, housewife
Ann	n.a.	economist*	retired*
Atanas	M.A.	engineer	active, runs own private company
Rodrigo	M.A.	artist	active, works from home

*mentioned in interview

Table 4 shows an overview of the individuals' residence changes of at least one year's duration, from one town to another. Ludmila, Steven, Tolga, and Martin moved from one town to another within one country. In the column, previous places of residence, only those that were related to a move between two countries are mentioned. As shown, all the interviewees have had experience with moving out of their country of origin and settling down in a second, third, or even fourth country. As a result of specific employment conditions in the IO, many swap assignments every three to five years, and this, in turn, is often related to change in place of residence. In addition, some of them frequently moved between houses within one town or country of residence. Martin, for example, said that since he left his parents' home to study in a different city, he has changed houses every one to two years, and he has never stayed in one place more than two or three years. Similarly, Reiner moved between four countries in Africa, and in each country he moved house very often. He said that, in the last twenty-something years, he has changed houses twenty-five times. Ann moved to and from the USA three times, each time to a different town.

Table 4. Places of residence

interviewee	Origin	current place of residence	current place of residence (years)	# of changes of residence before and after 18th birthday	previous places of residence and number of years spent there (x)
Samir	Northern Africa	USA	5 - 10	3, 4	n.a.
Reiner	Western Europe	USA*	15 - 20	0, 5	Africa (4 countries) (12)
Martin	Western Europe	USA	1 - 3	0, 4	WE (7), WE (1), USA (2)
Steven	USA	Eastern Europe*	3 - 5	0, 2	USA (22)
Tolga	Turkey	Eastern Europe*	3 - 5	1, 3	Turkey (8), USA (3)
· Lenka	Central Europe	USA	5 - 10	0, 2	WE (3), USA
Ludmila	Eastern Europe	home country	3 - 5**	0, 2	USA (1)
Sabah	Middle East	Western Europe (5)	0 - 1	5, 7	WE1 (10), WE2 (1), USA (5), WE3 (11), USA (5), WE4 (4)
Cecile	Western Europe	Western Europe (other than origin)	1 - 3	0, 6****	WE (n.a.), USA (25)
Diego	South America	Eastern Europe	2, 5 months	0, 9***	USA (10), SA (6), USA (2), SA (5), US (n.a.), Panama (n.a.), ME (3)
Ann	Western Europe (non-continental)	Eastern Europe	1	0, 7	USA (2), WE (1), USA (2), WE (n.a.), USA (5), EE1 (4)
Atanas	Eastern Europe	USA/Eastern Europe	10	0, 1	USA
Rodrigo	South America	USA/Africa	10 -15	5, 3	n.a.

* At the time of the interview, preparing to move back to his home country
** In the meantime, Ludmila was abroad for one year
*** As stated in the questionnaire (includes changes under 1 year, commuting between countries)
**** As stated in the questionnaire (includes change between houses)
SA stands for South Africa, ME - Middle East, WE - Western Europe, EE - Eastern Europe, a number next to it stands for a different country

At the time of the interview, the situation of three interviewees was about to change. Reiner was to retire and move back to his country of origin. He has already moved his belongings to a new house. He keeps a flat in the USA, as he plans to go back there often for job reasons and to visit friends. Tolga planned to leave Europe and move back to the USA, after a three-year stay and maternity leave. Steven had applied for a new assignment and, at the time of the interview, knew that he would move. As it recently turned out, he is currently in the USA. The next table shows an overview of the business travel destinations of the interviewees.

At the time of the interview, Tolga was on maternity leave and traveled for private reasons only. Diego had just undertaken a new assignment. He had decided to take this particular job because he wanted to avoid traveling. Except for regular weeklong trips to headquarters, and short (maximum three days) trips within his country of residence, he was not intending to travel. Cecile and Sabah travel for short trips to many Western European countries, but with no regularity in destination patterns. At the time of the interview, Lenka was about to change to a new assignment. She already knew to which countries she would travel: Rwanda, Burundi, and Congo. Steven was also to switch jobs, but he did not know any details of the next assignment and future destinations. Reiner was to retire, but was sure that he would still commute between Europe and the USA, to perform different short-term assignments.

Frequency and duration of business travel vary within the sample. The duration of travel depends on destination, work arrangements, relation to the client, stage of a project, personal situation, and tasks to be performed. As a general rule, overseas destinations require longer travel, not because of the distance but because of their costs. On the other hand, regular visits to the headquarters usually last only one week, even though they involve travel to/from another continent. The interviewees combine travel to different destinations for budgetary reasons. They travel for about a week to one country, and then go on to another, usually combining tasks in three or four countries. Such a trip then takes three or four weeks. Shorter trips are also possible, but there is a strict rule: a trip should not be shorter than one to two weeks, and not be longer than three to four weeks. Six weeks of travel is generally an exception. In the sample, Rodrigo travels for longer periods of time to Africa, sometimes even for three months. His situation is exceptional: he was supposed to move to Africa but, given his family situation, he has decided against and »replaces« residence there with longer temporary stays.

Table 5. Current and previous travel destinations

interviewee	current destinations	#	previous destinations
Samir	Central and Eastern Europe, former Yugoslavia	4	Central and Eastern Europe
Reiner	former Yugoslavia, Turkey, Central Europe, former USSR republic	4	former Yugoslavia, Turkey, Central Europe, former USSR republics
Martin	Turkey, Southern Europe, former USSR republic, Baltic Region	5	Turkey, Southern Europe, former USSR republics, the Baltic Region
Steven	Baltic Region	3	Africa, South Asia, Pakistan, India, former USSR republics
Tolga	(maternity leave)		Africa, Caribbean
Lenka	Central and Eastern Europe, Albania*	5	Central and Eastern Europe, Albania
Ludmila	Central and Eastern Europe	5	Central and Eastern Europe
Sabah	Western Europe	**	former USSR republics, Mexico, Africa, Arabian countries
Cecile	Western Europe	**	Central and Eastern Europe, Philippines, Chile, Africa, India
Diego	Europe	4	Jordan, East Africa, India, Pakistan, Haiti
Ann	Eastern and Central Europe	5	Central Europe
Atanas	Central Asia, Eastern Europe	7	Baltic Region, Eastern Europe, Central Asia
Rodrigo	Africa	1	Africa, Eastern Europe, Middle Asia

\# relates to a number of current destination countries
* soon to be changed to Africa
** on demand, more than five

Longer trips are usually less frequent. Depending on the year, Martin travels six to ten times per year. Lenka travels about one hundred days a year, Reiner spends one third of his time on travel. He describes this as »a lot, more than average« (I2: 11). He mentioned people who travel about two hundred days a year, but this is exceptional. When she worked in headquarters, Ann used to travel about one hundred seventy days a year. In one of his previous assignments, Diego was away from home for two weeks of each month. He estimates that he spent about forty to sixty percent of his time traveling. Steven belongs to those who currently travel relatively little. His trips are short, three days to a week, to neighboring countries. In the course of his assignments, he used to travel more, and for longer periods of time. When working in Africa and Asia, he traveled about four times a year, for four weeks each time. Ludmila's travels are usually five days long. She generally leaves on Monday and comes back on Friday, although from time to time she combines tasks in more than one country and spends up to two weeks abroad. She usually spends two weeks at home and two weeks away. She calculated that, in the eight months prior to the interview, she had taken thirty-six different flights. Ann had taken sixteen trips the year before. Sabah and Cecile often travel for one day at a time, to attend a conference or meeting in neighboring towns or countries. Often, their many short trips in a row add up to almost an entire month away from home at once. On previous assignments, they both used to travel much more. Cecile usually traveled for periods of two to five weeks. For approximately three years, Sabah regularly made a month-long trip to Central Asia. She later changed to a different region, and went on a three-week trip every two to three months. Rodrigo spends the longest time abroad when on business travel, up to three months at a time. Atanas combines business obligations with longer stays in his home country, to which, after several years abroad, his family has now moved back.

Most of the interviewees combine business and private travel to save expenses on flights, especially on intercontinental trips. At least once a year, they each visit family in his or her country of origin. Given the amount of business travel, it seems astonishing that so many of the interviewees also travel for pleasure. Steven, for example, often travels on weekends to visit friends in Europe: he goes, for example, to shop in Paris, or to the theatre in London. Steven, like Ann, also makes many weekend trips in the country of residence. Reiner spends most holidays with his family in Europe, while Martin divides vacation time between a visit to his parents' house and short holidays on a sunny island. In the last few years, Tolga has traveled mostly for private reasons: she visited many sites in the residence country, went on skiing holidays in the Alps, and took a trip to Egypt to »catch some sun«. She also took a driving tour through Southern Europe. In addition, she visited her parents-in-law in another European country. Similarly, Sabah regularly visits her country of origin, goes skiing in the Alps, and spends time with her mother in Southern Europe, her brother in the USA, and old friends in Austria. In the past few years,

Ludmila has had too much work and could not take holidays. Therefore her private destinations were limited to family visits. Only Lenka belongs to those who prefer to stay at home rather than travel during spare time. Both she and her husband travel separately for about a third of their time. They see each other only briefly or rarely, sometimes only once in six weeks, and thus they prefer to take every opportunity to stay together at home.

4.3. Mediating mobility

During interviews, the individuals were asked to describe how they entered the IO and what their previous occupation had been. Three of them entered the IO directly after university through the special IO's program for young graduates. Two others joined the IO as university graduates, starting on an irregular basis, until they were eventually offered a long-term appointment. The other interviewees joined the IO in the middle of their career. Four changed to the IO from another international organization, and the rest had worked in the private sector, or their national public sector, immediately before the IO.

Although no single pattern of mobility before entering the IO could be identified, in general the primary reason for the first change of place of residence was the wish to undertake studies or work assignments. Five of the interviewees moved to a foreign country to attend either school or university. One woman moved out of her home country for the first time to follow her husband to his oversees assignment. The rest moved for the first time to take up a job. It can be concluded that the choice of destination was not related to the essential qualities of the place; rather, interviewees primarily chose in the light of the facilities available. Unlike traditional migration, in which the choice of destination was based on the opening up of further possibilities, for the interviewees the facilities were the decisive factor in migration. For example, in the case of traditional migration, the USA is a destination for migration because it can be seen as a country offering better life opportunities (Goldberg 1992: 202). Those interviewed cannot, however, be called typical migrants. [39] The first movement was a tool that enabled them to achieve a goal: attending interesting courses at a university, or undertaking a dream assignment, wherever those were. Indeed, this form of mobility seems more like domestic labor force mobility than international migration. In all cases, moving abroad in the course of the career was an individual decision that was not an exact calculation of future gains, as most of the individuals did not have much idea of the destination country. They are also the first migrants in their families (with the exception of Sabah), and did not join any friends or relatives abroad.

The interviewees classify only short-term travel in the category mobility. Being mobile means to them being frequently, but briefly, on the move and traveling to another country. Some of them had undertaken regular business travels in their previous workplace, and some of them used to live in a foreign country. However, before entering the IO, none of these persons had traveled to such an extent. »Real« intercontinental and extensive mobility was a new experience for them (I3: 42). Many who had previously worked in other international organizations said that the frequency of business travel in the IO is greater. In general, the evaluation of the interviews revealed that the interviewees' extensive mobility is strongly related to working for the IO.

However, the IO does not require its employees to travel. Steven, with over twenty years service in the IO, says that, when he started to work in the IO, he did not travel at all (I4: 107). In general, new employees are not permitted to travel, because it is expensive, and requires a certain amount of experience in those who travel. The principle of cost effectiveness stipulates that employees travel only when necessary, and when means of communication other than face-to-face are not available, or are ineffective. Tolga explains that the IO has a very pragmatic reason for limiting the travel of newcomers: they lack experience, and it is not yet clear how long they will remain with the IO, and it may therefore be too risky to allocate budget to them (I5: 155). Moreover, the IO offers very different jobs, many of which require no travel at all.

It also provides facilities for distance communication, including its own satellite connections, e-mail, video- and audio-conference equipment, as

---

39 It becomes clear that here we are dealing with new patterns that cannot be explained using classical migration theories. Compare also Pries 2001, for the overview of classical and new migration theories.

well as secure diplomatic postal services. Employees are free to choose which means of communication best suits their tasks. Interviewees recalled the various facilities they use when preparing for travel and while abroad. Without these, extensive mobility would not be possible. The IO enables and supports extensive mobility. Entering technical and organizational networks makes people more mobile. I call this phenomenon a mobilization through existing networks. It means that individuals entering the IO are given the possibility of extensive mobility. The infrastructure is provided, and individuals can use it if they find it necessary to travel to perform their job well. As the interviewees often combine business and private travel, the IO's infrastructure increases both business and private mobility.

Travel destinations depend on the tasks assigned by the IO. However, it would be an oversimplification to say that individuals have no control over their mobility. Rather, the patterns of individuals' mobility are the outcome of mediation between various elements of the material and social networks (exogenous factors) and personal motivation and life plans (endogenous factors). There are two aspects here: mobility understood as short-term travel, and mobility understood as re-settlement.

4.3.1. Choosing and deciding: Arranging short-term mobility

The complex infrastructure of the IO mobilizes people. The IO can eliminate many obstacles, for example, restrictions on entering some countries, by issuing diplomatic passes or letters of recommendations to obtain a visa. The diverse complementary networks, which will be described in greater detail in the following chapter, simplify mobility. However, one should not forget that mobility in the IO is a mode of achieving a goal. Mobility is expensive, and therefore the IO provides multiple tools to limit it, including formal budgetary limitations, and various distance communication tools.

One reason why individual mobility forms change over time is related to undertaking a new assignment within the IO. However, entering the IO does not necessarily involve an obligation of mobility. Some interviewees did not travel at all during their first assignment, though two women recall having to travel extensively. This was not their decision, because at that time they could not choose how to deal with their tasks. Because various tasks involve mobility, a change of assignment is both the reason for mobility, and the tool by which to steer one's own mobility. Rainer says that one can apply for a job within the IO that requires no travel at all (I2: 55).

For those who have been in the job for some time, short-term mobility is, largely, a result of mediation within networks. A simple example illustrates this:

»I changed my assignments so that I have a chance not to travel so much and in addition I had increased responsibilities so that I am in charge of my own schedule. I am not dependent on others to follow their schedules and furthermore I am doing more and more also with IT communication tools, videoconferencing, and telephone conversations which also reduce the need for travel.« (I3: 30)

The purpose of a business trip is to communicate with counterparts. There are alternative methods of doing so: phoning, sending e-mails, or holding a videoconference. Whether travel is performed depends on the availability of the technology for distant communication. If, for any reason (for example, security problems), travel is not possible, physical mobility can be replaced with, for example, videoconferencing (I2: 65).

The infrastructure in the host country is an important factor. There are countries with which it is almost impossible to communicate at a distance. In such cases, a personal visit is necessary. For example, Tolga managed to conduct a small project on another country entirely from home, because it was possible for her to access all necessary data using the Internet and facsimile (I5: 13). Lenka was able to limit traveling, thanks to the good infrastructure in the countries in which she conducted projects. In contrast, her husband must travel a lot, because he works in a country in which distance communication networks are underdeveloped (I6: 22). Of course, other factors also play a role: the issue to be discussed, previous experience of distance communication or face-to-face meetings, even the political situation in the destination country, and the internal IO's regulations on security, may all mediate the extent of individual mobility.

Similarly, the duration of a trip is a result of mediation not only between a would-be traveler and his or her counterparts, but also between his or her family, other team members, the IO's procedures, the political situation, and the status of a project. Budgetary guidelines mean that the average length of overseas travel is between one and three weeks. The status of a project and the issues to be discussed decide the actual length of a stay abroad. This in turn relates to the counterparts. Organizing travel is more about coordinating with counterparts and colleagues on the timing and content of travel than ordering tickets and assembling proper business documentation. Given the numerous commitments everyone has, it is a challenge (I2: 29). One has to think in terms of a group, and to reach agreement by all the team members.

Mobility is often the result of a compromise between business obligations and private events. If a would-be traveler has a young family, he or she tends to reduce the number of days abroad. He or she may prolong the stay if it is possible to combine the business trip with private events, for example meeting friends, family, and so on:

»And then the other important part of preparations is of course also to agree with your family [...] for example if there is an important birthday or one of your children has graduation or wedding anniversary.« (I2: 31)

Business meets private obligations before a trip, when one must remember to pay the bills or the house cleaner. Ludmila complains that she must always pay interest on her telephone and other bills, because she never pays them on time. She keeps forgetting about them, and when away from home it is not technically possible for her to pay them (I7: 105).

The priority is clear: professional responsibilities come first, and private events are incorporated into the business schedule. For example, one can try to use a business trip to meet friends or family abroad when there is some spare time in the evenings or on the weekend, or even try to prolong a stay abroad in order to meet some private obligations. As Kaplan writes, when the family is scattered across the world, travel may be an essential part of family life (Kaplan 1996: ix). Such is the case of one of the interviewees, all of whose closest family members live in different countries (I8: 14).

On the other hand, many interviewees limit their stay abroad, to avoid staying away from their immediate families at home for too long (I3: 18). Martin says that one has to arrange private life around business travel. He himself reduced the number of trips and the duration of travel to spend more time with his wife and their small child. However, when his child is older, he intends to return to frequent traveling. Reiner says that one has to consider the impact of mobility on family. Business travel meant that he missed many family events, and gave his wife the feeling that she was left alone (I2: 31). In contrast, Steven does not have a family, and sees no conflict between his mobility and his personal life. His life partner fully accepts his mobility, and Steven travels whenever and for however long his tasks require him to do so. Similarly, Ann's husband, who is retired, follows her schedule.

The IO's labor market makes it possible to change position, and thus influence the extent of mobility and achieve the desired level of it. For example, pregnant women and young mothers make use of this opportunity. This option is also open to men, but »very few cases are there« (I2: 55). Often, children, not business obligations or the IO's policies, decide on the extent of individual mobility. However, in the group studied, the relation between mobility and family situation was not always obvious. Cecile, for instance, took her longest trips when her children were small, and that was her choice:

»I did it when the kids were very small and they could have stayed in France with my mother, I dropped them off and picked them up later on the way back to the USA, you know, but when they were in school I didn't do it. [...] I took them with me and on the way I was leaving them in France.« (I9: 84-87)

Sabah was also very mobile when her children were very small, but this was not completely her decision. She had decided to take the position in the IO, and she had known that it would mean frequent travel, so indirectly she chose to be mobile. Because she was mostly absent, her husband raised the children and she only supported him (I8: 45). She also changed her place of residence frequently, and she believes that this kind of mobility is very good for children's development. Tolga changed her assignment to a »residential« one before deciding to have children. The extensive mobility of her husband, also an IO employee, also influenced her decision. However, she thinks that long working hours are as problematic as mobility when you have small kids:

»Sometimes I had to work until eight or nine and my mother had to care about the kids...there were moments when I would see them only in the morning and then next morning because whole day working [...]« (I6: 81)

Ann, for example, is convinced that it is not good for children for their parents to be mobile, because children need stability in life. Although she worked, she was always physically close to them, in case they needed her (I11: 142).

Women who do not have children decide to limit their mobility for the good of their immediate family. Lenka decided to change to an assignment requiring less mobility because her husband travels extensively, and they were hardly ever together in one place. Such a life became a burden to her, and she was the first to compromise and restrict the extent of her business travel (I6: 16). In this regard, the desire for a corporeal presence can be a reason to travel, and a reason to stay.

Women's opinions and decisions about mobility and small children are very diverse. The men interviewed, in contrast, usually reduced their mobility, at their wives' request, when they had small children. Martin would like to travel more and he is not very pleased with this limitation (I3: 18, 40). Reiner admits that his extensive mobility led to many problems in the family, and that his wife demanded that he spend more time at home (I2: 31, 54). Diego's experience with his older children made him decide to abandon frequent and long traveling, to be able to spend more time with his second wife and the youngest kids (I10: 102).

While business obligations often restrict the opportunities to steer mobility in professional life, in private life the interviewees have their mobility fully under control. »Well, sure you can get tired of traveling, but then you just don't do it for a while«, says Steven (I4: 47). Neither having children (or not), nor being married (or not), has any influence on the frequency, duration, or destination of the trips undertaken. With or without children, the interviewees travel at least once a year to visit their family, and to relax briefly in the sun or to ski. Most of them use overseas assignments to visit new places in the area.

Some individuals abandon mobility to meet private commitments. Tolga, for example, wanted to be »a full time mother« to her two small children (I5: 5; 81; 103). Often, the interviewees speculate what reason might lead them to abandon mobility. One ground of Lenka's decision to travel less was her health, and she would also abandon it altogether if her health condition deteriorated. She used to have health problems when traveling; in addition, at home her immune system was often too tired to fight a simple cold (I6: 16). Ann was also glad to change to an assignment that did not demand extensive mobility (she used to travel one hundred and seventy days in a year), because her health condition had dramatically worsened and she needed time to recover (I11: 167). In her case, the cause of the problems was not bad hygienic conditions in the destination countries, but immense stress related to traveling.

One can try to avoid traveling to countries where hygienic conditions are very bad, or one can rely on medications and the recommendations of the IO's health department, and continue to travel frequently to these countries. This means that, without the infrastructure of the IO, the mobility of the individuals would be limited. Hence, if a certain condition increases or reduces mobility, it is mediated with other conditions.

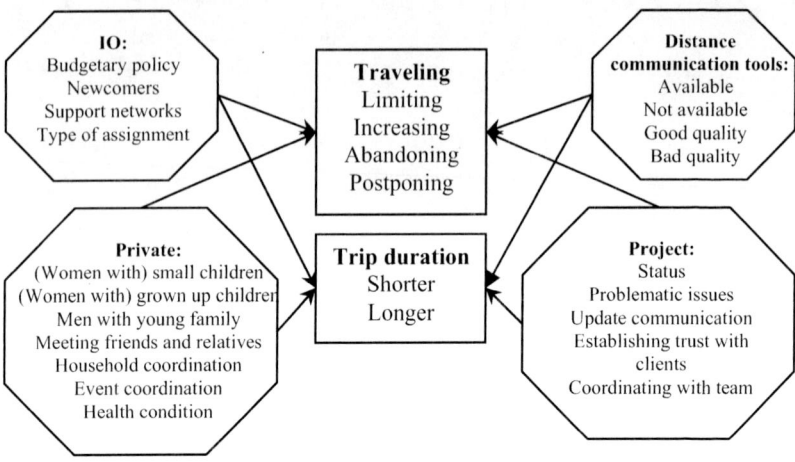

Figure 2. Mediation of short-term mobility between exogenous factors

The IO itself tries to create such infrastructure and conditions, which increase mobility even though conditions in the destination countries where its projects are conducted tend to hinder mobility. For example, if there is a very poor public transportation system, the IO allows its employees to rent a car to reach a destination far from the capital city. If there are unsafe hygienic conditions, it equips its members with medications, injections, and the appropriate information to overcome this hurdle.

In the next section, I elaborate on the endogenous factors mediating short-term mobility. I present the extent to which the particular interviewees' mobility fluctuated, and their main motives for these changes. I distinguish three issues: short-term mobility, resettlement, and long-term life arrangements. These issues are discussed under the perspective of the extent to which the individuals control their own mobility.

4.3.2. Value of personal experience: Endogenous factors of mobility

Urry draws special attention to the social organization of mobility. Corporeal travel results in intermittent moments of physical proximity to particular peoples, places, or events, and in significant ways this proximity is felt to be obligatory, appropriate, or desirable (Urry 2002: 258). He distinguishes three basic reasons for traveling: place, time, and social obligation. Therefore, the three bases of co-presence are face-to-face, face-the-place, face-the-moment motivations (Urry 2002: 202). The motivation to travel for business, rather than relying on distance communication, or choosing an assignment that does not require traveling, generally fits with the scheme described by Urry.

All the interviewees speak about the need to see things personally. Being in the country, traveling across it and meeting people, talking to those who live there and are experts, are all necessary to enable the interviewees to achieve satisfaction from work:

»You see what you have contributed to. You prepare project and then you see a bypass or a bridge built and people in a community coming and saying to you thank ›you very much for shortening our travel time‹, and it is so pretty and the environment was preserved and you feel satisfaction, you feel rewarded for what you have done.« (16: 40)

Travel is a tool for achieving better results and satisfaction from working, though a small part of the interest in traveling is just to get things done effectively (14: 70). To see people and places gives one a feeling of being needed, and of understanding the problems of one's counterparts. In return, it gives satisfaction, and enables better understanding of one's own role in a project. Such co-presence is located within time and space: participants travel somewhere to meet together. Meetings are multifunctional, for making decisions, seeing how one is heard, executing standard procedures and duties, distributing rewards, status, and blame, reinforcing friendship as well as distance, judging commitment, having an enjoyable time, and so on (Schwartzman 1989). It is also a way to get things done, to talk about difficult issues, to discuss and to show understanding. »A minimum amount of travel is necessary for this kind of job«, says Reiner (12: 55).

When difficult issues must be discussed, videoconferencing, in particular, although closest to a face-to-face meeting, is not a satisfactory tool. It is good for updating and informing people about the progress or problems. However, a critical issue can be successfully disputed only in a face-to-face discussion. When you need to convince someone, or a detailed discussion is necessary, you must go and meet this person (I3: 34). There is a difference in the quality of contact with counterparts via phone, e-mail, or videoconferencing, and face-to-face meetings. Co-presence affords opportunities to display attentiveness and commitment, and, simultaneously, to detect where others have little commitment (Urry 2002: 259). Personal contact is important, because it makes it possible to create a better relation with the clients. There are of course some practical reasons why corporeal presence in a country is desired. To work at a distance requires good co-ordination with counterparts, including those from a local office. In this case, one has to rely on the work of the counterparts and simply wait until one's request is realized. Sometimes a request by e-mail or post has no effect. In countries in which the working culture differs from that of the IO, in particular, written or oral requests from a distance are simply ignored. Many problems of this kind can be solved only through personal visits. Letters, memos, faxes, and e-mail are less effective in establishing long-term trust relations (Boden/Molotch 1994: 263 - 7).

»Go and see yourself« is a leitmotif of travel. No reports, studies, or accounts by someone else can replace personal experience. Co-presence is necessary to talk through problems, especially the unmediated telling of »troubles« (Urry 2002: 259). Reiner says that talking personally to his clients helps him to feel relevant. Close contact and discovering »the real« situation is possible for him only when talking to ordinary people, farmers, teachers, workers, and taxi drivers: seeing how they live, visiting their villages or towns to see their living conditions. These are the »benefits of the personal touch« (I4: 57). This kind of personal experience cannot be replaced by a conversation with high officials, who are formally Reiner's clients, or a visit to a capital. For him, a project's »real« clients are ordinary people, and he wants to discover their needs and problems. On the other hand, one can see the effects of the work, »see the impact of it«, and »how people in these countries need you« (I5: 25). Personal experience is important in getting to know the country in which one works. »Becoming the insider« and not to »remain at a surface« (I2: 127) is the aim of travel in such cases. Travel is desired in order to »create your own vision of the country« (I6: 107). Martin says that he took the job in the IO partly because he wanted to travel and to see »the other« with his own eyes. He sees travel as pleasure and not a burden, and he especially values exposure to different people and cultures. He feels privileged that he has a chance to be exposed (13: 42). People desire to know a place through encountering it directly. To be there for oneself is critical. This is a further aspect of co-presence – physical contact to places by walking, watching, touching, smelling, or hearing a place.

This is the motivation of face-the-place, which drives corporeal travelers (Urry 2002: 262). Distance communication disconnects people from their environments. In communication by phone or videoconference, each partner does not have an impression of how the other lives, because only physical presence offers this. One participates in the stories of the others better when in spatial proximity. Otherwise, the others are experienced as »caught in the moment«, immobilized in a particular time and place, and extracted from spatial and temporal contexts. In turn, spatial distance enforces emotional remoteness.

4.3.3. Grab the chance! Resettlement between plan and hazard

The previous section focused on short-term travel. In this section, long-term assignments abroad are coupled with general life planning and discussed. The focus is on changes in mobility in the course of the life of the interviewed individuals, and why the interviewees made these changes.

In summary, the following motives drive the individual decision about short-term mobility: new professional assignment or professional aims, educational opportunities, personal matters, and curiosity about the other culture. The same holds true for resettlement. Over the course of life, all of these motives occur, and create the mobility career of the individuals. For example, Tolga's first change of place of residence was related to studies in a foreign country. Subsequently she moved to take up a job. Finally, she followed her husband on an overseas assignment. Reiner and Cecile were interested in development issues, and their first change of place of residence was a consequence of these interests. Reiner's next moves were driven either by personal issues or by job requirements. Ann has moved mostly because of her family and children, but partly also because of her educational and career goals. Similarly, Reiner moved once to provide his children with better educational opportunities. For Sabah and Ann, the most important factor was to enable the children to grow up in a European culture, and so they left the USA, although it also fitted their job aspirations well. Diego's decision to move was a mixture of career development and personal reasons: on the one hand, he was aiming at an interesting assignment, and, on the other, at the possibility of attaining a more stable mode of life. Earlier, he had returned to his home country for ideological reasons: he wanted to help to restructure country's economy. However, he missed the institutional culture of the USA, and finally returned there.

»And then again, after five-six years I just found it too boring and started to look for something else. So it's been mostly my own decision and it's been mostly dictated by opportunities on the job market, the type of jobs available, that's certainly drove my earlier moves, these were times when I had no family.« (I10: 44)

In no case were the essentials of a place decisive regarding the destination of the move. In Lenka's case, it was a coincidence that she took part in the exchange program. The same applies to Ludmila, who was recommended to a university program by her employer, and to Diego, who decided to study in the USA because of the high respect the American university system enjoyed throughout the world (I11: 58).

The last but not least motive to change the place of residence is curiosity about new places, people, and culture. This factor remains, however, somewhat in the sphere of wishes and loose plans for the future. Some interviewees wish to undertake one of their next assignments in a particular country, because they are interested in its culture, habits, and people. Others imagine where they will once live when they retire. Usually it is their country of origin, but many would like to have a house in more than one country. Basically, the Europeans tend to imagine that, one day, they will go back to Europe. For some, the decision is dependent on the location of their children, or the general political and societal situation in some countries. Such plans, however, are rarely precise.

Mobility as resettlement is about taking opportunities – this is the clear message in all the interviews. It is about being in the right place at the right time, and about taking what life offers: for example, interesting educational opportunities (I6: 177) or job assignments (I8: 161). The location of such an assignment is secondary, both in terms of an organization and a geographical location. Many interviewees say they did not search for a job in the IO: rather, they took it because it was an interesting possibility at that stage in their life. The interviewed individuals set a general framework in life:

»I knew that I wanted to have an interesting fulfilled life so I would have to do a postgraduate degree, which I did. I was quite ambitious so I got a Ph.D. I knew that even though I was married and had small children I would never be going to be happy when staying at home. So even as early as my son was born, I knew I would have a different path, so in that sense you prepare. And you get yourself ready to take advantage of things which happen.« (I11: 54)

Often, the interviewees make an initial decision to study economics and specialize in international relations or development, and this structures their life decisions to a certain extent. Alternatively, they have certain wishes and desires and try to realize them. Some of them, for instance, wanted to travel and discover foreign cultures. Some aimed at performing an interesting job, and the IO offered them an opportunity to do so.

»Grabbing the chance« is a part of this life-plan, and also makes it mobile. It is short-term planning, living always with the option »we will see«. The IO enforces this way of designing one's own life. When they took their first assignment in the IO, many interviewees were not sure whether they would stay in it or not. They worked on a short-term contract, which was prolonged every couple of weeks or months. Even when they were sure of their employment, they continually changed jobs within the IO. Most assignments last between three and five years. This is the result of the IO's policy that aims at constant exchange of experience, best practices, and knowledge. This can be ensured by employees' mobility between departments, sectors of expertise, and countries (I5: 163). Most interviewees did not exactly plan their career path. »It's just happened« (I11: 52). Rather, they have an idea of what they want to do, and they seize the chance when it appears. For example, a month before the end of his current position, Steven was not sure what exactly his new assignment would be or, more important, where it would be. The most likely, he said, was in the headquarters of the IO, because »at my level and when looking at the opportunities it's more than likely gonna be there, but…but possibly not« (I4: 19). Diego found out what his next location would be only some five months before the move. This change was planned, as he had been seeking an assignment that did not require extensive mobility. This was his wish, although beforehand he did not know much about the possibilities that would be available to him. All of the interviewees »keep looking at the vacancy announcements, seeing what's possible« (I4: 17).

This taking-opportunity strategy is linked to no particular plan for life. Having a new job or undertaking studies is considered a temporary arrangement. The individuals always assume that discontinuity, such as change of job or residence, is an integral part of a person's biography (Bilden 1997: 241). Who knows what will come next, how long this situation will last, how long one can perform this job? Usually this temporal character of a new life arrangement makes the decision, whether to take a job and move to another country, much easier. Tolga says that

»[To move to the USA] was not difficult because I came as a student. I didn't have anything, just my suitcases of my dresses and I didn't have any plan if to stay or not to stay. I took it as it was, my purpose was just to do my master and after that we will see.« (I5: 63)

Lenka's contract with the IO, for instance, was first extended for some weeks, and then again and again, for some time. She moved to the USA, and she was then assigned to work on several Eastern European countries. This 25-day-job developed into a stay of more than ten years in the USA. Reiner also seems surprised that he has now lived outside Switzerland for over thirty years. Moving out of Switzerland was not his aim. He was interested in working on development issues, and moved to Africa to participate in the projects of a consulting company. His re-settlement to the USA had little to do with a wish to move to this particular country; rather, it was driven by problems finding a school, other than a boarding school, for his younger son. He applied for a job in the IO as some of his counterparts had suggested this option to him, and it just happened that his new assignment was in the USA. Short-term planning leaves space for any new project, which can then be included in the biography. There is no need, and no reason, to assume that one particular project will work out. Anything is acceptable: there is no reason for any particular development in personal life (Kraus 1996: 183). There are multiple life-choices and life-paths, and anybody can be the architect of his or her own biography (Bilden 1997: 237). One can decide to be mobile, travel frequently, or choose a place of residence. On the one hand, there is no general plan that the interviewees realize in their life. After all, who could assume some of the developments? It is much better to keep your eyes open and use whatever good opportunities life brings than to plan and be disappointed, as Ann elucidates. Anyway, planning does not usually work, she believes (I11: 52).

Life offers many possibilities, many different paths. It is one's choice which way to go, and one should always be aware that there are other choices possible, other opportunities waiting out there. All the interviewees see this as positive, as enriching and interesting. Life, and mobility as part of it, is thus less about planning and more about deciding.

Whatever

4.4. Bright side, dark side – costs of mobility

The individuals interviewed have no doubt that mobility is their own choice. However, although many desire it, mobility is often a burden to the individuals. Many of the informants stress the very positive role of mobility in their business life. Travel is a tool in achieving better performance at work. However, as the previous sections showed, individuals reduce the extent of their business travel when its negative consequences disturb their private life. The main reason for this is the lack of time for family, which starts to be a problem when there are small children. The following chapter will discuss when and how extensive mobility clashes with private life, and how the interviewees deal with this problem. Three areas in which mobility has repercussions on the private lives of the informants can be identified: these are related to family relationships, friendships, and the organization of daily life.

4.4.1. Being a part-time family member

As mentioned, mobility often interferes with the interviewees' private commitments. Business trips may be scheduled exactly when, coincidentally, their wife or child's birthday is to be celebrated, or some other private event is to take place. Reiner complains about missing many such events (I2: 31). It is particularly difficult when one cannot keep in touch with the immediate family when abroad. The situation becomes especially demanding when a family member is sick, or when urgent and unexpected issues at home need to be resolved. At such times, »it is a burden on family life« (I2: 53)

Men usually try to minimize the negative consequences of their extensive mobility by reducing the number and the duration of trips. Women, in contrast, often resign from assignments that require them to travel extensively. There are several reasons for this: some see such extensive mobility as a burden on their relationship, especially when both partners travel a lot. Children are the second reason. The third is usually health problems, and the psychological burden of mobility. Women see the collision between work and private life more as a conflict. They have problems managing the household and the relationship under the constant time shortages. They perceive their life as discontinuous, divided into periods of absence and presence (I6: 16). Lenka complained especially about being constrained by time squeezes, work, and her own health being affected by difficult conditions and unusual food in foreign countries. She was tired of missing her husband and her house, and feeling lonely when abroad, or when alone at home while he was away. Given that there are always many things to do in the household, the time to enjoy life together was, in their case, shortened dramatically. There was very little chance that her husband could change his assignment soon, so she changed hers. Shortage of time disrupts seemingly trivial personal contacts. Routine interactions play a significant role in the maintenance of close relationships and in defining the roles in each relationship (Duck 1998). It shows how important they are that Lenka, and some other interviewees, seek a position that does not require them to travel very often. Lenka has not decided to stop traveling, but she will limit it greatly.

Tolga admits that when she and her husband were traveling their relationship was complicated, but traveling became a real problem only when she and her husband had their first baby. Before this, she and her husband would see each other only once every six weeks or so. »Before you have children, you just close your door and you go« (I5: 79). She then changed her department, to take up a job that did not require her to travel. Nevertheless, long working hours were a burden on the family, and to being a »full time mummy«. Tolga decided to take a three-year-long leave and move with her husband to Central Europe, where his new assignment was based. For her, both her own mobility and, later, her husband's mobility were problems. It was a challenge to deal alone with all the problems at home, and with two small children. It required her to find a solution: she hired an *au pair*, and often used her mother's help.

It seems that Lenka's decision to change her assignment was a difficult one, and she reflected a lot on her life and mobility before taking it. She believes that mobility is much easier for people who are alone. Before she was married, traveling was not a problem. Not having a husband or a boyfriend means being free of responsibility for anybody else. It does not matter whether you are alone at home or in a hotel room – you do not miss anybody, except perhaps your friends:

»You live simply your life in the city - you rent a small flat, you don't own anything, you don't have plants, you don't have animals, you don't have a car to worry about. You own so little in terms of a relationship and material things so you don't have much to take care of it is much easier to take off and go away for long trips.« (I6: 117)

She believes the more relations one has – to material objects and to people – the more difficult it is to travel a lot. Even renting a flat or owning a house makes a difference. In the second case, you invest more of your emotions in furnishing and decorating it, and thus you create a relation to it. When you are away from it, you miss it and worry about it. It is even more complicated when you have a relationship and miss your boyfriend or husband. In the long term, it becomes very stressful, and traveling changes into a burden. The fewer ties you have, and the weaker they are, the easier it is to be mobile, asserts Lenka.

The interviewees differ in their judgments as to whether irregular contact with their other family members is destructive to the relationships and their intimacy, or not. Some claim that their family suffers from their physical absence, and that distance communication cannot make up for this. Others say that, no matter what, the family ties remain strong. Usually, contact with family members other than spouses and children is not considered problematic. Male interviewees, in particular, do not deliberate about their relationship to their parents and relatives. Sporadic visits to their families and more or less regular phone calls are sufficient to sustain contact. The interviewees easily bridge the distance to their parents. Ludmila says she became used to dwelling with her parents on the phone. She calls them regularly no matter the cost, because this way she feels comfortable – »I try not to set barriers myself«, she says (I7: 51). For those whose friends and families live in the USA, regular contact is even easier because it is cheaper, thanks to the IO's satellite system. One can call for free via the IO's satellite in the USA: calling a local number is then free of charge, and long-distance connections are much cheaper than via commercial networks (I4: 109). In general, women seem more sensitive about distance between family members, and often regret being far from their parents. Though this relationship is not in danger of losing its intimacy, they miss daily contact with their parents, they are worried that they are not there when something bad happens, and miss their advice and warmth. »You cannot call mum non-stop when you cook and you are not sure what to put in a pot« says Lenka (I6: 70).

Because of physical distance, individuals need to prove more flexible in their family arrangements. Every possibility for a face-to-face meeting needs to be used: many interviewees therefore combine business travel with a visit to their parents (I5, I11). Visits to the parental home of both parents are, on the other hand, arranged so that the time available is divided fairly between partners. Thus, these visits require a certain regularity and good planning. Many interviewees say that they always spend summer holidays in the husband's country of origin, and the winter vacation with the wife's family, and they try to arrange another week's holiday during the year, to be spent by themselves, or with the children only, in a third »neutral« country (I6: 135). For Reiner, regular visits to his country of origin, Switzerland, are a kind of obligation, though not a burden. Spending his only holiday each year in his home country is important for him, because of his children. He wants them to develop ties to the culture of their parents. The success of his strategy is confirmed by the fact that two of his sons decided to study at a Swiss university, despite never having lived there before.

4.4.2. Weakening of old friendships

To establish whether mobility influences relationships with friends and family (parents, brothers and sisters, cousins), the interviewees were asked to describe their group of friends, indicate where they lived and where they come from, and to say how they communicate with them. This revealed similarities in the social networks of all the interviewed individuals. They all sustain contact with old friends, and make new ones. Even so, many old friendships ended after a time because of changes of residence or other factors. All the interviewees note a difference in the quality of long-distance relationships.

Some of the interviewees acknowledge that changing country of residence is related to a certain choice: one either takes the opportunity to go abroad, or decides not to risk losing friends (I6: 70). Many friendships end because of distance; however, many interviewees had managed to sustain contact with university and hometown friends for a long time. Lenka says she would not be able to cut the ties; luckily, her closest friends stayed »loyal« enough to maintain a long-distance relationship. She keeps in contact, especially with those who have access to the Internet and those who have a phone.

For Steven, moving to another country made it possible for him to select the friends with whom he still wanted to keep in contact. Martin sustains relationships with many friends from school and visits them whenever possible. However, he admits that the contact is, in general, limited. Reiner states that he has lost contact with many friends. He finds it difficult to remain in contact with those whom he can see for only one or two weeks a year. One develops different interests and perspectives, and »after a number of years discovers not having much in common with friends and relatives« (12: 81).

Cecile writes Christmas cards to all her friends (19: 66). Like the other informants, she has very little time to keep in contact with her friends more regularly. Sabah admits that many of the personal e-mails she receives are not replied to for a long time: business e-mails are a priority and there is no time left to reply to friends. She believes that this lack of daily contact destroys friendships (18: 191). Tolga, on the other hand, maintains very good contact with her old friends: she claims this is because they have a special relationship connecting them. She went to a boarding school for very talented children from poor families, and grew up there with her friends. They were like a family for her, and for eight years they were together every day. They all keep in touch and have reunions, and, no matter where the reunion is, Tolga flies there. She also has regular contact with them via e-mail: they have their discussion groups and share pictures of their families. They are also active in an association that supports this boarding school and funds scholarships for new students. The school and the association have a tradition lasting 150 years, which makes for a special relationship connecting the old and the new students (15: 125, 141). Although Tolga maintains such a close contact with her old friends, she notices and complains about a difference in the quality of her contact with them. She is especially aware of the shortcomings of communicating by e-mail. She prefers to call friends rather than use e-mail, because she gets instant answers this way. She is too anxious to wait for an answer via e-mail (15: 73).

The other interviewees also prefer to call rather than write e-mails. Martin speaks about a general misuse of e-mails:

»That's the number of e-mail, the whole communication traffic is getting too much and it doesn't reflect the substance. It is really a hell.« (I3: 152)

He reduces the number of e-mails he exchanges with friends; he is tired of it. As long as he and his friends agree that e-mail traffic is overwhelming and accept that communication has to be reduced, there is no damage to their relationship. For the exchange of information, phone conversations or occasional meetings are enough. Martin states that it is very difficult to have a close relationship with friends because of »moving around so often«; but, despite not communicating very often, it is always very nice to see his friends face-to-face and then contact is restored.

For Reiner the telephone is no better than e-mail. He uses both forms of media only to exchange information:

»What you can communicate in terms of real serious communication by phone is very limited. Do you really talk about your emotions or really things that are important for you over the phone? You talk about the weather, how are the kids, pretty superficial things or logistical things. But not the real stuff.« (I2: 83)

In general, contact with old friends is sustained by all possible means. As »the best«, the interviewees indicated occasional meetings, usually once a year while on holiday in their home country or, whenever possible, in combination with business travel. E-mail and phone complement each other. E-mail serves to schedule face-to-face meetings or the exchange of pictures, interesting reports, and short pieces of information. Phone conversations are preferred for a more detailed exchange. The choice of media of communication may be related to the type of attachment connecting people (Döring/Dietmar 2004). The more intimate the private relationship, then the richer, more synchronic, and more personalized the medium chosen: for example, the telephone for family talks, especially when emotions are to be shared.

Typically, the interviewees accept that their friendships have evolved, and see this as a normal development. They believe that this is the price one has to pay when moving to another country. However, such »growing apart« is not confined only to relationships in which one or both friends are mobile. Many adult persons experience friendship as significantly structured by the challenges of everyday life: coordinating couples' activities, aligning family compositions, pursuing careers, and matching different schedules (Rawlins 1994: 285). Most adults, and also my interview partners, display resignation about this gradual and »natural« loosening of ties. However, the interviewees stress that the existing possibilities of regular meetings and communication media reduce this price they pay for their mobile lifestyle. None of the interviewees considers returning to their home country because of friends. Mobility simply requires caring about old relationships, and if one does not undertake this effort, it is, unfortunately, very possible that a friendship may end. The difference from »settlers« is · that mobile people have to »re-establish relationships to friends« when they come back (I4: 65).

Boden and Molotch (1994) maintain that since co-present interaction is fundamental to social intercourse, virtual travel (communication in distance) will not significantly replace physical travel. The modern world has not reduced the degree to which co-present interaction is preferred and necessary across a wide range of tasks. The analysis of the interviews with my informants confirms this in relation to friendship.

Mobility also influences with whom one has contact, and who becomes a new friend. Very often, new friends are expatriates or belong to an international community, connected either by thematic issues or by membership in the same organization (I3: 50). The problem of making new friends will be discussed in more detail in the following chapters.

However, the role of extensive mobility in relation to the social networks of the individuals should not be overestimated. Many old friendships do indeed weaken over the years due to increased mobility. However, many friendships also break up as a natural development, due to a change of interests and life-styles that is not necessarily related to mobility. Many informants stress that mobility has not really influenced their social networks: their circle of friends and acquaintances has changed because of long working hours or the the demands of family life, especially children. These results do not differ greatly from the studies of non-mobile groups of adults, who report having minimal time for friends because other responsibilities interfere with them (Sigman 1991; Rawlins 1992; 1994: 282). When children are born the circle of friends evolves. First, one has less spare time, is more constrained, or cannot stay late in the evening. Second, one chooses friends who also have children so that when meeting them, the kids can play together (I5: 73). Martin, the young father and the father-to-be for the second time, notes with some sadness that the criteria for meeting people are driven almost exclusively by children (I3: 92). On the other hand, when there are children, it becomes more important to maintain contact with the family in their home country. Although some ties may become weak, others are refreshed and reinforced. As mentioned before, many informants spend their holidays together with their children in their country of origin, to enable the children to develop a relationship to their grandparents and their family, as well as to the culture and the country.

Relationships under conditions of spatial remoteness are in fact relationships under conditions of temporal ruptures, which affect individuals most. The interviewees complain about irregularity, time shortages and squeezes, real or experienced (Southerton et al. 2001). Every travel fragments the time with family or friends, the time spent in physical proximity. Over the year, this time is divided into short periods, it discontinues. Further, time delays are a problem for the individuals: they render impossible that immediate reaction that affects the intimacy of the relationships.

4.4.3. Keeping chaos under control

Mobility not only makes it difficult to maintain contact with old friends. It also limits contact with those who would otherwise be in proximity, in the same place of residence. One is often away from home, and this makes it difficult to organize daily life. Social life can be handicapped by the amount of traveling. There is little time for being together with the spouse or friends. Frequent absences make it difficult to maintain friendships in a place or to develop friendships, to be a member of a club, or to participate in collective activities (I2: 99). Such simple things as meeting friends, or going to the cinema, may be disrupted by extensive mobility, says Ann, who took sixteen trips last year (I11: 72). Her social life is disrupted, and her husband's is too, because he waits for her before meeting their common friends.

Your family will wait for you, but many of your friends may not be prepared to wait months until you are back and have time to meet them. It is complicated to maintain contact to »just friends«, because »people do not understand« and »only the true friendships keep« (I7: 101). It is difficult to find a girlfriend or a boyfriend because you have little time to spend together with another person in one place, which is very important, especially at the very beginning of a relationship. The interviewees feel isolated from other people, who do not understand their way of life:

»Nobody of my friends has such a way of living […] they are really tired of setting up the dates for our meetings or parties exactly when I happen to be in town, it is unpleasant to them because I have no chance to keep my promises. The problem is that I have so many friends, a large group. And I have only half a year in the country, there is not enough time to meet all of them.« (I7: 101)

Similarly, it is hard to plan any other activities, for example, attending a language course that requires regular attendance. Although many business trips can be planned well in advance, most of the informants are away from their place of residence for some two weeks a month. Often, however, trips are not planned more than a month in advance and already-scheduled events must be postponed. Ludmila managed to meet her private language teacher only once a month, and later only once in three months. Finally, she resigned (I7: 105), as both she and the teacher were too stressed and disappointed with the situation.

It is no wonder that the informants have few hobbies and that most of them just go to a gym, which does not require them to plan: they pop in to a gym during lunch break or immediately after work. It is a hobby that does not require regularity and can be exercised anywhere, including in a hotel while on a trip. Some do similar things outdoors, for example, power or Norwegian walking, biking, etc. Extensive mobility means that spare time activities are individualized. A favorite hobby of many informants is to be at home: to spend time together with the family, do some work in the garden, cook together one evening, take care of the household.

The single informants in particular complain at length about how difficult it is to organize their own household. Simple little things are rendered problematic by mobility. As mentioned before, there are bills to be paid, and often they remain unpaid for a longer time because of a trip. Small household repairs are difficult to arrange when one is home only at weekends. These things are much easier for those who rent a flat than for house owners. In many situations, one has to rely on the help of friends, family and hired people, for example *au pairs*, house cleaners, housekeepers, etc. The female informants all complain that their household is not in the condition they would wish, because they simply lack the time for housework. Tolga managed to keep her household under control only thanks to the help of her mother and an *au pair*. Sabah relied on the help of her husband and a nanny.

Health problems are a direct consequence of mobility. Many interviewees complain about bad hygiene conditions in the countries of their destination, as well as diseases, and unusual food that affects their health badly. In addition, the change of time zones, long hours on planes and connection time at the airports, extremely long working hours when abroad, general stress related to work, and changing conditions all have an impact on the informants' health. The problems continue when at home, and so they need time to recover after each trip, and this in turn reduces the time they can enjoy at home with their families. Each informant has developed a strategy to protect his or her own health: they have obligatory injections against tropical diseases, carry medications for diarrhea and food poisoning, care about hygiene, and carefully avoid eating unpeeled fruits and drinking unboiled water. They rely on the experience of travelers, on the formal advice of the Health Department, and on their own instincts. Even so, many become very sick each time they travel, and in some cases the only strategy left is to search for an assignment that does not require them to travel.

The sections above have revealed some of the difficulties related to extensive mobility. First, mobility requires individuals to organize their personal life around it, in a way that minimizes some elements, while others are supported by various networks. For example, maintaining close relationship to family requires extensive use of tools of distance communication, such as e-mails and phones. Most informants call their families at home every day while they are abroad. They also limit many activities in order to find more time for their families. For example, Diego likes playing golf, but he gave up this hobby to spend more time with his small daughters. Reiner bicycles to the office and so uses the time effectively, by exercising while on the way to the office. At weekends and in the evening, he can dedicate all this spare time to his family. However, although mobility is highly relevant, a lack of time for family, hobbies, household, and friends is not exclusively a problem of highly mobile people. As the example of Tolga shows, she had exactly the same problems both when mobile and when just working in the office. Some problems increase with mobility, and do not disappear despite more regular working hours. Most of the interviewed individuals work long hours in the office. Also, the discontinuity of the interviewees' friendships cannot be clearly assigned to mobility only. Rather, the challenges of adult life, multiple commitments, and pursuing one's career are responsible for weakening friendship ties.

Mobility is also relevant inasfar as it leads to a temporal shift in the social practices of the interviewees. The greatest difficulty about mobility is its irregular character. It makes it difficult to arrange a meeting with friends, to take part in any group activities, and to be a member of any association. It is especially a problem when one has to invest time and attention in a new relationship, or develop trust with new friends or a new partner. Some complain that the other cannot understand their mobile way of life, and have little patience for them. Many do not tolerate constantly postponed meetings, and arranging their time to fit the informant's travel schedule. Perhaps this is why four of the informants' partners also work in the IO, and are themselves mobile. Mobile individuals have to make an effort to re-integrate in their environments each time they come back home.

It is believed that distance communication mitigates these effects of mobility and spatial ruptures. However, the literature has focused on the geographical and spatial aspects, as in discussions of the networked society. The interviewees in the group of mobile transnational professionals use distance communication tools as part of their daily activities. They do »network« daily, they bridge the spatial distance by communicating. If communication has to proceed, there are few limitations to it. The barriers to communication lie not in the accessibility of technical media, but in the comfort and quality of their usage, time shortages, and language. However, although the interviewees have access to the most modern media, they are rather traditional users. They use stationary telephones, they rarely use the Internet, and none of them indicated that they used chat rooms or instant messaging programs. For them, emails and phones are a mean of sustaining contact with parents, siblings, and friends, and when they enlarge their networks they rely entirely on face-to-face interactions. It is possible that their physical mobility hinders their »virtual« mobility.

While focusing on the interviewees' practice of communicating over distance, I observed a split into two separate worlds, in both of which my interview partners dwell: a virtual world, in which business and coordination are managed (even if often with some difficulty), and a real world, in which intimate or difficult matters are shared. This division is not identical to that between private and public, or between private and business spheres. These worlds are not interchangeable. The division between them is marked by a change in the content and quality of the messages transmitted. In the virtual world, messages tend to »disappear« in the huge information traffic. Many remain unanswered, and although the flow occurs, communication often does not. In this world, certain functions are exercised: coordination, document and information sharing, updating, scheduling, etc. The choice of tool depends on the type of task to be performed: e-mails for co-ordination of meetings, audio-conferencing for agreeing with a group of people, videoconferencing for solving minor problems and updating, phone for exchanging reactions, etc. Location matters little here. »Real« life is handicapped by extensive mobility. When a person relocates over a long distance, there is an anxiety that the intimacy of relationships with those left behind will deteriorate. Distance communication tools are a poor replacement for physical proximity, because they do not offer the same »richness« of communication (Jaffe/Aidmann 1998: 180). In this world, physical and temporal proximity gain importance as factors influencing intimacy in the relationship.

Distance communication tools are an important component of each remote relationship. However, their power to mitigate the physical distance is imperfect, because they do not diminish sufficiently the temporal aspects of the social practices of mobile individuals. They may have the power to »reduce« the geographical distance between family members and friends, so that geographical distance does not necessarily mean loss of intimacy and emotional detachment. However, the temporal aspects of each relationship remain affected by physical distance, which is a threat to intimacy and emotional proximity. Remote relationships are more affected by time shortages and temporal ruptures, which require more effort in coordinating and sustaining synchronization than in bridging the physical gaps. The temporal aspects decide on the individual's membership in social groups, both small-scale networks and larger communities, which require participation in their spatio-temporal trajectories more than being physically present in a particular place.

PART 3
SPATIAL RELATIONS RECONSIDERED

5. Mobilization and disembedding processes

5.1. The IO's networks

Let us have a closer look at the IO itself, to understand the context in which this extensive mobility takes place. The structure of the organization includes different departments operating inside the organization. When preparing to travel, the interviewees contact the infrastructure of the IO, which helps them to take any necessary actions. Organizing travel is simple. One contacts the in-house travel agent, who deals with tickets, bookings, and a visa, if required. In this case, the infrastructure consists of procedures, material equipment (for example, booking tickets via e-mail, or using electronic forms sent directly from the respective web sites), and people (3: 20-22). The health department is also a significant part of the infrastructure (12: 21, 19: 106). It monitors the situation in those destination countries where various dangerous diseases occur, issues warnings to employees, and provides them with any necessary medications.

The IO has its internal job market, which functions alongside the external one. This enables employees to compete with each other for assignments within the IO. Tolga explains that she found her current job in this way (15: 100). Changing assignment within the IO leads to the exchange of experience and individual promotion. The interviewees think that this makes the IO an interesting place to work, as one is able to enjoy a diversity of topics, tasks, geographical locations, and people.

The IO has offices in over one hundred countries all over the world. Having worked in Europe, you have a chance to work next in Africa, Asia, or South or Latin America. Changing assignment involves a different scope of responsibilities, a new environment, new colleagues, and new destination countries. Many use a change of assignment to direct the amount of travel undertaken and to control their own mobility.

For the re-settlers, the IO also provides financial assistance, including below-market-rate loans available for a variety of purposes, for example the purchase of a first home. A mobility premium is also available. It assists staff members and their families with the general costs associated with expatriation. In the case of temporary assignments abroad, another set of allowances and benefits applies. However, it is one interviewee's personal opinion that these benefits are no longer a major factor for seeking overseas assignments, because they are no longer as high as they once were (I5: 103).

The IO's employees' organization also gives advice on how to make the process of moving household and family less frustrating and less time-consuming. It deals with overcoming the differences between the countries of origin and settlement. Its services include advising on schooling for children, spouse career, housing, and child and elderly care. The IO supports several voluntary networks that provide guidance to assist new settlers. One network advises spouses and life-partners with job search and employment in the USA. A housing advisory network provides information on issues relating to short-term and long-term housing options, including interpreting and negotiating rental leases and sales contracts, and referrals to real estate agents. A childcare advisory service helps in evaluating and selecting quality childcare, infant care at home, and pre-school. Similarly, schooling advisory provides assistance in understanding the national educational system, choosing public and private schools, and provides information on any special programs for children with behavioral problems. When one is assigned to another country, a special team can provide information on the living conditions, cultural customs, and religious beliefs and practices of the host country. It mediates between the families of IO staff members already residing there. The IO also offers language training. Other facilities or procedures supporting the mobility of the employees include the systems of distance communication, the standardization of procedures and working conditions worldwide, and mobility rewarding systems.

On business travel, the interviewees use the support of various technical networks, including computers, telephone messaging, post, and satellite connections. The IO offers traveling employees the use of special rooms in their offices that have been prepared to accommodate visiting staff. There they can use computers and satellite connections. It is also possible to check e-mail for private purposes, and talk to family. Re-settlers can also connect to the satellite network from home (I5: 73). The satellite connections are used for both business and private purposes, as is e-mail. Most interviewees do not have separate private e-mail accounts and they use the IO facilities to communicate with family and friends. Cheap and convenient telephone connections have improved greatly in the last few years, and the mobile employees appreciate this immensely (I2: 83). It matters less now that you are away from home, because it is now possible to stay in contact (I4: 109).

Another mobility-supporting mechanism is the system of points-trips. Reiner explains that this is a system of points rewarding extensive mobility. For every two hundred days an employee is on travel, he or she can take his or her spouse on a business trip (I2: 75). The IO sponsors spouse travel. Given the number of days they travel, every mobile employee is able to take the family on a business trip every eighteen months.

The obvious example that comes to mind, when thinking about mobility and networks, is the existence of the IO's offices all around the world. Although the local IO office is not the first destination of most traveling employees, he or she always contacts it. There is no standard design of the offices but many look similar. Some newer offices have similar furniture but they differ greatly in size. There is a huge difference between the main office and the local offices, mostly because of the type of work performed in them. Their equipment has to meet different needs. There are also great variations in the size of these offices, and this influences their architectural inner design.

All the local offices have a designated contact person for the traveling employee, to support him or her, and to co-operate on specific tasks. Many offices have special rooms for visitors, with computers and telephones at the disposal of travelers. However, this does not necessarily meet the needs of the visitors, as Reiner explains. Usually it is much more comfortable to use the laptop in a hotel room than in a crowded and noisy visitors room (I2: 43). Most IO mobile staff members travel with laptops and have access to all documents, e-mails, and other tools independently of the IO's network. Some of them use docking stations in their home offices to work stationary, and before leaving they update files (download software, replicate databases, etc.), in order not to have to do it in local offices (I2: 31). Most interviewees admit dropping by local offices to use the phone. Abroad, they hardly ever use a mobile phone, because it is the most expensive option, and often impossible for technical reasons. The IO has its own satellite connections that make phoning much cheaper. The travelers use them both for business and private reasons, rather than phoning from hotels, which used to be very expensive, especially some years ago. At present, employees can call their family once when they arrive, at the expense of the IO. Otherwise, many use the satellite connection from home, which reduces general phone costs significantly (I5: 73).

5.2. Supplementary networks and routines

There are also networks external to the IO, which are not the IO's property but do have a complementary role in supporting the mobility of the IO's employees extensively. The IO has special agreements with other networks: for example, hotels, airlines, airports, translators, etc.

Local offices are very important for the IO, but they play little role for employees during and before travel. Many of the usual trips are to meet counterparts in the country, and these meetings are scheduled directly by the traveler, before arrival, from his or her main office per e-mail or phone. The local offices help only when coordination with the local team member is required. The first destination after arrival is thus a hotel. Hotels are a part of non-IO networks that are complementary to the IO, and they are a very important component of travel. For most interviewees, they are not only a place to sleep but also to work, especially in the evenings and over the weekends, when they provide a quiet place offering comfort and privacy (I6: 44).

The majority of the interviewees place high value on the choice of a hotel. A room has to be comfortable and large, and have a good Internet connection. Equally important is its location: it should be close to the IO's local office, and also in an area with many restaurants and attractions within walking distance. When the interviewees find a hotel that they like, they try to stay there on every trip (I3: 110), but of course this not always easy or possible. There are towns where the tourist infrastructure is very poor and there are no convenient hotels: they are too small and often fully booked, or their infrastructure is insufficient.

A very interesting network that supports extensive mobility is the network of language interpreters and translators. The inability to communicate abroad could hinder mobility. Therefore, the IO pays interpreters to enable communication with the native citizens (I2: 61). Like a satellite connection, an interpreter is an essential tool in communicating, and in making further conversation possible. Usually English makes mobility much easier. It is sufficient that people »understand enough for you to survive« (I11: 66). Of course, this is not yet the case in every destination, but at least in the IO's offices, and in hotels and airports, one can communicate reasonably well using English. It may be any other language, of course. When no common language is available, some interviewees rely on alternative communication skills, for example, body language (especially in informal situations), but more frequently other people:

»Sometimes important people, for example a minister, don't speak any English and then you communicate through their people, their deputies, assistants, etc. or what I also do very often is a conference call. I have the interpreter on the line and the person I would like to talk. So the interpreter interprets it as in a real meeting.« (I2: 61)

Here people and language very visibly constitute one network. If one uses one's own language skills rather than relying on interpreters, the degree of independence changes. Many new settlers have to build on local office employees, advisory networks, groups of expatriates, new acquaintances, international schools, etc. Such a network can be very complex, and in the case of resettlement it usually includes all these elements.

Other complementary networks include airports, airlines and ground transportation systems, restaurants, television, etc. The interviewees use chain hotels, fly and take planes, and make stops or arrive at airports. They find themselves in different infrastructure networks that sometimes connect distant points of the world. Moreover, the interviewees normally choose the same connections and the same cities to change flights (I2: 43).

The basic importance of these networks lies in providing similarity independent of the location. This in turn enables routine behavior. Networks offer the same conditions in different places. Despite regional differences, one can expect similar equipment in a hotel, a restaurant offering international cuisine, service in English, etc. Regardless of which airline one chooses, a meal will be offered in the plane, as will newspapers and video (I2: 41). Furthermore, there is certainly a business lounge at the airport, as well as some shops and restaurants. English is also spoken there. The same is true of re-settlement: the individuals spend their time in networks of expatriates, their children go to international schools, they shop in self-service stores that lack the »local fleur«, watch non-dubbed English movies in cinemas, watch cable TV in English, etc. No matter where one is, one can rely on networks and expect their nodes to be similar. The interviewees certainly do. They appreciate networks and use them, because they make travel easy. »There is no problem« is the most frequent judgment in relation to networks.

The technical and organizational networks of the IO make people mobile. Their personal motivations to travel are accommodated and supported by the IO. Individuals also work out their own methods of sustaining mobility, to make resettlement easier, or to avoid the negative consequences of being mobile. Such techniques are complementary to the institutional assistance, and the individuals use them whenever the IO's support does not exist or is insufficient. They help to deal with being mobile, with facing new sites, new problems, new people and places. If a network does not provide enough similarity, or where there is no network, the interviewees themselves produce similarity through routines.

Even at the preparation stage, every step is routine. Without difficulty, the interviewees can explain in detail how a typical trip looks, as all trips are similar. One communicates with the counterparts in a destination country and agrees on a date for the visit. The date is then coordinated and agreed upon by the team members. The next step is to prepare all the necessary documents, and to agree the detailed agenda of the visit with team and the counterparts. One should not forget to replicate the databases on a laptop. At the same time, one contacts the in-house travel agent electronically. The itinerary is stored in a computer database, and the Health Department is automatically notified; if necessary, it informs the traveler per e-mail of medications or injections required for the trip (19). Packing is an important part of preparation. It is an experience driven by routine to pack proper clothes, medications, vitamins, etc. One takes little things to make the stay in a hotel room nicer, for example, thick socks (16). This routine may be partly disturbed by the weather conditions in the destination country: depending on these, the set of clothes may differ (12). Most interviewees travel on Saturdays or Sundays in order to start the week with meetings, and to have some time to overcome jet lag beforehand. On the day of departure, one takes a taxi to the airport »and ... off you go« (12: 39).

The entire schedule of a stay abroad is standardized. One arrives at the airport, takes a taxi or shuttle to the hotel, depending on the destination town (I2: 43), and follows the regular agenda. Reiner says he always sleeps for two to three hours because he is badly jet-lagged. Only later does he go to any meetings in his timetable (I2: 43). Others take a sleeping pill and sleep overnight despite being tired, or go to a gym to avoid falling asleep (I1). The following days resemble each other: there are a couple of meetings with clients, some short and some long; but, whatever the precise issues or project, the working day starts at 8.00 in the morning and ends late in the evening. At the end of the day, there are usually issues to discuss with colleagues, documents to read, and many e-mails to answer, as Lenka (I6: 40) and Reiner (I2: 45) complained. There is very rarely spare time to relax in the evenings or on the weekends.

Even when there is some, spare time is also a matter of habit. Reiner, for example, always does power-walks through the city, usually taking the same route (I2: 47). This does not change from trip to trip. In this way, his stays abroad somehow resemble ordinary days in the USA, where he bikes regularly to the office and back (I2: 89).

The repeated actions that have to be undertaken when preparing and when traveling make being mobile easier. The interviewees often reflect on this, saying that after many years of traveling one has to develop a routine. One is used to packing, or »one stays packed in a way« (I4: 63), one knows how many shirts and suits to take. Routine helps to minimize the risks and stress related to travel, and to mitigate many difficult situations that arise in private life because of extensive mobility. Feeling lonely abroad can be minimized by making yourself comfortable in a hotel. Knowing how to achieve this feeling is a matter of experience. Routine actions minimize the stress related to preparations and being abroad. Routine also helps during travel, when waiting at airports, for example. Thanks to routine, one knows when to leave home for the airport, not to come too early, and to wait for a shorter amount of time (I6: 161). Having routines is seen as natural, a way humans are. People always follow »a standard program« (I6: 42) because they eat breakfast, dress, go to work, eat dinner, and so on. Travel routines are no different. Importantly, having routines means knowing how to make oneself feel comfortable away from home, how to organize a day in another place, and not having »to improvise« (I6: 42). It means one feels secure, thanks to routines. One knows what to expect and how to behave in a situation.

Often, travel routines also relate to interviewees' private life. Usually, they standardize their holidays: for example, by going to the same place every year, or relying on standard packages (I3: 72). They use other networks and networking agents, such as a travel agency, justifying it by saying that it makes life easier.

Networks and routines play an important role: they create similarity and familiarity in every location. In every place in the world, the practices of the individuals are similar. For the individuals, networks and routines enable mobility and make it easier. They reduce its negative consequences, mainly the effort and stress related to frequent adaptation to new conditions. They also mean that locations matter less; they do not influence the individuals' practices to the extent that they would if the networks and routines did not exist.

5.3. The non-spatial principle of fixation

External job posting ads state that »The IO offers an internationally competitive compensation package including pension, health insurance, and other benefits«. Inquiry at the IO's web sites sheds more light on these benefit systems: the IO has its own retirement plan, comprised of insurance for retirement, death, disability, and withdrawal upon termination. It also offers various resettlement benefits and termination grants. The various staff programs include internal and external training, childcare, discount vision care, exercise facilities, periodic health examinations, etc.

Special rules apply to the taxation of salaries. Employees are paid on a net-of-income basis, as most staff members are not subject to taxation on income received from the IO. An employee of the IO is no longer subject to any state taxation policy or social insurance system. In addition, the IO's property is by law »immune from search, requisition, confiscation, expropriation, or any other form of seizure by executive or legislative action«. Employees of the IO also enjoy immunities and privileges. Those who are not local nationals are granted immunities from immigration restrictions, alien registration requirements, and national service obligations. Those with »a problematic nationality«, for example Pakistani, which could cause problems when entering India, or Iranians, are given diplomatic passes enabling them to enter any country (I9: 523). The existing agreements between the IO and the nation-states guarantee not only the immunity of its employees and properties, but also a special status equal to that of an official of the country. This relates for example to travel and communication. Any official communication of the IO enjoys the same treatment as an official communication of a nation-state.

The IO is a thus comprehensive organization. Alongside its well-developed network of offices, it has a well-developed technical infrastructure, including equipment for data transfer, video and audio conferencing, e-mail, laptops, etc. Several institutions, such as the in-house travel agent, the various advisory networks, the Health Department, and many other programs, enable and support the mobility of its employees. An individual who undertakes employment in the IO joins a complex system.

This has two main consequences. First, many who enter the IO move from their home countries to the USA, where the IO headquarters is located, or to another host country if taking an overseas assignment. However, they do not migrate from one nation-state system to another, but rather enter an exterritorial organization. All these measures put the IO in a position that is similar to and competitive with the national welfare state. In certain respects, the IO assumes the functions of a nation-state. Its employees are disembedded from a nation-state system and are integrated into the IO system, with its own labor market, pension system, medical care, etc. The analysis of the context of their extensive mobility leads to the hypothesis that the interviewees cannot be considered as »external to each state« (Deleuze 1986: 49-53), but are rather located within the non-state structures of the IO. They are disembedded from the territorially-bound structures of a state, but at the same time fixed in the social space structured by the IO.

The IO has the power to detach the individuals from their bonds and mobilize them. It assumes some of the functions of national welfare states. The difference between these two organizations lies in their relation to space. Unlike a national welfare state, the IO does not follow a territorial principle of fixation. It does not aim at excluding any part of the space for itself and can co-exist with various organizations, including national welfare states. Its relation to space is based on the functional principle. It creates and locates offices in order to perform its tasks. However, often its direct presence is not needed to exercise its functions in a country. No local binding is necessary to create a bond for its members.

The question is what kind of consequences this has for individuals who are mobilized and disembedded by the IO. Following Simmel's argument, that every social fact finds its spatial reflection, we suspect that the fact that the employees of the IO are fixed in its structures has a spatial reflection. How the processes of re-embeddedness and, consequently, re-territorialization happen must be investigated. Given Simmel's recognition that not every relation to space has a necessary character, and that a non-territorial principle of fixation applies to many social formations, a question arises: do mobile individuals fix themselves following a non-territorial principle, for example, the functional one? What is their logic of fixing? Is it territorial? Do individuals choose their locations? Under the conditions of extensive mobility, it seems unlikely that the primary logic of fixation is territorial.

The interviewees were asked about their experiences of living abroad and being at home. In addition, questions on their plans for the future, mobility decisions, and life course helped to reveal the principle of fixation. Given the powerful context, it was expected that the individuals would indicate their job as a primary factor in deciding on their location. Indeed, when asked about their plans for the future, and in particular where they would like to live, all the interviewees answered that »it all depends on the job« (I4: 69). They choose particular tasks that seem important and interesting, and take them further in their personal development and career, and they do not »have anything against moving to another country« (I4: 69). As to their reasons for changing place of residence in the past, the individuals mentioned interesting programs at universities, particular courses offered at schools, language training, and the possibility of undertaking desired assignments in various companies or organizations.

The majority of those interviewed see their future within the IO. For them, the choice of residence is closely related to an assignment. The IO has not created any privileged locations, despite the clear distinction between headquarters and the field offices, which might suggest this. None of the interviewees expressed the wish to work in the main IO's office, or in any particular office. Thus, although the geographical structure of the IO predetermines the scope of locations for its employees, it does not add any system of preferences to it. Individual interest in performing particular tasks is the decisive factor in choosing a particular location. If one likes the current place of residence, any move must be driven by a job that is »something special« (I8: 69).

As described above, the IO offers sufficient possibilities to enable employees to control their own mobility. Despite this undertaking, a particular assignment may be related to extensive travel and change of residence, and anyone who opts for this must sign a contract, including a clause about readiness for mobility. It is always possible to choose an assignment that does not require extensive travel. When mobility becomes a burden to individuals (in the case of women, this is usually when they have children), they take the initiative and change their job within the IO. As Samir says, nobody forces you to travel (I1). As a result, mobility is generally not seen as enforced by the IO. It is a part of everyday life, and one can control it by taking opportunities. In this process, the choice of location is a secondary issue (I4: 67). The primary choice is functional. The spatial logic plays a secondary role.

We are looking at the following process: the IO, although in principle indifferent to space, creates the system of offices from where its operations are led. It has thus its spatial manifestation. For individuals who follow the functional principle of location, the office location of the IO becomes the focal point for their business and private life. At these focal points, the individuals construct their homes. They move their family and their belongings to a new location. In this way, an old location becomes mobile (I9: 82). All the belongings that give you a feeling of being at home, as the interviewees say, are transferred to the new focal point. Over time, the process of re-embedding is completed. The new focal point becomes the location of home, with all its features – a network of friends, favorite restaurants, places to exercise, hobbies, etc.

Fixing is a process. The role of time has two dimensions. On the one hand, the individuals stress the temporality of their life arrangements. They do not make long-term plans. It is precisely this temporality that enables flexibility. The motto for life is Grab the chance, as shown in the previous chapter:

»I didn't have any plan if to stay or not to stay. I took it as it was, my purpose was just to do my master and after that we will see.« (I5: 23)

For Tolga, this lack of planning resulted in her spending over ten years in the USA. Because she had never planned to do this, she had no problem accepting a move to another country some years later. With the same flexibility, she agrees with her husband's plans to move to Germany, or to

Belgium, or to the Netherlands – wherever he finds an interesting job for himself.

On the other hand, they note that time is needed for embedding. It takes time to get to know the place and to meet new friends:

»Well, over a passage of time it became home here you get used to place you're living you get used to shopping and the places that you shop.« (14: 97)

It is understandable that many years are needed to establish a bond to a place. However, all the interviewees displayed the ability to adapt quickly. Many overseas assignments last between three and five years, and this is enough to enable them to achieve a feeling of being at home.

However, the relativity of fixation is not unrestrained. There are two limits to it. The first relates to the substantive qualities of locations, such as climate, inhabitants, armed conflicts, and diseases. Most interviewees would prefer not to move to countries in which the domestic political situation does not guarantee security. Some would consider such a country, but only for a short time. Some have had such experiences in the past, for example, in Africa: they faced very poor hygienic conditions, and they would not like to return there. Either they feel too old for such adventures, or they wish better surroundings for their families.

The second limit relates to the symbolic, if not the sentimental, value of a place. Many interviewees stress that, when they retire, they would like to go back to their country of origin. Those who come from Europe would choose any European country as a possible location when retiring:

»In general I am big European fan and I am hoping that that's the place...I mean when I retire I go back to Europe.« (13: 136)

The greatest difference is whether one makes plans in one's professional or private life. In professional life, location follows the non-spatial principle almost exclusively. Individuals position themselves primarily within the socio-technical structures of the employing agency. Re-embedding and re-territorialization follow the focal points of the organization. Similarly, private locations depend on different networks of infrastructure (for example schools and universities) and the social networks of family and friends. However, in this case individuals set clearer limits to their choice of location. The substantive qualities of places take on importance, and favorite places do not have to serve any purpose:

»Everywhere where there is sunshine I like to go and it is depending of course on the memory of the trips I have. If I had extraordinary good time there and you have good memories then you want to go there again.« (I5: 117)

Perhaps the words of Samir, one of the interviewees, summarize this best. According to him, there are four components of life: family, community, work, and friends. These are not equal components, but one has to keep them in equilibrium. By community, he refers to city and neighbors. The city is also important, and one must like the city he or she lives in: otherwise it is not possible to have a good quality of life. The proportions between these components may differ and are not equal. They are subject to change over time, but they must always be in equilibrium (I1). Three of these four components of life, as specified by Samir, are not spatial. The individuals fix themselves within socio-technical structures, trying to find a balance between work, family, and friends. The qualities of a place are of secondary importance for the individuals.

6. Placing

The description of the sample makes it clear that the research group is characterized by geographical promiscuity. Many interviewees have moved several times between continents. They speak more than one foreign language at work, and often their families too are bi- or multilingual. Some actively participate in host communities, and are engaged socially to ensure that they do not lose ties to their home communities. Some have changed their citizenship. Their life courses are inconsistent with the assumed isomorphism of space, place, and culture, which has dominated research in the last decades (Ferguson/Gupta 1997: 34). Such a presumed convergence of culture (language), identity (origin), community (participation), and territoriality (place) is at the basis of studies within methodological nationalism (Martins 1974: 276; Smith 1983: 26; Beck 1997a: 116; 2004a: 21; 2004b; Wimmer/Glick Schiller 2002).

The following chapter addresses the problem of spatialization under conditions of extensive mobility, starting at the level of the most private socio-spatial interaction, meaning those spaces called home. Mary Douglas writes that we think of home as a kind of space, defined with such terms as »here« and »where«. It is a localizable idea. The question is not »how« nor »who« nor »when«, but »where is your home« (Douglas 1991: 289). Home is a structure in space and time. Much of the literature considers home as a fixed location embedded in a broader cultural, ethnic, or national environment. Thus, mobility is seen as a danger. Gupta notices that anthropology has been based on the unspoken premise that »home« is a place of cultural sameness, and that difference is to be found abroad (Gupta 1997: 32). This convergence is very doubtful in the light of studies on the mobility of images and information, which leads to the separation of space and culture, and community and territoriality. However, the authors are not sure about the extent of mobility's influence on the idea of home (Rapport/Dawson 1998: 27).

The second part of the chapter focuses more generally on the question of attachment to places, under the condition of extensive individual mobility.

6.1. Attached to a detached home

Home is traditionally understood as a source of individual identity and as a place. The word »domestic«, derived from *domus*, carries its Latin sense of both a physical and affectionate place of residence and reproduction (Immerfall 1998: 176). The formation of individual and collective identities begins at home, understood as a place (Ong/Nonini 1997). Short (1999) writes that home is a key site in the social organization of space. It is a meaningful and active moment in time and space, and in the creation of individual identity, social relations, and collective meaning: home is where »space becomes »place«. Home is thus considered a fixed environment: being at home means being stationary, centered, bounded, fitted, engaged, grounded (Rapport/Dawson 1998: 21). Home is considered a stable unmoving center from which the world around can be perceived, conceived, and experienced, and, thanks to which, ethnic and national identities can develop. Clifford (1998) postulated that the research aims to look at the processes, rather than at the essences that are involved in present experiences of identity building. However, the anthropological and geographical traditions would rather tie the issues of Being (Heidegger), belonging, community, collectivity, and the existential issues of the self, with home as something subjective, located, and placed. Such a defined home is opposed to space, which is open, meaningless, and enables motion. Most of the research employs this distinction and bases its arguments on the essentialist view of places.

The notion of home is idealized and emotionally loaded. Home is linked to the past, the history – of a person and of a place. On the one hand, time is needed to develop a bond to a place; on the other hand, for those who have left, for migrants, home becomes a point in the past, the place they used to occupy, as it used to be, as a stopped history (Massey 2005: 123). Travelers and migrants re-establish the feeling of homeness by repeating daily activities, for example eating the food that they had when at home, bringing the past back in (Clarke 2005: 314). Therefore, mobility is seen rather as a danger to personal well-being, and mobile people as uprooted. Although recent decades have seen a growing interest in the mobility of people, goods, money, and information, the concern with losing one's stable point of perspective has increased rather than faded, because movement was mythologized in anthropology as enabling fixity (Rapport/Dawson 1998: 22). For many authors, exile, emigration, labor migration, and tourism are the central motifs of modern culture, while being rootless, displaced between worlds, and living in a fluid present are the most fitting metaphors for the modern consciousness (Nkosi 1994: 5). Mobility is said to take people out of their places of origin. Mobile people are rootless, have no ties to any particular place, and their identity is apparently de-territorialized (Ferguson/Gupta 1997: 39). Having no roots, binding, or home has been pathologized in »the national order of things« (Malkki 1997: 62), in which the nation, its territory, and the imaginative collectiveness are the source of any individual identity. In this approach, any migration is considered to occur between the containers of nation-states, and mobility thus levers people out from the identity-building structures. Within this pessimistic (postmodern) perspective, mobility leads to the emergence of »non-places« (Augé 1994: 92ff), space with no identity and history, in which mobile people spend most of their time, and with which they do not have any relationship. On the other hand, it creates people who are lonely and live only in the absolute present. They do not have a point where the past, the present, and the future could meet (Heller 1995: 2).

Some authors recognize that the idea of home involves mobility. Ferguson notices that the notion of »home« as a durably fixed place is in doubt, although certain aspects of life can remain »localized« in a social sense (Ferguson 1997: 39). Urry observes that contemporary forms of dwelling always involve diverse forms of mobility (Urry 2000: 133). People dwell in and through being at home and away, through the dialectic of roots and routes. In other words, one dwells not only at place (Heidegger) but also when on the move, in travel (Clifford 1997: 2). Conceptualizations of home thus require a broader perspective of pluri-local attachments. Home should be seen as something that individuals can take along as they move through time and space (Rouse 1991: 8). The idea of home undergoes a change. For a world of travelers and journeymen, home comes to be found in a routine set of practices, in a repetition of habitual social interactions, in the ritual of a regularly used personal name (Rapport 1994).

Home also involves mobility in another sense. Home is a place that one leaves and returns to. Home is thus a turning point of movement, not an exit. It is not given, but established by movement. The home may well be a place, but feelings of being at home are activated by movement back and forth (Westman 1991: 20).

Social psychology stresses the role of security and familiarity in the constitution and the meaning of »home« (Hage 1997). This aspect is especially important in relation to people who were involuntarily displaced, and are forced to live in exile. For them, home comes to be found in a routine set of practices, a repetition of habitual interactions, in memories and myths, in stories carried around in their heads (Berger 1984). Often, home is constructed around religious practices, which connect an individual with a community and place of origin, and offer emotional support during the trauma of resettlement (McMichael 2002).

In contrast to these groups, mobile transnational professionals do not constitute a community: a unit of belonging with clear boundaries that provide a source of common identity (Kennedy 2004: 161). Unlike cross-border migrants, they are not bounded by ties of family and kinship, land, ethnicity, race, nationality, religion, and language. Therefore, the problems and life situations of migrants and mobiles, despite certain similarities, are different. While migrants are told to integrate with the host society and »find their second home« in the host country, mobile people, who re-settle every couple of years, or spend half the year in hotel rooms in various countries, are often considered as uprooted, or they develop multiple roots (Rushdie 1983). Migrants are very likely to sustain extensive connections with their home countries. They may belong to both the country of origin and the host country, and be socially well anchored in both locations. Such connections may induce the creation of international migration networks, and increase the flows of people between the two locations (Chaney 1985; Boyd 1989; Fawcett 1989; Grasmuck/Pessar 1991; Durand/Massey 1992; Wilpert 1992; Portes/Sensenbrenner 1993; Espinosa/Massey 1997). The migration systems (Zolberg/Smith 1996; Faist 2000) or transnational social space, which are a source of individual identity similar to a single homeland, may be constituted on this basis (Glick Schiller et al. 1992; Basch et al. 1997; Pries 2000). There has as yet been no investigation into how chronically mobile people, disembedded from the context of nation-states, maintain their relationships to diverse localities. Little attention has also been dedicated to their informal and smaller-scale yet expanding transnational networks, consisting of interpersonal connections (Dezalay 1990; King 1990; O'Rian 2000; Colic-Peisker 2002; Hannerz 2003; Kennedy 2004).

Mobility means meeting the unknown and often the insecure. For »chronically« mobile people, it means that each time they encounter the different anew. It seems that, under these conditions, security may play a great role in their lives. For a mobile person, home may be a place where it is safe. This is not only the security of staying: there is also the security of being free to come and go. If we start from the assumption that, to be mobile and to stay mobile, it is necessary to have a stable point of reference guaranteeing security, then we have to ask how this feeling of security and stability is achieved. In analyzing the empirical material, I therefore ask about the possibility of achieving security and familiarity under the conditions of extensive mobility. Are they guaranteed by the spatial binding of home? I am also particularly interested in how individuals constitute their homes, where their homes are located, and whether homes are necessarily spatially bounded.

The notions of »home« and »mobility« unavoidably involve the concepts of space and place. Traditionally, social science assumed that mobility is performed in space, and home is bounded to a place, as described in the previous section. To understand the process of constitution of home, under the conditions of mobility, it is thus necessary to re-conceptualize the idea of territorial bounding, and to consciously consider the notions of space and place. I propose to look at »home« differently. Using Simmel's terminology, »home« can be considered a focal point for certain kinds of relation. The spatial binding of a person leads certain forms of relations to gather around this person (Simmel 1983 (1903): 229). By choosing a certain place (a flat, a room, or a house), a person creates a focal point of her/his relation to objects and persons. As discussed above, the choice of this focal point is functional. This does not exclude non-functional relations coming to dominate later in this functionally space-bound focal point. Simmel stresses the role of physical distance or proximity in the form of social relations (1983 (1903): 232). Binding in a certain locality, in physical proximity, induces a certain type of relations (Simmel 1958: 7001). For example, people living in a house can undertake certain activities together, and manage a household together, in a way that those who are spatially separated cannot. Fixation or location has also another importance: a place, not as a commodity, but as a location, is important in realizing the idea of »home« (Simmel 1958: 700).

Under conditions of extensive mobility, it is more than likely that home is constituted in daily practices. The question is how individuals construct home for themselves, and which processes lead to the establishment of the feeling of being at home. What do individuals understand when they mean that they are at home?

Many of my informants pointed to the need to construct home:

»I guess you need to create your own home when you leave the house of your parents. And then depends: it can be very easy if you don't live very far from the rest of your family, your parents and grandparents…depends. And it's like mixture, it is the same thing more or less because you live so close but when you live far and when it is over the ocean then it becomes quite difficult.« (16: 70)

This lack of spatial proximity to the primary family makes it necessary to work out one's own concept of home. Distance from the family makes it more difficult to replicate the example of the parents' home. Residence in a distant place offers new examples and patterns of what »home« means. It opens new horizons, and makes it possible to adapt different models of furnishing, of organizing objects and subjects within a place that is to become home.

This quotation points to a certain dualism in the understanding of home. Home can be, at the same time, an emotional place of origin, the place where one grew up in a family, and a point of departure for the rest of one's life. At the same time, home is something that one constructs: not a place any more, not a particular location, but rather a set of elements. It involves work: it is not given, and it is not chosen out of all possible places. It is not a location one chooses to live in, but a result of a process of working out what »home« means to an individual.

Not all the interviewees speak about »home«. Many refer rather to a point:

»Yes, you need a focal point, you need the point which for you is a point of stability, which makes it easier, at least for me, to deal with all the flags of mobility, when I travel I like to come back to my apartment.« (19: 142)

This is very far from essentialism. A focal point is something »less« than home in the understanding of social psychology, and it does not assume that emotions are involved. It has little to do with the issues of Being, but rather with dwelling, organizing, arranging your life. It is a way of dealing with mobility, a counterpoint to the constant movement, a little piece of stability.

Having a focal point, a point of reference to which you come back, and from which you can depart for your next trip, becomes an urgent need when children appear in the family. All the interviewees who are parents note that children, in particular, need a stable point in their lives. It is necessary for their development. Mobility can be exciting for children (I5: 107), but it is the obligation of the parents to provide them with a home base:

»Now the point of reference is here but we all miss a little bit a point of reference there because it used to be for all the years the point of reference for my children.« (I9: 144)

To become home, it has to be a shared point of reference, a shared focal point. It is not the place that makes it home but the social relations that orbit around this focal point. The immediate family itself, spouse or partner and children, located, physically present in a certain place, is a focal point for mobile individuals. The immediate family is therefore so very important because it gives a feeling of security that results from the stability of arrangements.

Where is such a point? When asked where their home is, many interviewees do not give an answer that localizes home in geographical terms. When asked about where they feel at home, most interviewees first talk about their families. »My home is where I and my family are«, says Martin, »no matter in which country we lived I felt home there« (I3: 120). Despite strong feelings toward the country of origin, Ann says

»Well, it's my home too because it is where my husband is, it's where my pictures are, it's where my current set of clothes is, it's home and I think about when I am coming back think about coming home when I am arriving at the airport I always exhale – I am back.« (I11: 156)

It is interesting that the women interviewed first mention their immediate families, but then speak about different objects, which are for them equally important in feeling at home somewhere:

»[…] home it is your house it your own place that you furnished the way you wanted that you share with your family that's the home.« (I6: 70)

Another interviewee does not really feel at home in her new place of residence, because, due to the weight limit, she couldn't take everything from her house. The things that she was able to take are not enough to make her »feel homey« (I5: 61). She misses her house, which she furnished herself, and where she was surrounded by carefully selected objects, such as paintings, kitchen equipment, et cetera. It is evidently the task of women to construct the materialities of home. Reiner mentions, for example, a table around which he and his family gather for dinner together, and to talk about all that has happened during the day. This table is a central object at home for him, but as a symbol of being together with the family. It could be any table that allows them to sit together, eat, and chat, not this particular table. Importantly, home is less about the essential quality of objects than about relations between them and the individual. For Ludmila, for example, it is very important to own things – her home is where the objects are her property (I7: 31). Similarly, for Tolga, home is full of her pictures, her furniture, her pots (I5: 61). Family is also about the relationship to the people, which makes them different to any other people.

Men either do not take care of the objects at home or, at least, do not care about transporting them to a new destination:

»[…] in our case it was a very conscious decision that we are not going to move around with many things so we tend to very pragmatic people when it comes to that and we basically move around with our cloths.« (I10: 16)

Perhaps it is the task of their wives to care about organizing the move to a new place of residence and furnishing it. Some claim to have not yet found any piece of furniture that they would like to have with them always. Their home is based purely around people, not objects.

Home, however, cannot be limited to a single point, a place, a location, such as a house, a room, a flat, or an apartment. Being at home goes beyond the boundaries of »four walls«. Not only are the objects in the house important in making somewhere feel like at home, but its surroundings too are equally important. The individuals mention infrastructure as an important component of being at home. At this point, a broader sense of »home« emerges from the interviews. Although we usually mean a single house when we call a place home, this place is a part

of a larger infrastructure, and fixation within that infrastructure is central
for the feeling of security. Such infrastructure as schools, restaurants,
parks, places to exercise one's hobbies, cinemas, et cetera, makes it
possible to feel at home in every corner of the world. They are like a
landscape in which one can move freely, where every hill and path is
known. Many individuals claim that they could not move to a place where
such infrastructure is absent, because they could not feel well there, not as
if they were at home (13, various lines). The networks of infrastructure
allow similarity, exactly as do the objects at home that mobile individuals
move from one place of residence to another. They replace time in the role
of assuring familiarity. Reiner, over fifteen years in the USA, says that

»I feel home here because I know the place…and I know it because I spent there
so many years…« (12: 97)

Steven, for example, felt in New York as he did at home, because he had
lived there for over twenty years. Since moving to Hungary, his life has not
changed much because, there too, he found the infrastructure he was used
to in New York. Thanks to this similar infrastructure, the period of
adapting to Hungarian conditions was very short, and after a year Steven
was talking about Hungary as his home (14: 27).). Home-feeling includes
freedom, of movement from and to, as well as freedom of choice about
where and how activities can be performed, within larges spaces. When it
is not possible to go out and live life outside an »immediate« home-place,
the individuals feel restrained. In consequence, they do not feel at home
despite having a focal point.

Recapitulating, home is thus a place where interaction is most
important, where one meets the nearest and dearest, a place that one leaves
and comes back to, a turning point in mobility. Home is where social
relations are based on physical proximity. It embodies social relations and
materialities of certain kind. The same is true for objects: where things that
one owns are close, there it is home. Yet home stretches beyond direct
proximity. Feeling at home can be assured only within a familiar
environment, within infrastructure like schools or cinemas. Not only the
materialities but also social networks assist the feeling of familiarity. As
Steven mentioned, you meet people in the new place of residence. In
another part of the interview he says that

»I lived there for twenty-two years before moving here so it was my home, it was where all my friends were [...]« (I4: 13)

Cecile stresses, in the interview, that home is where you have friends to interact with, and this is so important to her that »it is the personal relations that make the decision« (I9: 60) whether and where to move. She has friends all around the globe and feels comfortable everywhere. She is able to produce familiarity and similarity for herself everywhere on the basis of her social network. Having friends around, being able to interact with people one knows well, makes every place not so very different from that other place where you spent time before. It means that, no matter where you are, you can spend time in the ways you are used to: go to the cinema or theatre with your friends, have dinner with them, invite them to your house for a party, etc.

The same applies to daily routines. As long as working time is the same, as long as the type of work is similar, as long as there is the infrastructure that enables the smooth and usual course of the day, any place can be familiar and support the feeling of being at home. To feel at home means to be in a familiar environment, to have owned and known objects around, and to interact with family and friends, and one can therefore create a feeling of being at home at any time, for any time and in any place. A hotel room can be such a place. On trips, some interviewees take with them a bunch of things that makes them feel more like at home: for example, thick pajamas, pictures of the nearest and dearest, computer with all data, et cetera. Although no hotel room can become home within a week or two (I6: 42), such techniques help people to avoid feeling homesick when on business travel.

Home, as described by my informants, is thus a part of social and material networks. To feel at home means to feel comfortable in the networks: to have friends to interact with in physical proximity, and to be able to communicate with the locals, to know the environment, to be able to use the facilities of a town, etc. It means being surrounded by familiar items. They are familiar because they are known, or because they are similar. Either you know the people and the environment because you have spent time there, or because these are the same people (or the same kind of people) and the same facilities (or the same kind of facilities) that you experienced in the previous place of residence. For someone who has never lived in a community of expatriates, the new place of residence, in which social contacts are limited to this particular group, does not provide the feeling of being at home. For someone who had a small house furnished with care, a new house that is large and luxurious but rented, and equipped with modern commodities to which one has no emotional relation, is not a home (I5, numerous passages). This is the point at which the need for similarity and familiarity is perhaps closest to the nostalgia of the essentialist parental home or *heimat*: the only place, the particular location, the primary experience of things and their essential qualities.

Yet the empirical evidence from my study does not allow us to accept this interpretation. Indeed, many individuals do seek similarity and familiarity, but in a self-appointed home, not in relation to their childhood place. This is where they differ from migrants: they did not lose their home, but rather chose to leave it and to establish a new one nowhere else. They are also free to go back, and many of the interviewees indeed do so. They travel regularly to their parental homes and »dive« into their environment, eat local specialties prepared by their mums, talk to old neighbors, exchange gossip, etc. Because they can do so, they do not miss it. Mobility disconnects them from their old home but enables regular returns. They can go back, even to their past.

The above shows that this self-appointed home is located not in a particular place but is a part of a network. It can be anywhere and everywhere and, what is more important, it can move with you because it can be renegotiated and reconstructed. Home constituted in networks is mobile. Another perspective also opens up here: homes are open spaces.[40] They are neither homogeneous nor closed entities. Homes are heterogeneous parts of broader networks of elements and relations between them. Yet they can also act as single entities, because access to them is clearly defined. People, objects, and relations between them are carefully selected to become a part of this open, mobile space. These particular relationships grant them a common identity, its own essence. In terms of topological metaphors, home is a region in which difference and heterogeneity are suppressed to define the place (Hinchliffe 1997: 205).

---

40 Massey (2005: 179) speaks about home as a relatively open and porous space in comparison to, for example, a laboratory, which is governed by many professional rules restricting access to it. Yet her sense of openness differs from mine: as acceptance of intrusions, or the impossibility of complete closure of spaces, which are necessarily relational, and thus its borders are renegotiable. The exit point of her analysis is an already existing space (home) and not its establishment »out of nothing«.

These three qualities – heterogeneity, openness and interconnectedness – make home mobile.[41] Its location in a network is a result of defining relations to the diverse elements constituting networks. Home does not have to be constructed anew in every new place of residence but it can move with an individual. It can be easily transported in the networks in which travel is being performed. Distance in a network is not an obstacle to mobility, because a network is a series of elements with well-defined relations between them. In a network, proximity is not metric but has instead to do with identity and relations between the elements (Mol/Law 1994: 649). Places with a similar set of elements and similar relations between them are close to one another, and those with different elements or relations are far apart.

To imagine and understand home as a part of heterogeneous networks, and as a network itself, helps to explain why the interviewed individuals have so much difficulty in locating their homes in geographical terms. Many informants, when asked where their home is, answered like Cecile:

»I don't know, I think my home is in the middle of Atlantic. I feel home in the USA and in Europe.« (19: 82)

Home localized in a network is not a territorial entity. Its material components have spatial extension, but home is not a place, nor an object, but a network. It can be manifested in one particular territorial location or in many:

»I wouldn't move to one place. I would until my I could sort of physically afford it and financially afford it I would start with three places where I would spend a few months each.« (18: 121)

Being mobile is not necessarily detached (Ahmed 2003: 1), but at the same time attachment does not have to have a spatial character, as we usually assume it: fixed and static. Nor must the opposite spatial character to

---

41 Yet conceptualizing the mobility of home relates to a certain problem: when the elements of home do not change, and the relationship between them is not altered, then, from the perspective of networks, home is rather an immutable mobile (Mol/Law 1994: 649). It is definitely immutable in the case of those individuals who decide to move with a certain set of objects, and with people with them. However home never stays completely unchanged: there are always new elements, new objects joining, and some old ones leaving the network. What remain unchanged are the relations constituting home. Homes are mobile only from the perspective of the metrically defined space in which movement takes place between »points« in space, between clearly defined and exclusive units (regions). More about regions and networks follows in chapter 7.

attachment be spatial solitude. One can be at home in more than one location. There is no reason to assume that home is only one, single, and rudimentary. As Fortier shows, home does not necessarily have to be a place of origin, but rather a point of destination (Fortier 2003). In the researched sample, home is neither the point of origin nor of final destination, but it is here and now, with the individual. It connects many locations and the past and the future in the here and now point of presence. It is a very real construction, not a place from the past or the future for which one feels affection.

6.2. Steady relationship or one-nightstand? On relationship to places

The non-territorial principle of fixation and attachment to a spatially non-fixed home that we identified does not conflict with the fact that the individuals are physically present in a place. The question arises, what does it mean to be in a place? What kind of relationship does a mobile individual have to a place? Given the mobility of »home«, are these individuals attached to any place of residence at all? What do they understand by being in a place and being related to a place?

In the literature, place is associated with a particular territorial unit, and encompasses the materialities and people physically present in this unit. The concept of place is commonly used to signify an entity that is experienced and perceived as meaningful by a person or a group of people (Groat 1995; Canter 1997). Place attachment refers primarily to affective, cognitive, and behavioral bonds between individuals and one or several places (Altman/Low 1992). Therefore, the research concentrating on place often assumes that the consequences of not being socially and psychologically committed to a place are negative. The lack of attachment is considered to represent a loss of community, to threaten individuals with alienation, and neighborhoods with disorganization (Putnam 2000). Opinions about the relationship between people and their places fall along a continuum, from theories that posit internal, psychic sources of attachment to those that find the source of attachment in social structure. For example, some traditional ethnological analyses hold that attachment to place is rooted in a »territorial instinct« (comp. Ardrey 1967; Berghe, van den 1974). Cognitive approaches state that a sense of place is necessary to maintain psychological stability. A bond to a place is considered crucial for individual well-being. Sociological tradition argues that attachment to place is founded on the type of social relations individuals have in a particular neighborhood or town. »For most city dwellers attachment to the local means to the neighborhood« (Immerfall 1998: 179). Classical community theorists focus upon the material interdependence of individuals in a local area (comp. Hunter 1975). Others see the locality as a creation of the larger society (Leeds 1973). Mobility is seen in contradiction to place attachment, and is regarded as deviation and associated with disintegration (Relph 1976; Altman/Low 1992; Hay 1998), and mobile people constitute a threat to the local communities to which they do not (yet, or no longer) belong. In recent years, the increasing number of works on global cities, which consider the effects on urban life of flows (of managerial and financial elites), have expressed concern about the negative influence of temporary and invisible migrants (Doyle/Nathan 2001) on the city, its organization, and people (comp. Moulaert 2003). Recent social research raises important questions, and casts doubt on the role of place attachment in the era of mobility. Some authors contest the strong ties between a community and place, and show that an individual can be strongly related to a distant or even a virtual community (Calhoun 1991, Albrow et al. 1994, Rojek/Urry 1997). Nevertheless, many interpret this occurrence as ambivalent for the inhabitants of a place. It is assumed that length of residence is significantly related to intensity of attachment, and therefore mobility will hinder, or even prevent, the formation of affective ties with places. Further, place and community remain interconnected in the research. Relationship to a place is addressed as a relationship to a community. Few studies address both perspectives, by focusing on mobility and on place bond, as two sides of a coin (Feldman 1990; Gustafson 2001a).

Two theses have been discussed in the literature. The first relates to a compulsory move or forced dislocation (Brown/Perkins 2002). A bond to a place actually surfaces with greater clarity when people move, particularly when the move is compulsory (Giuliani et al. 2003: 111). The second thesis says that voluntary mobility, however, may result in new possibilities and gratification in one's life that balance the lack of attachment (Fried 2000).

When associating place with community, researchers say little about place. Often, place is opposed to absolute space, and seems to merge with people and infrastructure that are located somewhere. Attempts have been made, in various disciplines, to distinguish the components of place in order to define its importance for individuals and groups. Psychologist Canter (1977; 1997) developed a model of four interrelated facets of place: functional differentiation, place objectives, scale of interaction, and aspects of design. Geographer Relph (1976) speaks of three components: physical setting, activities, and meaning as constituents of place. Agnew (1987), analyzing the concept of place within social sciences, finds three major elements: »locale«, the settings in which social relations are constituted; »location«, the geographical area encompassing the settings; and sense of place, the local »structure of feeling«. More recently, there has been a trend to research places as dynamic constituents, as processes, and to stress their interconnectedness (Massey 1994; 1995; 2005). Usually, the research focuses on a single element of place, and the researchers tend to share the conviction that the most difficult thing to grasp is the meaning of places.

To understand what a place and being located mean to the mobile individuals, I follow the »indicators« to which the interviewees themselves pointed, rather than focusing on particular predefined locations. These indicators are the social networks and environment (material networks) that constitute the most important reference points. I start from the assumption that arises from the exploration of the informants' mobility: namely, that their attachment to place is subject to mediation. People choose to become attached to places in different ways, depending on their personal needs, opportunities, and resources, and on the characteristics of the places in which they live. People do not choose from endless possibilities: social and economic constraints define and limit the alternatives that are available to them. It is therefore suspected that, for example, language skills may influence the building of social networks and involvement in local communities. Therefore, in addition to the social networks of the interviewees, I consider the following factors: language skills, family and job situation, hobbies and spare time, knowledge about local conditions, and participation in community. In consequence, the meaning of places is subject to mediation. In this respect, the three-pole triangular model of Gustafson (2001b: 9ff) seems most similar. According to him, the meaning of places is situated between three themes addressed by the researched individuals: self, others, and environment. I also keep in mind that commitment to the local can take two general forms: social involvement, and subjective feeling, and both these categories are suspected of taking several forms (Gerson et al. 1977: 39). I now proceed to look at both these main forms.

I am less interested in the subjective meaning mobile people attribute to particular places; rather, I try to work out their relationship to various places. I focus on actions rather than narratives, and consider the conditions of these actions. I do not select a particular place, but rather a particular situation in which an individual is at a certain moment. Four different situations can be distinguished. The first is when an employee moves to the USA to undertake an assignment in the IO's headquarters. The second is when he or she moves to undertake an assignment in any other country. The third is when one travels regularly to a country to work on a project there, and stays there for a period of up to two weeks. The last is the relationship to his or her place of origin. In each case, the conditions that may determine attachment to place are very different, and I discuss them separately. Common to the first three cases is the temporary nature of assignments (however, someone taking an assignment in headquarters usually has a longer job perspective than someone moving to a third country); in relation to the place of origin, there is physical absence. As discussed in the previous section, the individuals move within a network of the IO's offices, and the principle of their attachment is, with some exceptions, functional. Closer investigation of the IO, described in the chapter on the context of mobility, shows that the IO itself supports its employees actively in the process of re-settling, and provides them with »first help« in a new residence place. This should also be taken into consideration in the subsequent sections.

6.2.1. The international crowd. Moving to HQ

All the individuals interviewed had lived in the USA at least once, while undertaking an assignment in the headquarters of the IO's. However, at the time of interview only four of them worked there. Atanas had lived there with his family for ten years. Recently, however, they decided to move to his home country, but he has kept the flat in the USA, to have a place to stay whenever he has to work at headquarters. Most of the interviewees had experiences of living abroad before moving to headquarters, or had already lived in the USA. Steven is American and there was little problem for him to move to headquarters. Tolga studied in the USA and obtained a job in the IO immediately after graduation. She did not experience the move as any great change. Diego had also studied in the USA, and it was already familiar to him when he undertook an assignment there some years later. Similarly, Ann had previously lived there. Reiner welcomed the move with pleasure, as he and his wife had, for a long time, been intending to make it. They had previously lived in Africa, and in the USA they were able to enjoy the infrastructure to which they were accustomed in their home country, Switzerland. Ludmila worked in the headquarters for only one year, the shortest time of all the interviewees, and during this period she traveled to Europe frequently.

I distinguish between change of residence to headquarters and to a third country because, according to the interviewees, the location of the IO's headquarters is very distinctive. First, it is a large, multinational city, »like a motel«, where people come and go and »you never know who will be your neighbor next week« (I6: 66). Second, beforehand, most interviewees already had some idea of what it was like to live there. Tolga, for example, knew a lot about American culture from the media. She read about it and saw it on TV when she still lived in Turkey. However misleading some of information might be, American culture already seemed familiar to her, and she was not anxious about moving there (I5: 63). Of course, this does not mean that life there is a dream, and the interviewees are aware of its negative aspects: people come there to work intensively, spend long hours in the office, and, in the evening, drive home to the suburbs, leaving the centre abandoned. Many criminals and poor people live downtown. Some newcomers have problems adjusting, especially when renting a flat in the city centre. On the other hand, they appreciate the chance to meet people from all over the world. It is exciting to learn about many cultures. Perhaps because it is a melting pot, the city has adapted itself to many different foreigners and created a »user-friendly« (I6: 66) environment for them.

Language is also part of it. Although English is not their mother tongue, all the interviewees have spoken it fluently for years. English is the language spoken in their office environment: it is one of the official IO's languages, and knowledge of it is a formal requirement for a job. Some of the interviewees had completed their studies and graduated in English. Others had worked in an English-speaking environment before entering the IO. For those who currently live, or used to live, in English-speaking communities, language is not a barrier to social contacts.

All this might suggest that the interviewees encounter few constraints on participation in community life, and experience few difficulties in developing their social networks by enlarging them with local inhabitants. However, a closer look at the social networks of the informants does not confirm this supposition. All the interviewees have very diverse and multinational groups of friends. Many of them live in mixed marriages and get to know new friends through their spouses. However, most friendships are made within the IO. All the interviewees keep in contact with their old friends from school or university. Martin estimates that some two-thirds of his friends are his countrymen and the rest »international« – people he met on the job in different countries (I3: 56). Most of his friends are spread all over the world and he has irregular contact with them, per e-mail, telephone, or personally when he happens to be in their country. Some of these friends are also his neighbors. He enjoys this »kind of international crowd in this apartment building« (I3: 96).

Similarly, Lenka's friends are mostly international: they are either colleagues she met in the IO, or from »outside«, embassies or the neighborhood. (I6: 84). She complains that it is difficult to maintain friendships, because people come and go. She has »lost« many friends because they moved back to Europe (I6: 84). She notices that »somehow foreigners stick together« (I6: 85-88). She believes that the reason for this is that foreigners simply have something in common because they are foreigners (I6: 86). She has observed a tendency to gather in national groups:

»[...] when you are from Russia you have friends from Russia, you get together to go for lunch, for dinner, discuss, but it doesn't mean that you're gonna be good friends because the personalities are so different and the fact that you are from the same country doesn't necessarily mean that you are going to be excellent friends. You can be a much better friend with someone from the USA or...some other European countries or Latin America. It is all about personality.« (I6: 88)

The situation described here relates to the IO. People leave because they have changed assignments within the IO. Having lunch together also takes place within the IO. In this case, the foreigners sticking together are all employees of the IO. Clearly the IO's headquarters plays a major role in defining the social networks of its employees. It is the first place one enters after arrival, usually directly from the airport, and even before check-in at a hotel. The assignment in the IO is the reason for the change of residence. The IO is huge and thus provides an individual with many possibilities for meeting new people. They all have something in common already: they are the IO's employees, and many of them are foreigners. From the beginning, they can exchange their experiences in the country, when moving, finding a house, school for children, etc. The IO also provides the necessary infrastructure for meeting – a cafeteria and a gym, for example. The individuals spend most of their day in the IO's buildings: they work on average some ten to twelve hours a day, and many use the common facilities before or after work, and also have lunch inside. Then the drive home takes at least an hour, and they sleep some six hours, which means that they have a maximum four hours a day for meeting friends and spending time with the family. In addition, many of them travel extensively on business: they are away some 100 days a year. As Lenka says, »when you travel so much your favorite place is home« (16: 98). There is in general little spare time, and when one is away so often, one prefers to spend this time at home, with the immediate family, and doing all the necessary household chores, such as looking after the garden, cleaning, washing, etc. The same is true for those who live in a third country, as I will discuss in detail in the next section.

At the same time, the IO is a world on its own, and it has the power to stipulate the collective behavior of its employees. First, many of them are foreigners who share similar problems. Second, they do comparable types of work. Many have had a similar education, either in technical subjects or economics. Third, they have similar background experiences, from education to migration. For many, this job has always been their dream job, and they are very happy and proud to be an employee of the IO. Many have also previously worked away from their home country, including in developing countries. This interest in development issues connects them, and they »feel that (they) are all a community in the IO«, they »feel (they) are making a difference« (15: 25). All of my informants were very proud of being a member of the IO community. Many of them stressed the importance of the work they do; the others enjoy the international environment and the chance to meet people from very different cultures. They emphasized that it is never boring in the IO because of the diversity of people and tasks. In this they see the IO's advantage over other employers. One can find everything within it: a new job, new friends, and new adventures with foreign cultures.

However, in spite of being embedded in an international environment, the interviewees often complain about the limitations on the development of personal social networks:

»[...] Most of my friends were from the IO and most of them have friends in the IO, so it is an interesting issue because I was at many parties and these were not any typical business events but for example birthday parties or on other occasions and practically all the people were from the IO. Perhaps it is because all of the people are immigrants, even if they are there some twenty years anyway they have friends in the IO only, so at most of the parties everyone talked about the IO and only sometimes it happens that a spouse of someone is from outside the IO and this is already a great thing, though most of them have anyway a spouse in the IO.« (17: 33)

Some informants perceive this as a disadvantage, because they feel that they are not able to integrate with the locals, because nobody there is a local. Interestingly, the interviewees do not live in typical expatriate communities; but although their neighborhoods are some ninety percent American, about ninety percent of their friends in the neighborhood are foreigners (I12: 46). The interviewees see the HQ, and the city in which it is located, as a multicultural motel where people are always on the move, and stay there only for a while to do their job, then leave again. Perhaps this impression is true of other foreigners in the city as well; perhaps it is a result of immersion in the IO, and seeing the city through the IO's windows.

Ann, who had previously lived elsewhere in the USA, and compares these two places, says that this motel-like character is a huge advantage of the HQ location: in some small communities in the countryside she, as a foreigner, although a native English speaker, was not accepted, and could not integrate with the local community. She felt unable to accept how different the locals were, their lifestyle and opinions, and vice versa. This was one of her reasons for returning to her home country. In the HQ she never faced such problems. The others also feel comfortable there, precisely because in such an environment they are not a minority: they are not labeled as expatriates (I5: 113), or members of any particular national or ethnic group. The individuals experience such labeling as disadvantageous and limiting, because it results in immersion in exclusively foreign or ethnic groups.

Their involvement in social networks is nevertheless limited to informal, sporadic meetings. Apart from one interviewee, who used to be a member of a national association, no one else is a member of any organization. Interestingly, the interviewee who for a time was a member of an association contacted it thanks to the IO. One day some young people involved in the association, who were also IO employees, contacted her and asked if she would like to join, and she did (I5: 141). The type of tasks she performed resembled her previous involvement in her home country. In this respect, she is an exception in the sample, the only one who maintains a very close and semi-formalized contact with her fellow citizens. She is an active member of the graduate association of her old school, supports the current students in the school, travels regularly to the reunions, and visits her school friends who live in third countries (I5: 125). She is also spatially close to her family, as she lives in the same city as her mother and her siblings (I5: 51).

The temporary nature of stay of both many work immigrants and IO employees obstructs not only participation in associations, but also friendships. Contact with foreigners and the IO's employees, in particular, is easiest, and the most effective in terms of time efficiency. Time restricts the interviewees in multiple ways: on the one hand, their job requires most of the day (I3), and the family and the household fill most of the spare time. In addition, many interviewees travel extensively. The time available to them in the location is thus broken up into periods of presence and absence. As Reiner says, this periodicity of presence makes any kind of formal group involvement almost impossible (I2: 99). This irregularity and lack of time enforce individualized forms of social involvement. As result, the interviewees choose those forms of contact that enable them to control timing: infrequent meetings with friends in the location, sporadic meetings with friends during business travel abroad, and telephoning or e-mailing family and friends abroad. For the same reason, they prefer sports and hobbies in which they can participate together with their immediate family (I10: 82), at home (I6: 129), or on the way to the office: biking (I2: 89), physical exercise in a gym (in the office or, when abroad, in a hotel) (I3: 86), cooking (I1), or going to the cinema and theatre (I11: 72). These hobbies do not require any special time management and can fit in any schedule. They can be exercised at almost any time and anywhere, even when abroad for a short time, or in a new place of residence.

For the interviewees, HQ's location town is very distinct from all other places. It is not its architecture or infrastructure that make it different, but rather »the little things«. When asked »what is the place like«, the informants talk about how their life is there. They talk about the climate (I7: 31), the motel-like character of the city, empty downtown, long working hours, an international group of friends, their lifestyle, including high mobility, their concentration on home and family, but also user-friendly services, and finally the IO itself, which plays a central role in their life. This picture of a place is analogous to Lefebvre's consideration of the city:

»[…] the urban is a form that of the encounters and gathering of all the elements of the social life, from the fruits on the earth to the symbols and the so called cultural works […]« (Lefebvre 1972: 206, quoted by Martins 1982:170).

It is a place that is lived and perceived rather than conceived (Soja 1996: 78). Although this place seems to be so well known and so convenient, or perhaps precisely because it is, the individuals do not try to get to know it in depth. They spend their time predominantly in the IO: they do not know the local inhabitants, and their social networks remain »the international crowd«, which is not bound to this particular place. The individuals are able to avoid any conflicts in this location, as they do not immerse themselves in the local environment.

6.2.2. Luxury of a regulated exposure. Moving to a third country

In third countries, structural conditions play a similar role, but different factors and outcomes can be observed. Language is expected to limit rather than enable active participation. Most of the interviewed individuals currently live in a country in which the official spoken language is not their native language. In non-English speaking countries, the possibility of socializing depends on how widely English is spoken. For example, Diego compared two countries – Saudi Arabia and Slovenia – and said that it was »easier« in the first, because more people in shops, and in services in general, spoke English. This was important mostly for his wife, who stayed at home and cared for the household. On the other hand, cultural differences may play a greater role. The temporary nature of a stay has to be investigated more closely, especially regarding social networks. The IO is expected to be an important factor in mediating between the place and the individuals.

In the analysis, I first looked closely at the process of settlement in a place. Earlier in the book, I described the interviewees' search for a new assignment in the internal job market. When they are accepted for a new position, they ease into the new job slowly. In the case of an assignment abroad, this means, for example, that they visit the destination country and meet their future work colleagues, see the office, and search for accommodation (I10: 32). Even before that, one tries to get into a job and reads many documents about the country and the prospective job. For a couple of months, one does a double job, in both the old and new positions (I10: 34). This is the most difficult part of the moving process, according to the interviewees. The transition period between the old and new assignment continues after the move, as »for at least a month or so you'll still be getting requests from the old job« (I10: 18). The other part of moving is easier. The IO provides support in choosing a house and accommodating to new conditions. One takes individual decisions on housing but »when you do it for the IO it is easy« (I11: 152). One has to transport one's belongings, but everything goes smoothly with the help of specialized companies, and thanks to the interviewees' own experience. One already knows what things to take, which things are important in creating a new home, etc. The first step in a new place of residence has been taken. One has a house with one's own things in it, one has a job, an idea about the new tasks, and has met the new colleagues. The children are enrolled in an international school, and normal life begins.

Normal life means that one goes to the office in the morning, works nine or ten hours a day, and goes back home. Normal life means also that, from time to time, one travels on business, usually to neighboring countries, for two or three days. This does not, however, mean that this normal life is exactly the same as life in a previous place of residence. As a newcomer, one has to work out social networks, get to know how to deal with daily routines, like shopping, learn how to exercise old hobbies, and perhaps try something new. Every place offers certain possibilities. Given that the IO's offices are located in capital cities, the scope of possibilities, regardless of country, is large:

»I think, what is happening today is that you are able to go to most...yea, certainly again it is my experience...that you are able to go to countries as diverse as this [Saudi Arabia and Slovenia] and if you do not want to be exposed to any of these differences, if you are not someone to deal with them, there are ways to completely shut them off.« (I10: 48)

Certainly, there are cultural, religious, and societal differences between places, but it is also possible to ignore these. There are, for example, western compounds in Arabic countries, and a Western European can actually spend time exclusively in them, except for work. There are communities of expatriates with their facilities and infrastructure like clubs, school, shops, cinemas, etc:

»So this is something what is open nowadays, you can go almost anywhere and you could completely avoid the local. If you're gone out you know that this is not a very good thing to do because this is really a missed opportunity, but the fact that you can do this means that you are able to almost consciously decide how much exposure do I really want to have to local things« (I10: 49)

To decide to expose yourself to the local means being ready to accept a certain risk: the risk of being misunderstood when communicating, or feeling less comfortable as a stranger among the locals. It is, however, possible to regulate the degree of immersion in the foreign environment: during the stay. One may take »a break« from this exposure and spend more time in a group of expatriates. One can acclimatize slowly and initially avoid exposure, and later become more familiar with the hosting country. It is »a luxury« (I10: 49) that one can afford nowadays:

»If you are smart enough you will recognize that this opportunity is there, you will make a use of it but without necessarily having necessarily to put your family and your world up side down, you can regulate that.« (I10: 49)

Are the interviewees »smart enough« to immerse themselves in the local environment, to get involved, to be exposed, or do they take the opportunity to avoid this risk? No matter how open-minded and eager to take risks my informants are, they all face certain problems in realizing the wish to participate in the locality. The first limitation is language: hardly any of them know even some basics of the host country's language. Ann remembers only one person who learned the language and spoke it in the host country, but »he is a very rare exception« (I11: 62). She herself can manage in a taxi or in a shop, »and after all the shops here are mostly supermarkets anyway« (I11: 62). So she is not afraid to deal with the linguistic barriers: they are not barriers to her, because she does not necessarily need to know the local language. However, because she lacks the language skills, in her job she has to rely entirely on IO office colleagues. She notices that she never actually comes into direct contact with the locals, because someone translates everything for her. Business issues are translated by professional interpreters, paid by the IO. Her colleagues help her with personal problems. She is not very proud of this:

she would like to understand more, but does not think that, at her age, she would be able to learn another language. Her motivation to do so is rather low, because she will leave the country in some two years. She can communicate with people, though only in English, and she can shop and manage her daily life. The other informants tell the same story: they manage the situation. They learn the basics of the language, as Steven did, for example, and they can understand a simple conversation. Or they do not see any need to learn it: as Martin points out, »Everybody speaks enough English for you to survive« (I11: 66).

Language skills play a greater role for those wives who also move to a foreign country. They find things »more difficult«, especially in countries where the community of expatriates is rather small, (I10: 24), and especially in respect to shopping and house services. However, after only two months in their new location, Diego's wife had already found new friends:

»To get to know people and to make acquaintances, that is not a problem, that is very easy, very quickly through the school actually…in the first two days of school the school has already arranged for some ladies to show my wife around the city and not only some ladies, but actually they arrange for some ladies who are Spanish speakers so it hasn't been a problem from that perspective. I guess Ljubljana is as any other capital in the world, it has a large number of expatriates and you can easily find people who speak any language so it hasn't been a problem.« (I10: 26)

What Diego considers an advantage, some other interviewees see as a barrier. They complain that all their friends are exclusively expatriates. They believe that the barrier to integration is not the language, but different needs:

»In the school there are three or four families which speak English but the conversations are very limited – they don't want to open up their mind or…or just to arrange dinners together for example, we expatriates we meet somewhere and then lets go to dinner or lets go for coffee so you just try to make your donation and…Maybe we need more one another, we are more in need for people or friends than Polish people who already have families and friends, maybe they don't need new friends.« (I5: 69)

However, the lives of those who do not speak the language of the host country are organized slightly differently from the life of those who do speak it (I11). They prefer to shop in supermarkets, and go to the cinema, not the theatre. However, when it comes to their social networks and how they spend spare time, there are very few differences.

The social networks of all the informants are very international, and they do include the locals. The interviewees insist that whether a friendship develops or not it mainly a matter of »chemistry« between people. One does not try to get closer to someone simply because this person is a local. There is no reason to do so. However, if this person is interesting, has similar interests and problems, and if one's wife and children accept this person (I10: 94), then you become friends. Similar interests and problems usually imply that friends are also expatriates. Nobody excludes the locals because they are the locals, and nobody includes the expatriates because they are expatriates. Even when one knows the local language and there is no formal barrier to communication, there is no guarantee that one will make new friends in this place. Sabah complains that the older she becomes, and the less time she has, the more problematic it is for her to meet new people, and to keep in contact with them. This problem is independent of location. Most of the interviewees admit that the majority of their friendships originated in their school or university days, when they had time to socialize and to work at a friendship. They did not have a job, they did not have a family, and they spent more time with friends.

Even if the social involvement of the interviewees in the locality is, for the reasons described, rather poor, they are open to the local environment. They sometimes have a surprisingly good knowledge of the history of the country. They obtain a very detailed picture of the country, thanks to the many business documents and meetings. They have the kind of insight that many of the natives or long-term inhabitants do not. They are up-to-date with the country's political situation. On the job, they meet country officials, they know the problems of the local economy, and they have a good sense of social problems. All this is part of their business obligations. They are very aware of criticisms of the IO and its employees, and they fight the negative stereotypes of them, as foreign experts trying to influence the political and economic situation of the country, of which they are not a part. Their personal assessment is that they do know well the country in which they work and live.

They feel pressure to use the time that they have in a country in the best possible way, to get to know the place. This is important because of the quality of work they do, and to challenge the negative stereotypes of international elites detached from localities. One way of doing so is to obtain a picture of the country, its situation and problems, and inhabitants, that is different from the one provided by official documents, meetings, and counterparts. In comparison to those interviewees who work in the HQ, they travel less on business and more on private occasions. My informants thus »go to the field and research«, to use the ethnographic metaphor. They often take weekend trips, and find interesting destinations from books and maps (I5: 55). Traveling around is one of the main leisure activities. Often private trips are induced by business visits. One rushes through places on the business site visits, talks mainly to officials, and has no contact with the inhabitants and the places. This can be made up for during holiday travel (I11: 102). However, private destinations are not limited to the country of residence. In Europe, everything is near at hand, and many people take the opportunity to visit other countries over the weekend. They »jump« from Budapest to London or Paris, from Geneva to the Alps, from Ljubljana to Rome.

The question arises: What does it mean, in this case, to be attached to a place? »Knowledge« of a place, and its events and inhabitants, has an important role in the process of creating a bond to this place. [42] As described, the informants' friends tend to be expatriates. But they also know native inhabitants: their colleagues in the office, their counterparts and clients. They study documents and reports on the country's economic situation. They have a direct insight into national politics. They attend conferences and talk to experts. This means that they have a very different kind of knowledge of a particular country than the majority of its citizens. The interviewees acquire it not from TV programs, not during private chat with friends, but during official conferences, when talking to politicians and experts. This knowledge differs from that of the native inhabitants, who read newspapers or watch the news on TV, rather than speak to the minister to obtain information on the law most recently passed in the parliament. My informants observe rather than participate, because they do not know the language spoken in the country. They have to rely on their office colleagues and on other foreigners, who have perhaps been in the country longer, to learn about the problems in the everyday life of the

---

42 As Urry points out, it is difficult to establish the sociological significance of »knowing« or »knowing of someone«. »Knowing« may have no significance for the patterning of social life or the forming of »imagined communities«. »Knowing« is subjective and one-dimensional, it means a person may believe he or she knows someone, but this does not have to be reciprocated (Urry 2004). Therefore the category of knowledge used here relates to the reciprocated knowing of people (repeating or regular interaction) on the one hand, and the subjective conviction of the informants of being familiar with the events, history, and geography of a place.

locals. They make more trips to the countryside than the average native inhabitant, because they are fully aware that their stay is temporary, and that they should use the time well. It would be a pity to spend it watching TV. Their attachment to the place of residence is therefore full of contradictions.

6.2.3. Missing the complete picture. Business travel

Another type of relation to places can be developed on the basis of regular business visits to a country. All my informants either travel, or used to travel, to various countries on business. They usually conduct projects over a couple of years in their different stages, and they participate simultaneously in at least three or four assignments. Typically they travel to more than one destination and combine tasks. The question is whether it matters for the interviewees to which place they travel.

The interviewees were asked to describe how they prepare themselves for trips, and whether this preparation differs, depending on the destination. There is a difference, say the informants: one has to prepare a different set of documents and clothes. A destination is about the weather and about the type of meetings there. If one has only official meetings, one needs to take a different set of clothes than when preparing for many site visits (I2: 29). A suitcase is also packed according to the climate. Depending on the destination, one should also carry medications (I9: 106).

There are many similarities in travel, regardless of destination. No matter the place, a business stay is limited in time (from one to three weeks) and very intensive. A typical day abroad »starts at 8am with a breakfast meeting with the team«, then there are meetings with counterparts until 6pm. Many interviewees then go to a gym or to rest, have a dinner meeting, go to the hotel, make some phone calls, and reply to e-mails (I3: 100). There is very little or no time left to go out of the ministerial or office buildings or the hotel, to discover the place. Very few, only those who understand the local language, can use a taxi ride to talk to the driver and learn about the newest events and problems of the country. Site visits in the company of business partners and interpreters leave the interviewees no opportunity to get to know the place. Spare time is usually reduced to a weekend, if one is lucky (I3: 60). One is expected to work all day long, seven days a week. Breakfast and dinners with the team are also working time, because even if your colleagues are your friends the conversation ends up on business issues (I2: 45). One has to fight this pressure and manage some free time for oneself, even if it is only an hour a day (I4: 73). The interviewees try to use this time, by, for example, meeting friends or exploring places they have never seen before (I3: 62). Given the constant drive to work, and the temporality of the stay, any program of »exploring the countries« is modest and starts with the smallest things, like walking to the office or meeting instead of taking a taxi, jogging instead of exercising in the hotel, or turning down dinner with colleagues and going to a new restaurant downtown, or perhaps even meeting the locals, »because that is the best way of learning more about the country, by having informal chat with friends« (I2: 47).

Of course, this is not always possible. Some interviewees complain that they had been in a country many times, yet they never managed to see anything of it. One reason for this situation is the duration of a travel: if a stay abroad is limited to five working days, then these days are full of meetings and there is no time to go around (I7: 47, 107). It also depends on the team. There are teams of people who are more interested in the country, and are convinced that to go to the opera, or visit a town, is just as important as the working meetings. A team leader may than decide to prolong the stay and manage some spare time for its members (I7: 109).

»[…] most of the time we are at work and when we don't work we try to see around then we meet other people […] Just to have the feeling of the country the country is not the hotel room and it is also not the office in a ministry, half the country is just like the immediate things that you see some natural beauties as well as the level of development of the country.[…] I am curious as a person and also because it is a great opportunity to see when you are there and we always try to make at least one or two trips to the countryside to see the country then you have more feeling about otherwise you are like a tourist in a hotel room.« (I5: 27-31)

Although they are experts on the country, and in their job deal with its most important problems, after hours the interviewees are tourists, who can for the first time admire the exotic landscape, shops, and a street market. They visit the main tourist attractions, enjoy nature, climb the mountains in a national park, go shopping, etc. (I4: 75), all depending on the country and what it offers. As Steven notices, there are also countries where there is nothing to do in the spare time, because there is hardly any infrastructure for visitors. In such cases, the interviewees concentrate on work, keep themselves busy with business obligations, and leave the country as soon as possible.

Once again, their knowledge of the countries they work in is full of contradictions. They are experts and tourists at the same time. Their working day during travel is similar to that in their main office, except that it also includes a business breakfast and dinner with their colleagues. They also interact with different people during meetings with their clients. They see this as an advantage over working in the HQ, where they basically sit at their desk and meet the same group of colleagues daily (compare the chapter on motivation to travel). To a certain extent, they lead their normal daily life, as in their place of residence: they work intensively, they try to find some time to exercise their hobbies, they dedicate some time to their families – a long telephone conversation with their family is an important task in their busy schedule. They organize their hotel room as a mini home, where they can work and feel comfortable during the stay. They spend their free time as any tourist would: they sightsee, they try out restaurants and bars, they enjoy the specialties of a country – its landscape, culture, shopping possibilities. This very special mixture of being an expert and a tourist, being abroad and yet continuing to lead their everyday life, makes their business travel exceptional:

»That traveling as the IO staff member spoils you or has spoiled me for traveling as a tourist. Because whenever I travel as the IO staff member I become so much an inside of that country or that place I travel to that I hate to travel as a tourist where I remain at a surface or there I remain an outsider, I remain a tourist. […] And I get a lot of insider information […] Contact and information a tourist never gets. Whenever I travel to our client countries I learn so many things I become part of that country and can never achieve it as a tourist.« (I2: 127)

The interviewees have a feeling of knowing well the countries in which they work. »I've been working there now for over ten years. And I know Russia very well at this stage«, says Ann (I11: 80). However, they are also aware of limitations:

»I think I know them well from the perspective which is relevant for my work but I feel that what I don't know very well this kind of totality.« (I3: 64)

Their relation to the countries is thus one-sided and temporary: as long as they are experts they are attached to the place. They visit it regularly; they are interested in its issues, and develop an understanding of its problems, culture, and people. This is not a pure business relation – the interviewees have an emotional link to it. However, this relationship is formed by their business mission, and this means that they owe the same attention to every country in which they work or will work. Every place requires their involvement and their attention, and once their work there is completed, they »move on to another country, [they] just concentrate and move on« (I5: 121). When the business obligation has been fulfilled, there is usually no reason to go back to this country (I11: 106). Life goes on and it is a very busy life, and there is little time for returning to old places. »There is trade-off between going back and seeing something new, doing something else« (I9: 126). Many interviewees, however, remain interested in the development of the places they used to work in, and keep themselves informed by colleagues who still travel to these places. They learn of the latest political and economic changes, or trace the course of the IO's projects. They have a general idea of what is going on in these places, whether it be a new minister appointed, or a new restaurant opening close to the IO's office (I8: 59).

This attitude is certainly supported by the IO. Overseas assignments last from three to five years. The projects conducted abroad last longer, but usually one participates only in one particular stage and then switches to another project. »Normally, the IO wants you to change after every three, four years«, otherwise »you continue to bring the same each time and you and they need something different« (I11: 82).

In the IO, things never stay the same (I5: 103), and an employee should also move forward, develop, bring new ideas, and new energy. Therefore a change of an assignment is very positive: it enables variety and fresh opinions. It makes it possible to share experiences and gain new ones. This is also what makes working there so exciting: there is always something new. For most interviewees, part of the motivation to work in the IO was to explore new cultures, to meet new people, and to travel to many different countries. They do not want to stay in one place, they are curious about how it is somewhere else. They move on and, on the new assignment, develop a new relationship to the next place.

A mobile individual is no longer a persistent element in a place; rather, multiple places become important parts of the individual. A certain shift can be observed from »I am a part of« towards »This is a part of me as well«. For a certain time, the mobile individuals become a part of a particular place and they may influence it: in this sample, for example, by co-designing the economic policies regulating life in this place. In general, however, they influence places by their presence or absence, rather than by direct actions. Each place becomes a permanent part of them, their experience, and their identity. All the places they once related to (through their longer or shorter physical presence) are a part of their lives.

The interviewees are connected with various places, and each of these
· relationships is shaped by different mediators: the relationship to the place of long-term residence (as in the case of those who moved to work in the IO's headquarters) is mediated by the characteristics of a place (its motel-like character), and by the IO's environment, in which the individuals are predominantly immersed. The relationship to a third country is dictated primarily by the temporality of a stay. The persistence of the relationship depends to a large extent on business obligations.

6.2.4. Dream places – favorite sites, desired locations, destination goals

In Chapter Five, the non-spatial principle of fixation was discussed. As was shown, there are certain limitations to this principle, and they relate primarily to the dream place and favorite place. The questions about individuals' favorite places and preferred destinations, when they were free to choose, were an important part of each interview conducted. The interviewees talked about places in which they like being; shopping, dwelling, eating, and relaxing. They also talked about the places to which they would like to go to work, on holiday, and to live.

To a certain extent, the individuals can choose the countries in which they want to work: they can apply for a position in a particular department, and in this way decide on their travel destination, or they can apply for a particular assignment abroad. Some have very clear ideas about where they want to work, and when a job opening occurs there, they will grab the chance (18: 162). Yet most possibilities for freely choosing the destination remain in the private sphere. The interviewees can decide freely where to go on holiday, they can deliberate on where they want to live when they retire, and of course they have their favorite places. The drive to discover »the new« can be observed in their private mobility behavior, and one does not generally »go back to the same places over and over again, « except when »visiting friends« (14: 45).

However, the choice of private destinations may also be limited. At least once a year, the interviewees spend some weeks with their families –

parents and siblings – in their home country. Often they have a certain schedule of private trips: for example, they spend the longer or summer holiday in their home country (or, if their spouse is from a different country, they visit both), and they also go for a week »for pleasure only« to a popular holiday destination: an island (I3: 68), the French Riviera (I5: 45), the Alps (I8: 183), etc. Otherwise they take short weekend trips, usually to easily reachable places – typical tourist sites or big cities, like London or Paris (I4: 29), or in the neighborhood – destinations within two or three hours by car (I6: 137). Ludmila, the only single in the sample, visits her friends all over Europe (I7: 125). Very often the holiday destination fits the needs of the children: parents tend to choose sites that are children-friendly (I5: 95), or which are chosen by the children (I9: 90), or they try to secure the relationship of their children to their extended family (I2: 79). The discovery of new cultures and new places thus often remains in the sphere of wishes, or can be realized only in a limited version, over the longer term (one holiday a year is dedicated to visiting a new location, if at all), or combined with a business trip (I4: 75), or planned for the future (»when I retire…«).

What makes a place a desired location? The choice of the next location is usually well motivated by practical reasons, whereas the further in the future, the less role realistic factors play. For example, Sabah would next like to work and live in China, because she has read a lot about the country, is convinced that its economy is very interesting, and that, due to its very different culture, it would be an enriching experience for her and her children. However, when she talks about where she would move when she retires and can choose freely, she says that she would not move to one place:

»[…] until I could sort of physically and financially afford it I would start with three places where I would spend a few months each, and these places would be probably either Paris, maybe Paris, but just as I am talking about retirement age, when I don't work any more and I am not anchored […]« (I8: 121)

The next location for living is usually either closely related to an assignment (»It would only depend on the job and which job I would want to have. I don't have anything against moving to another country« (I4: 19)); or it is a matter of a well-thought out decision driven by, first, the security of a place, in terms of both peace and high-quality living conditions, with a good infrastructure in which to raise children (primarily schools), or well-being (friends and a tolerant environment). Ludmila says that, for her, the choice of residence place is related more to feelings than a calculation; at the same time, she mentioned school, possibilities for personal development, friends, or a relationship as factors influencing her decisions (I7: 87). Often the choice is negative: some places are excluded as possible locations in any case, for example, those that are unsafe due to a war (I6: 141). Usually the choice of the next location is very general. For example, the interviewees coming from Europe would like to live in Europe, regardless of the country (I7: 83). Those who are about to retire usually know very well where they want to be: in their home country. They plan to move back to join their families (siblings). Often their country of origin is the place of residence of their children, and they want to be close to them (I9: 72; I11: 158; I2: 93).

However, the further into the future, the more freely the interviewees pondered about where they would like to go, and the less specific the location and the reason for its choice. »Somewhere in Europe« (I7: 85; I3: 136), »everywhere where there is sunshine I like to go« (I5: 117), »probably either in the United States or probably in Europe« (I9: 58) are the typical articulations. Short-term trip destinations and their choice are also imprecise, for example:

»I would be very keen on going to India or to Asia. I mean I just like...for me it is more exotic, this kind of culture religion is different and so very attractive.« (I3: 66)

Places are attractive because they are supposed to be very different from the place where one grew up or currently lives. Their attractiveness is based usually on very stereotypical opinions gathered from the media. Thus Steven wants to visit Sri Lanka, because he saw it on TV and he hasn't been there yet (I4: 81). Very often the ideal is to stay mobile, to travel or to be located in a couple of places (I9: 138). In the extreme case, the future is not related to any particular location, but rather to a type of activity, for example, traveling, painting, reading, »enjoying life« (I6: 123).

Some of them mentioned that they liked some places very much, or found them interesting. Yet nobody said that he or she has a favorite place to which they would like to go back. When asked directly, the interviewees usually said that they do not have a single favorite place. Favorite places are specialized places. No single place fulfils all needs and wishes. Rather, one has a favorite place to shop for suits, another to buy souvenirs, and another to go to the theatre. One has a favorite place for short holidays (usually an easily accessible sunny island), and another place to walk, another to eat, etc. »It just depends on the objective«, says Steven (I4: 79).

For example, Paris »is the best city in the world, and London is terrific for theatre, so is New York« (I4: 79). Sometimes a favorite place is related to very special positive memories (I5: 117), or to people (I8: 119), but there can be many such places.

6.2.5. The point of departure. Relationship to the place of origin

Traditionally place of origin is understood as a part of a homeland, its territorial component. Homeland encompasses two other dimensions: psychological and biographic-temporal. The spatial component relates to a familiar and trusted environment: landscape, town, village, city quarter, or a street. The temporal dimension understands homeland as a part of an individual biography – a place of origin. From the psychological perspective, homeland guarantees well-being and confidence, because of familiarity. It gives the feeling of belonging (Schiedeck/Stahlmann 1999: 79-85).

Mobility and globalization question the togetherness of these elements (Appadurai 1998). As shown in the previous section, confidence and well-being can be achieved in a detached home that is primarily based on the immediate family and a minimal set of material belongings, pinned down in any location. Under the conditions of extensive mobility and a certain homogenization, familiarity can be found in networks, and a trusted environment can be placed anywhere in the world, not necessarily in the place of origin. As Schiedeck and Stahlmann (1999: 85) show, homeland can be compensated for by various types of communications technology. Homeland can thus be spatially detached, and limited in time. In the case of enforced migration, individuals can re-establish their homeland by working actively on new cultural and social bonds (Keupp 2003: 31). Similar tendencies can be observed in self-chosen mobility (Clever 2005).

In the course of the interviews, it turned out that the individuals clearly distinguish between their current or past places of residence, and their home and homeland. There can be many places of residence, the individual home can be located anywhere, but there is always a single place of origin. It is a place of birth and, regardless of a later mobile biography, this place remains important. However, on the basis of the interviews, it is often not possible to distinguish where the difference between a place of origin (cognitive definition) and homeland (emotional bond, usually to a whole country) lies. The interviewees use these terms interchangeably. Depending on the context, they mean a town or a country as their homeland and/or place of origin. The scales shift. For example, when they talk about visiting their family, they mean a town. When they talk about general cultural differences between their current place of residence and their place of origin, they mean rather the whole country.

The importance of a place of origin is compound. In the multicultural environment in which the individuals dwell, the name of the place of origin is a person's label, an attribute of distinction. Independently of the strength of the relationship to it, the individuals give the name of the country where they were born to identify themselves to another person. Place of origin as a label becomes important in a context: when meeting a foreigner, and while in a place outside the country of origin. What is understood by this label is open: only in the course of the subsequent conversation is it clarified what it means to come from Germany, India, or Morocco. In some contexts, a place of origin (usually described by the name of the country) can be »enlarged« and become a synonym for culture and cultural habits. Those interviewees who live in the USA state that their home(land) is Europe, not a particular country in Europe. In comparison to the USA, Europe is, to them, a homogenous cultural space, where a certain set of values and a common history united people and distinguish them from the Americans:

»We are Europeans; we see Europe as our home.« (I11: 46)

»At the beginning I missed home of course and not really the country, my home is Europe.« (I6: 66)

The interviewees point to the common working culture in Europe (I6: 68), the quality of products (they usually shop in Europe despite residing in the USA – I3: 80), and a rich history reflected in architecture (I7: 32).

Usually the country of origin matches the citizenship of the individuals (especially in those countries in which citizenship is based on *ius solis*). In the case of »enlarged homeland Europe«, citizenship turns into an empty legal category. Sometimes, however, when, for any reason, citizenship does not match the country of origin, citizenship is less important in the self-description than the place of origin (I8: 10).

A place of origin is for the interviewees an important part of their biographies (I9: 12). It is for many a place where they grew up and made friends, where they completed their education, and where they had their first job. It signifies a certain distinct period in life: for example, it is characterized by greater immobility, lack of responsibility for one's own life and family, more spare time, development of one's hobbies, etc. It is, however, possible that a new place of residence has a great emotional meaning to an individual who finds there all these elements that for him or her are the necessary elements constituting what one usually means by the term homeland: for example, family, friends, possibilities of personal development, etc. (I5: 113). Family and friends, in particular, seem to be the most important elements of such a »homeland«.

In the present period of their lives, the interviewees return to their place of origin. However, the individuals stress that the relationship to their families and friends, rather than to familiar landscapes or culture, makes them travel regularly to this place. People turn out to be more immobile than some elements of culture. For example, one can cook dishes from the home country in the new place of residence, but one cannot experience people over distance as one can in physical proximity (see also the chapter on mobility and its consequences). Often it is possible to share these elements of culture (for example language) with other immigrants from the same country (I6: 85). Again, due to mobility, the conglomeration of culture, place, and its inhabitants disappears.

As long it is possible to visit the home country and to experience it regularly, there is no need to idealize it and to miss it:

»I mean the one thing that is Venezuelan without the doubt is the food and that's I like but again I can go without Venezuelan food for fifteen years and I wouldn't notice and when I go to Venezuela for twenty days I can eat Venezuelan food for twenty days and that is quite peculiar.« (I10: 68)

As long as it is not »lost«, the place (country) of origin is thus not a unified and homogenized place where landscapes, habits, people, culture, and language melt into an imaginative idealized conglomerate. One negative example seems to confirm this thesis. One of the interviewees, due to the political situation in her place of origin, cannot freely go back there to live. Since she was a child, she has been extremely mobile and has lived in many countries. She has also changed her citizenship, and members of her family live in many different countries. She says that

»I really feel like a citizen of the world I don't feel that I am one nationality or the other but I with age it's funny with age, elder age I get much, much more attached to my country. And...you know, I don't love the government there, I don't even have a place to stay there, because they took everything from us, I don't really have anything there but I in my heart I feel I have to go back, I go back at least once a year to I go to my home town at the sea and I just spend there a few days and sort of resource myself and I come back I don't know what it is but as I age you know I fell the attachment much stronger than ten years ago and twenty years ago. I haven't been there for twenty years when I went back, you see, I had a long time passed without even wanting to go back now I go back every year.« (I8: 10)

On the one hand, (home)country can be re-established in a new place of residence (I5). On the other hand, for many interviewees (home)land is there, a stable part of their individual biography. Its importance is about its presence, which does not mean that many of them would like to go back there and live there. Some make it dependent on the political situation in the home country, or on their personal and family situation: some would prefer to be close to their children and not in a particular place. In any case, place of origin is a resource. It is not really a resource of familiarity: it can change itself when an individual is absent (I2), and be less familiar than a place of residence. Place of origin is rather a resource of another kind. Place of origin is an exit point for any later experience. It is a point of exit for mobility, and the individuals compare with it each successive location and every subsequent experience. It is a zero-measure in experience with new people and their habits, new landscapes and new conditions. Living in a place similar to the place of origin requires a different kind of adaptation work from that required in a place that is very different (I2: 105). One's own mobility can be interpreted positively or negatively, depending on the comparison of the new place of residence and one's situation there, and the situation in the country of origin (I6: 181). Place of origin constructs the horizon of one experience with the other.

It is questionable whether it is possible to speak about homeland in this case, at least not in the sense common in the literature. The meaning of a place of origin, which is equated with homeland, is important in this sample, but it does not involve emotions that would justify a comparison with »home«. Place of origin (a town, a street or a country, depending on the context of discourse) is no longer »the home« of the mobile individuals. They do not lay claim to this particular place as »homeland«: the taken for granted connotations of the place of origin, and of the homeland, cannot be assumed. Nor is the current place of residence necessarily the »home« place. Place of origin is also not the idealized or imagined place to which one would like to go back. It is usually not a place for one's own future. It does not have to be a single country, but may be just one town or village – all depending on the context and the scale of comparison. It can be experienced independently of place of residence, and no matter the individual biography, it remains an important part of it. It is an exit point for mobility. It is a label in contact with »the other« and it is a perspective from which one experiences »the other«.

6.3. Redefining places

From the analysis of the interviews, the following components of a place and of a relationship to places are apparent. In each place, the relation of an interviewee to this place is about consuming the place, influencing it, experiencing it, and being influenced by it. By consume, I mean a functional use of what a place offers: this usage is thus mediated partly by the materialities of a place – its landscape, natural resources, infrastructure (from buildings and streets to shops and cinemas). To influence a place is to make a difference, mark one's own presence. By experiencing a place, I mean experience of place-specific qualities. In each place, three major components can be taken into account: the inhabitants, the political organization, and the materialities of a place (landscape and infrastructure, for example, its architecture). By being physically present in a place, an individual has to do with all three components, but to each of these he or she may have a different relationship.

The table below presents the situation. The first two columns relate to the general identified components: elements of places that are important to the informants, and the type of relationships connecting individuals to these elements.

Table 6. Places, dwelling, relationships

Elements of a place	Types of relation	Real places	Types of dwelling
Social (inhabitants) Material (infrastructure) Landscape Organization/ Political rule	Influence it Experience it Be influenced by it Consume it	Origin Residence Destinations Dream places	Absence/Memory/Presence Presence/Absence Temporary presence Absence/Memory/Wish

The next two columns show the types of existing places to which the informants travel, or where they live, respectively. The last column shows physical involvement in these places. The type of dwelling in a place is characterized first of all by temporality. The individuals are mobile and therefore often absent from their place of residence. In other places they
· are predominantly absent. As described in the previous sections, different relationships connect the individuals to different elements of the places in which they are present or absent. For example, in the places in which the individuals conduct projects, and to which they regularly travel, they influence their infrastructure (for example by co-designing and conducting projects sponsoring a construction of highways, bridges, or investment in agricultural development). They are influenced by their places of origin even though they are currently absent from these places. They may experience the different landscapes of places in which they are predominantly present. They are related to a place of residence through work and friends, to a favorite place by its functionality and their positive experiences and memories of it, to a wished-for destination by their imagination of it and curiosity, to a dream location through desire for a particular life and life-style, to their homeland because of their families, friends, and as the perspective-setter.

A relation between an individual and a place depends on both the individual and the materialities and inhabitants already in this place. For example, a political organization that occupies the place (a local government of a city) may exclude the individual, by law, from active political participation in the place. This is the case of migrants who are not given a right to vote in community elections, for instance. The form of attachment to place may vary, depending on whether one lives in a small village or a big city. The example of Ann (I11) shows this clearly: she acclimatized perfectly in a big city in the USA, but she had problems being accepted in a small community in the Mid West. Both the social and the material networks present and absent in these two places determined her relation to these places, and in the end also the duration of her stay.

When we consider the materialities of places, we first see the difference that they make to individuals (Hetherington 1997: 184). Some places, for example, transit places, such as airports or train stations, define the nature of the relationship to a greater extent than other places. They fulfill a function: they enable smooth transportation. Independently of how complex such places are, and although they now include more and more functions (for example, shopping, rest, entertainment), the relation to them is defined by the temporality of stay and their standardization. These places are sites in the sense of Augé (1994), »non-places«. Their character limits the scope of possible relations with an individual. They are designed to enable people to leave them. They may make the stay more or less pleasant. An individual knows the kind of features such a place has, and is prepared for them. My informants, for example, use time at airports to read, work, or play on their computers. It is highly likely that, at airports, many people shop, or look at the products in the exhibition windows, eat a snack, and do the same things as my informants. This limited character of such places and their orientation towards a certain function makes them either neutral or negative places: my informants feel uncomfortable in such places and minimize the time spent there. They either influence such places or they do not; but they do not experience them, because they are standardized and there is no difference in the experience of each of them.

A city is a much more complex space and it is multifunctional. It is a dwelling place, and it provides entertainment, education, work, and social networks, and it has a certain landscape, architecture, etc. The more possibilities a place offers, the more likely it is that individuals relate to it in some way. My informants feel more comfortable in, and are more likely to choose, a place that offers them a greater range of possibilities for personal development (educational and employment), enlarging social networks, leisure, etc. They feel bad in, and leave, places in which, for example, their social contacts are limited to a group of expatriates, or where they cannot realize their hobbies or dreams. They avoid insecure places affected by armed conflicts, and places in which the political or economic situation disables their mobility, both geographical and social.

Individuals can turn a place into a site if they use it in a limited way, functionally. For someone who arrives at a place, takes a taxi from the airport to a hotel, works in an office, and leaves the place after one or two days, the relation to this place is most probably one-dimensional and restricted to a function. Such people are considered to lack any relationship to a place. This purely functional and one-dimensional, superficial relationship to a place makes the individuals comparable to bits of information or objects transported through the infrastructure networks around the globe (Castells 2001: 470). They are excluded from social life in these places. The predominantly negative valuation of this situation in the literature relates, in particular, to the fact that individuals who dwell in homogenous networks do not experience the difference of places, the particularities of the location.

The picture that emerges in the course of the analysis of relationships to places in my sample is much more complex. For my informants, a place is not a unified homogenous entity, but rather a multidimensional togetherness of different elements. The individuals are aware that any place in which they are present is a complex system that they cannot experience completely. They are aware that certain aspects of a place are inaccessible to them. Usually it is a problem of the duration of a stay in a place. During a business trip, an individual has too little time to visit even the tourist attractions, not to mention achieve closer contact with its inhabitants. In a place of residence, they are able to sightsee the place but cannot vote in local elections, for example. The temporality of a stay results in the place losing its unified character: its aspects separate in the partial experience of a mobile individual. Positioning becomes ambiguous: different aspects of places – economic, social, political, everyday practices, and identities – do not cohere.

The borders of such a place are difficult to define: they differ from one aspect to another. The political boundaries of a nation-state co-define the place through complex laws. Another border is constituted by the economic situation, both official regulations and »everyday economics«: prices, opening times of shops, etc. The next boundary is set by the availability of diverse products: food, clothes, etc. Architecture, landscape, and climate do not coincide with the other borders: they may overlap with them or cross them. Social networks may stretch between and beyond these boundaries. Such a place may be as large as a region or a nation-state, or as small as a street, village, or town. A place may include units separated by political organization, for example, a town and its non-urban surroundings, or a section of a city and a farm in the countryside.

Here Simmel's consideration of the Stranger comes to mind: place does not have to be bonded to a particular territory, as it is shaped not only by physical proximity but also, to a great extent, by what is far. The social and physical boundaries that once marked the limits of local relations are, as a result of mobility (of information, images, and people), more akin to thresholds across which communication and other forms of distant interaction may take place. »The inside« and »the outside«, »the belonging« and »the excluded« change into new constellations. There is nothing like a stable, territorially fixed, cozy, local world of everyday life: rather, the cozy world moves with an individual, and a particular territory is re-shaped to include these multiple cozy worlds of the mobile individuals.

Places are dynamic settings. The »how« and the »who« are intimately tied to the »where« that gives them a specific content. Place establishes a concrete situatedness in the common world. This emplacement is as social as it is personal. It has a collective character. This complex collective concreteness is embodied in place-names. Place-naming (which Simmel called individualization of places) is the institutionalization of a geographic and historical setting (Casey 1993: 24). Place-naming distinguishes places from their surroundings. Place-naming ultimately seals the seemingly amalgamated aspects of a place: territory, inhabitants, and a binding rule that orders the »how« that unifies under the common name of this place.

This everyday process is also reflected in the theoretical and empirical studies on locality. The traditional correlation of community and territory assumes the understanding of places as distinguished by their political rule. Any part of a territory on which a unique rule applies is a place, whether it is inhabited or not. For example, a village is a place: a togetherness of territory, rules governing it, its inhabitants, and the material and social outcomes of their activity – houses, streets, schools, and problems. The distinctiveness of a place primarily follows its political exclusiveness. Some authors contest these clusters in respect to the amalgamation of community (and/or culture) and territory. Using, above all, the example of migration, their studies show that a community can stretch over several such units. A local community is thus a translocal community, with strong ties to two or more spatio-political units (comp. Albrow 1997; Glick Schiller et al. 1997; Pries 1998). A community of immigrants re-creates their host place by reshaping their neighborhoods to correspond more closely to their needs and values (Castles/Davidson 2000: 131). Such place-making cannot be recognized in the sample discussed. My informants experience the place rather than change it actively. Their indirect influence on the place relates to their consumption and is, supposedly, long-term (it may be that the more foreigners in the country, the more »foreigner friendly« the place will become: the interviews with the HQ's employees seem to confirm this thesis).

Despite the heterogeneity and multiplicity of settings and their occasional character, places seem to be an entity. They tend to look like a homogenous concoction of a territory, social groups and its habits, cultural expressions, language, and political organization. It is taken for granted that an airport is a place. Its name already suggests the unity of all its elements: a single label encompasses all the elements that constitute an airport, and isolate it from its surrounding. A city is distinguished from its environment by a political rule, although its borders may not be noticed when walking from the centre towards its peripheries.

Actor-Network-Theory (ANT) would say that this is an effect of punctualization (Law 1992: 385). It is efface of heterogeneity and the illusion of unity. Something unusual must happen to split this seemingly homogenous unit into parts, and reveal the heterogeneous network behind its agency. For example, a television is a coherent object with relatively few parts, but when it breaks down it rapidly turns into a network of electronic components and human interventions (Law 1992: 384). Certainly, some networks are easier to punctualize than others. They are network packages, routines, taken for granted. The claim of ANT is that such networks are more widely performed than other networks. They are counted as resources. They may take a variety of forms. Punctualization is always precarious, and it faces resistance. Punctualized resources offer a way of drawing quickly on the networks of the social, without having to deal with endless complexity (Law 1992: 385).

Punctualization is part of an ordering process that the ANT calls translation. It generates ordering effects, such as devices, agents, institutions, and organizations. It implies that one thing, for example, an actor, may stand for another, for instance, a network. One of ANT's empirical conclusions is that translation is contingent, local, and variable (Law 1992: 387).

Some networks survive longer as punctualized actors than others. They manage to avoid being de-punctualized; they manage not to reveal their heterogeneity. Some translated gatherings are thus more durable than others. They maintain their relational patter for longer. In particular, those sets of relations that are embodied in durable materials are the most stable. A relatively stable network is one embodied in and performed by a range of durable materials. However, durability is also a relational effect. Any durable material may have a different effect in another set of relations.

If we look at place from the perspective of the ANT, we can see it as a punctualized heterogeneous network. Place is an ordered set of elements. It is embodied in durable materials: landscapes, buildings, streets, bridges, etc. It generates certain effects that are calculable, and in turn increase its robustness (Law 1992: 388).

What has to happen to reverse the process of translating a heterogeneous network into a single unified place, and to turn that place into a heterogeneous network that can be re-translated? In other words, what processes of resistance re-order places? The answer that emerges from the empirical research is mobility. For my informants, places are first of all heterogeneous. They are all certain that their own experience relates only to certain aspects of places. They know that a place is not only a territory. They know that that may be physically present in the territory of a city, but still know little about its inhabitants. Or they may have a close relationship to an inhabitant, but not know where he or she lives, nor the landscape in which this person walks, nor his or her routes through the city. They know that they may influence the economic situation of the place, but they do not speak or understand the language spoken there. They have this knowledge of heterogeneity of a place because of mobility. They are mobile. This means that they are in places for only a certain limited period of time, and then they move on to another place. Mobility is about the temporality of experience. A limited time spent in a place makes impossible the holistic experience of that place. A place no longer translates to a homogenous entity. However, such re-translated places have an effect, a power. They can nevertheless behave like agents: they do not lose their integrity completely. They do not collapse as agents: they stay effective. However, for the mobile individuals, they change their meaning. Their power is re-defined.

For someone who has spent his entire life in his place of origin, this place is »the place«: in such a situation, any enforced mobility would be a displacement. A mobile individual settles in places, but only for a while. A mobile individual dwells in many places, none of which has a clearly privileged position. Any place in which mobile individuals stay for a while is not »the place« but »a place« – one of many. At the beginning there was only one place of origin – the place. The mobility experience changes the character of this place. It becomes one of the places in which the mobile individual dwells. Each successive place is important, and for many mobile individuals it is just as important as the place of origin. The place (of origin) thus turns into »a place« or »the place« among »the places«. Places lose their character, their exclusiveness. This does not mean that they lose their divergence, or that they become gradually more and more similar to each other. It does not mean that the meaning of each place has the same quality for the individual. The array of spatial experiences supports the situatedness and the particularity of each place-setting. Indeed, what makes a place is the particularity of its setting, its exceptionality. Let me recapitulate the argument. Places are heterogeneous dynamic settings. However, they seem to constitute a homogenous spatial unit. Several processes lead to this. The ANT would call them translation. Place-naming, and the amalgamation of political rule over the territory and its inhabitants, play a part in translation. Places are embedded in diverse materials that support their durability and stability as homogenous entities. As such, they possess power: for example, they are seen as a necessary component of individual identity. However, because of mobility, their homogeneity is challenged. Mobility means periodicity and partition of the individual experience in places. It hinders the holistic experience of places. Places appear to a mobile individual as a set of aspects, each of which may be experienced (influenced or consumed) separately in a certain period of time. Places appear as a setting of different elements. Therefore they may be as large as a country (political unit) or a climate zone, or as small as the route from the house to the office. They may stretch over different political units and include physically distant individuals. Such de-translated places lose their privileged position. »The place« turns into »the place among other places«. However, they remain empowered. They are reference and focal points for mobile individuals. Being »implaced« remains intrinsically particular. However, a shift from »I am a part of« towards »This is a part of me« can be observed. Mobility and the temporal character of experience stress the particularity of place-settings. Place is no longer about the co-presence and amalgamation of components, but about the exceptionality of a setting. These settings are dynamic. There exist dynamic and fluid possibilities of renegotiating positioning. Such places are a-historical but not a-temporal: they do not bind the past of the mobile individuals, but they are in a constant temporal process of re-constitution. The past of a place is not a subject of the discourse.

There is a second aspect to this dynamic constitution of places. Places develop, they progress, they have own trajectories. Places participate for a certain time in the life of the mobile individuals, for example, for the duration of the project that they conduct in a country, or the period for which they are employed and reside in a particular town. As soon as a person leaves a place, this place remains in his or her memory like a snapshot, immobilized in time, made static. In the spatial imaginations of the travelers, they become parts of the past, points on the map: immobile, always there where you left them, looking as they did when you left them. The wish that my interview partners expressed, to visit the same place again and again, means the wish to take part in its further development, and thus acknowledge the changing character of each place. The mobile individuals admit that places have their own trajectories and that, when they are absent from these places, they do not participate in their stories. These go on without them. To go back to them means to go back to their trajectories, and to become part of them, to develop with them.

It is interesting however, that my informants go back to certain places for a certain period only, after which they never return again. They are not even curious about how these places have changed in their absence. This is important, considering that, through their practices of travel, mobile individuals link places into their single story to produce their spaces. They link events and people (happening in time, thus dynamic), yet this linking is episodic: after the dynamic period, some dynamic elements of this linkage are »moved« to the past and immobilized, and they become static although still part of the linkages. Spaces constituted in their practice are thus also temporary arrangements, and dynamic in time: they are on-going stories.

7. Spacing

The previous chapters showed that the principle of placing does not have to be territorial but may be, for example, functional. They described how mobile individuals constitute their private place – home – and how they locate it in networks. They demonstrated how places are de-constructed by the mobility of individuals, and how each element of a place in turn gains independence. They pointed at the ambiguity, for the mobile individuals, of positioning the role of particular places, and the distinctiveness of places with respect to their ability to bind individuals. They outlined the elements that make a difference to the individuals in their relationship to places. The following chapter deals with what marks the difference between one place and another. In other words, it deals with similarity and difference, and asks about the role and constitution of boundaries between different elements, and the relationships between similar ones.

The previous chapter discussed the strategy that the individuals employed to regulate their exposure to the components of places. The individuals decide whether they want to experience those elements that are new and different for them, or to avoid the risk of misunderstandings by leading their lives within familiar networks. The interviewees point out that, in every location, some elements are different from those that they have already experienced in other locations, whilst others are similar:

»[…] my own experience moving across these very different countries has been that on the one hand how similar they are and on the other hand that as similar as they appear to be on ninety five percent of the issue, how different they can be on the other five percent. Yes, they are different, yes, they are not as different one thinks they are, 'cause on most things they tend to be quite similar but for that small percentage that are different, differences are big.« (110: 46)

The aim of this chapter is to consider in detail these differences and similarities, to examine how significant they are, and to examine the extent to which they depend on geographical location. In other words, it asks the following: if something is somewhere other than here, is it different, and if not, why not? Also, what does this mean for the constitution of boundaries between »here« and »there«?

The words »different« and »difference« appear frequently in the interviews, almost four hundred times. However, few words are as imprecise as »different«. Often it appears together with a country, and then it means a particular unnamed country: not the USA, not the country of origin, not the country of residence, but any other country. »Different« is here a label, applicable as a replacement for a name: not particular but »different«, »other«, or »all the other« countries. The interviewees use the same label in relation to places: »in different places« means »not here«. »Different« appears often in relation to religion: the different religion is either »not the one I have, « or »not the major religion in my home country/ place of residence«, or it is a synonym for Islam. It is less apparent what »different« means in relation to people. Sometimes it stands for individual characteristics, sometimes it relates to group characteristics, and sometimes it is a synonym for the inhabitants of a particular country. It is even more ambiguous what »different culture« denotes.

»Different« in the interviews was related also to parts of the world (geographical locations), the IO departments (the ones dealing with certain topics, like economics or environment, or geographical regions, like Asia, Africa, and so on), the circumstances and situation of countries (economic structure, problems), the interviewee's own situation, etc. »Different« is used in direct comparisons, not as a general category of description. For example, the interviewees very often say that working in the HQ and in a field office are different: the elements that they compare in this case are access to people and information, time available to them for managing tasks, the tasks themselves, the number and type of meetings, and the course of the day in general. They also compare their own situation in terms of opinions, skills and professional knowledge, pace of events in their life, etc. What make them »different« from many other people, including old friends from school or university, is their experience of mobility: it is extensive travel and exposure to the difference.

7.1. The five percent of difference

It was said in the previous chapter that mobility makes places specialized: there are, for example, places where the interviewees only shop (London or Paris in I4), where they only spend holidays (often an island in the Caribbean), and where they only work (business destinations). In this chapter, I am interested in the differences between places, and how the mobile individuals perceive them. I relate to the differences that the mobile individuals see and experience at the moment of arrival, and to which they react. I do not intend to follow the development of places, respectively not how mobile individuals change these places or how the locals shape their policies to have influence on such mobile people.[43]

Not every difference is relevant, not every difference »makes it different«, and not every difference has the same meaning for the individuals. Out of this »jungle« of »the different«, four main types of difference can be distinguished: trivial differences, deterrent differences, those that provide an exotic touch, and those that require adaptation. This typology relates to the possible reaction of the individuals to these differences, in relation to their mobility. The existence of exotic differences motivates the individuals to mobility. However, differences that require adaptation skills from individuals diminish the extent of their mobility. Deterrent differences lead to their rejection of mobility. Trivial differences are, for the interviewees, the least interesting part of being mobile. These are the differences that one »lives with« in each situation. They are neither difficult nor exciting and the individuals can ignore them.

7.1.1. Deterrent differences

The interviewees often point to these differences, which they consider factors influencing their decision on mobility. As already mentioned, the individuals do not want to travel to countries in which the political or living situation is dangerous. They do not want to, or try not to, travel to countries where there are armed conflicts, or where criminality is very bad,

---

43 Such research has been done in relation to global cities that attract global flows of capital, humans, goods, etc. (compare also Sassen 1991; 1994; Allen et al. 1999; Body-Gendrot/Martiniello 2000), and holiday destinations like the Caribbean (comp. Shields 1991; Sheller 2003; Azaraya 2004).

or where their life would be in danger. Here they mention some African countries and Chechnya (I2: 137-139). Next to war, hygiene is the most important factor preventing mobility. Bad hygienic conditions, and the high risk of food poisoning and other diseases, made some interviewees limit their mobility (I6: 38). But it is also limited by the whole infrastructure available during travel, which makes it either more secure in general, or at least possible to deal with problems like sickness or armed conflicts. It may differ from place to place, and become an important factor in deciding whether to travel to a country (I6: 36). Some of the interviewees talk about their dangerous adventures:

»[…] planes are not safe, the airport is not safe […] the transport from the airport to the city is extremely dangerous, there had been hijacking, I was involved in an accident […] we lost the wheel it was not very pleasant because for two hours we were standing in the middle of the sun on a very dirty road and dusty and I feared for my safety but then….Recently a very good hotel was constructed but before we stayed in an awful one which did not have running water which didn't have proper light, no air conditioning, no heating, and I've been poisoned a number of times...« (I6: 36)

Security is usually the main consideration in choosing a new assignment abroad. One »needs to strike a balance« between the interesting job and »the issue of security« (I10: 28). Infrastructure plays an important role in guaranteeing security. Shabby hotel rooms, bad roads, lack of hot water, and ugly surroundings directly affect personal security and intensify the feeling of constant danger, so that the individuals try to avoid staying in such places (I11: 96-98). The general political situation in a country is also a deterring issue. There are two possibilities: either the political regime negatively influences living conditions in the country to such an extent that its inhabitants cannot lead their life as they would like to (for example, they cannot enjoy religious freedoms or travel freely, or they are forced to undertake certain societal roles – I8); or the political situation makes life in this country »unattractive« (I10: 86).

Sometimes seemingly unimportant factors play a role in the decision about the place of residence, because when one has a free choice, one becomes meticulous:

»I am not so keen on going to central Asia countries […] I would miss to go to some restaurants…I would miss going to some movies.« (I3: 124-126)

The deterrent differences can be thus described as those that involve possible dangers to the lives of the individuals (extremely bad hygienic conditions, food poisoning, accidents, armed conflicts, crime and violence); and those that limit the individuals in their freedom (politically, freedom of belief, freedom of mobility, and personal development: choice of occupation and hobbies).

7.1.2. Settle in the difference

Not all the differences detected by the interviewees are, in their opinion, deterrent. Many differences between places seem »unpleasant« or make their life more difficult, but one can adapt to them. Poor infrastructure in a politically unstable country, in which hygienic conditions are extremely bad, is an important factor, and may lead the interviewees to reduce or stop travel to such a place. However, a poor infrastructure in a generally secure country is something one can get used to, or at least can tolerate for the duration of travel, although »it is an issue« that cannot be easily ignored. Sometimes quite surprising problems occur:

»India is a very tough place to visit because it is so crowded, you can't ever get away from the crowd of people either in the country side it would always be one village after the next, there are always people on the road and you cannot get away, so you are always sort of pressed in, so I mean this can be an issue.« (I4: 69)

Most interviewees talk about infrastructure that is different from what they are now used to, either in their home country or in their previous or current place of residence: »Not better, not worse but different« (I4: 41). Different in this context means unfamiliar, unknown, new. It is the infrastructure the places offer in everyday life, like hotels, houses, streets, shops, restaurants, schools, theatres, cinemas, concert halls, public transportation, and access to information. Different might mean that in one town one always takes a hotel bus from the airport, whereas in another town one uses a taxi; or, in one place, hotels offer a full service for business clients, including good lighting, a desk, and Internet connection (I7: 119), whereas, in another, one is lucky to have warm water and clean bed sheets (I6). These are all differences to which the interviewees become used when in a new place of residence, or destination of business travel.

Social relationships in each place also make a great difference to the individuals. In three situations – a stay in the USA, an overseas assignment, or visits to one's home country – three different patterns of social networks can be identified.

Table 7. Social networks development

Relation	Situation		
	The USA	Overseas	Country of origin
New	International neighbors, IO Employees with families	Expatriates: int. school, embassies, Local IO staff	-
Old	IO colleagues	Visitors from previous location	Family, school friends

Social networks in the country of origin are, for the majority of the interviews, in stagnation. They are limited to close family and some old school friends. Over time, many friendships erode. In addition, business contacts are lost (I13: 86) and the interviewees become more firmly anchored in social networks abroad.

In a sense, »one takes what is there«: in the USA, in the neighborhood, the interviewees easily learn the style of meetings used by their neighbors, who are often very international (I12: 46). In his neighborhood in the USA, Atanas, for example, came to understand the type of party he calls »take a drink, take a talk, take a go« (where everybody comes, takes a drink, talks a while, and leaves). He quickly adapted to this style, which is very different from the way of hosting and being hosted in his country of origin, and he learned to like it. Ann believes it is normal that her social networks and the type of meetings are very different abroad from those in her home country:

»Here we have a lot of visitors who come to stay, I run a guest house, I am booked solid, all my guest room is full, all the coming summer and it was like this the whole last summer so we are never alone. But we see people one at the time, we have smaller dinner parties, we go less to other people's houses. But I think this is normal. We get to meet some new people but it tends to be always the same group, you know, the UN, some of the embassies. Then I have nice friends here in the office and that's very nice. But it is not what you would call a big circle or a diverse circle [...] it is some less heterogeneous group of people.« (I11: 68-70)

The social networks overseas are usually more homogeneous despite being more international than in the country of origin. Most of the new friends are in the same situation, they are expatriates, and they get to know each other in two homogeneous contexts: in an international school, or in the

IO (in the USA especially). Overseas, many spouses of the IO's employees »dive« into the social activities supported by the international schools that their children attend. These differ greatly from their social networks back home or in the USA (I5), and this difference is not always experienced as enjoyable, interesting, or easy; but for a certain period of time they all accept it. Very limited access to social networks in a place (to a single group, for example, mothers in an international school, or only IO employees and their families) may thus be a reason not to choose a particular place as a place of residence (I5, I7).

The type and content of a social network determine how one spends spare time, and how one's life in a place looks. With one's family, one would rather spend a lot of time at home, chatting at the kitchen table, and eating (I10: 65, 80, I2: 89). With one's old school friends, one spend hours talking and exchanging the news, sharing problems and impressions (I5), perhaps at home, or in a pub with a glass of beer. With one's new international friends, one drinks a beer at the sixth barbeque party one's been to in the last few weeks, or one meets them at an official dinner in an embassy (I11). In the business travel destination, one has no time for meetings apart from professional ones, business breakfasts, and dinner with team colleagues, and so on.

Similarly, the infrastructure shapes life in the place: if there are no cinemas and theatres, one may take up gardening as a hobby. Social networks and infrastructure have a mutual influence: if one has no friends in a new place of residence, one may go to the cinema or to a concert more often, either alone or with only his or her spouse.

For the interviewees, what they do makes a difference, not where they are. Many statements support this thesis:

- Venezuela it is very different to the USA – there your life is less hectic, you live slower, you do not work at such immense speed (I10).
- The USA was very different – I had to stay at home with my children and if I needed a book for my thesis, I had to drive two hours to the nearest library (I11).
- In the business trip destination it is different, because there I work from early in the morning till very late in the night, including business breakfast and dinners with the team colleagues and writing e-mails when already in the hotel room (I3, I6).

- In Nigeria it was different because there I had problems to phone, it was expensive and of a very bad quality. I could not communicate often with my family (I2).
- Kenya was very different to Switzerland – there we had ourselves to organize the school for our children and all the families were meeting very often, for the whole weekends, we grew together there very much (I2).
- In China it would be different; I would have problems communicating with people (I3).
- Tanzania was different, there were many interesting tourists' sites, we went on the weekends to national parks (I4) and in Pakistan, we went hiking, and it was different (I4).
- France was different; there I studied (I8).
- In the HQ it is different, there I have the infrastructure and access to the resources and I meet people internally and have time to read and write. In Croatia I work the whole day long and meet many officials, talk more to people outside and have no time to write and read e-mails (I13).
- My life here and in the USA is similar; there is not really a difference. I do the same; perhaps what is different is with whom I do it (I4).

In this way, differences are reduced to differences in life-style and activities. Thus, there are places dominated by work activities, there are places dominated by family relations, there are places dominated by tourist activities, etc.

7.3.3. The Exotic Touch

One reasons why the interviewees want to travel is to experience something new and unusual. If everything was the same, they could stay at home. If they could not travel, they would miss »the smell, the food, the air, and the people«, because »the world consists of so many different sides, to be able to see a few of them is enriching« (I9: 132). However, not all differences are exciting. When working in an organization that standardizes its procedures all over the world, when performing similar tasks in cooperation with people who are not locally bound, when staying in a place for only a short period of time, and when living within expatriate communities, etc., it is difficult for the interviewees to discover and experience something surprising, something one remembers forever, something that makes one say »Wow«, and tells one's friends about. When mobility and exposure to the new and unfamiliar become a part of everyday life, such impressions rarely occur, and are therefore even more desired.

When the interviewees are asked to say something about their experiences with mobility, they usually start their story either by complaining about the difficulties and problems related to extensive mobility, or they describe the most unusual and surprising things that have happened to them while traveling. When they are asked about their travel destinations, they first list the places that impressed them, in a positive or negative way: for example, countries where they were sick, or those they liked most, and the most unusual ones. Sometimes only at the end of the interview, and almost accidentally, they mention that they also traveled to some other countries, which they have not mentioned because they are too similar and too familiar to remain exciting. Here the case of Atanas is representative. When we scheduled the meeting, he said that he was the perfect candidate for an interview because he was very tired of mobility. During the interview I returned to this topic, and he replied thus:

»It is surely very difficult because of all the tiring things, because one has to sit in one position more than ten hours in the place, and of course, there are no great attractions on board, and a relieve from this monotony are, when being already in the field, the excursions to the sites, a kind of safari, when I spend hours in a land rover or in a Jeep driving along the steps and the desert, sleep in a tent among the shepherds and walking there from one place to another, this is a kind of relief, entertainment which I have there [...] There are huge distances and to control my project I have to drive one and a half day, then sometimes I have to horse ride or walk. But I say: this is the nice part, you can forget for a time about civilization, places, hotels, airports, computers, and simply for a short time immerse in the life of people who live there and simply disconnect from everything.« (I12: 76-78)

What may seem an inconvenience – a stay in the desert, without a toilet (I12: 84) – for him is a relief from a routine of frequent travel. This is the kind of experience that makes these trips unusual for him, and very different from a stay in many other countries. Similarly, as Reiner describes,

»The bigger the difference to your previous place...when we moved for example from Europe to Africa, Africa it was really in the bush this is like the difference like between living on the planet Earth and living on the moon.« (I2: 105)

When he later moved between two African countries, the difference between them did not seem very great. Therefore, the whole story about his experiences in Africa was limited to these first, most different, and most exotic impressions. He described at length a stone house without electricity that they lived in: using gas lamps and a gas fridge, their problems with water supply, wildlife around the house, mosquitoes screens in the windows, muddy roads along which a car could hardly move after rain, and so on:

»It was indeed a very exotic place at that time [...] Sometimes we had to leave our car on the hill and walk the last two three kilometers. And of course it happened that we found big snakes not only in the garden but also at one point there was a big snake in the kitchen.« (12: 107)

Both stories concentrate on a combination of unfamiliar nature (desert, snakes, and insects), housing and infrastructure (no houses but tents, no roads or bad roads, no electricity, no toilets, etc.). Reiner's and Atanas' stories were positive. All the differences they came across enriched them. Other interviewees encountered differences that they consider rather challenging, for example in »troublesome« Albania, the »Muslim country«, unfamiliar, where people are »extremely different from the European« (I6: 46). Yet in this story, the cause of differences was not primarily the religion, but the dictatorship:

»[...] because through forty five years they were isolated from the rest of the world so the notion of mafia...you know associations crime and extreme linkages between families this was totally new to me.« (I6: 46)

Similarly, the interviewees experience Russia as a country that »cannot be described rationally« (I11: 90). The extreme contrasts between the capital and the rest of the country are striking. Moscow is a city of power. It gets richer at the cost of the regions, and so the imbalance increases steadily, and sharpens social problems. Some towns seem to be run entirely by mafia: they are corrupted, and have a very poor infrastructure. However, the country can be fascinating, a real challenge due to such extreme inequalities and poverty (I11: 94-98). The tremendous contrast between rich and poor also surprised Tolga:

»When I went to Abidjan, I felt like...like miniature Manhattan...the buildings, so developed and then I saw all these shadows, in the hotel I asked a receptionist to take me to their bazaars to see what people are saying how they're behaving and it is completely different, different world...On the other hand I went to Belize there is a huge difference between cities: they have two main cities Belize city, by the way, Belize is a country of two forty hundred thousand people and most of people live in Belize city, but they have created the artificial capital Belmopan in the middle of the rain forest and only six thousand people are living there: only ministers and their families.« (I5: 36)

· Sometimes, the »wow! effect« is induced by the gap between expectations before travel and experience in the place: Tolga did not expect to see skyscrapers in Abidjan, nor European architecture in Cape Town, nor such extreme poverty in Latin America. She had associated such poverty with Africa (I5: 37).

The exotic character of a difference is a function of contrast. Three types of contrast can be distinguished. The first type relates to the expectations of a mobile individual (the »African« example). This includes two further types of contrast: the internal and the external contrast, meaning the contrast within a judged object (the »Russian« example), and with the already known object (Atanas' story).

The »exotic« difference is challenging: it requires the individuals to work out a new scheme of understanding, and induces further investigation of the reasons why things are as they are. However, the individuals adopt the role of an observer and commentator on these differences.

7.3.4. Trivial differences

There is fourth type of difference, to which the individuals pay a surprising amount of attention, although they do not necessarily react to them. For example, rather unexpectedly, the interviewees care a lot about the differences in climate between places. To a great extent, weather determines their preparation for travel. The time of the year and the temperature are for them as important as the type of meetings that they will have at the destination (I2: 35). Weather may even be an important factor in choosing a place of residence, although none of the interviewees would reject an assignment in a country where it is »too hot« or »too rainy«, but even so it is a difference that distinguishes places. For example, Ludmila complained about the water and air in the USA, which she blamed for her skin problems, and said that »such things I do not have in Europe« (I7: 31). The food is not without importance: it can greatly influence daily practices, for example, in those places where food or water poisoning is rather common. The interviewees pay great attention to what they eat, and avoid certain kinds of foods, for example, fruits that cannot be peeled, etc.

Unexpectedly, the interviewees place more importance on the weather in a place than on the religion or habits of its inhabitants. It seems that the mobile individuals can more easily avoid the latter than rain or food shortages. The individuals can »close themselves« within the expatriates' community to »shut off from the different«, but they are still affected by storms. Their relation to these differences may have a submissive character.

The following table summarizes the findings.

Table 8. Differences: mobility, aspects, relations

	Differences			
Reaction	deterrent	settle in	exotic	trivial
Mobility	rejected	diminished	increased	stand still
Aspects	hygiene; political regimes; economy; crime, violence	infrastructure; social networks	contrasting structural conditions	weather food
Relation	participatory	participatory	observer	submissive

Finding differences is only one side of mobile practices: finding similarities is the other. The first makes mobility interesting, but the second makes it possible. One could say that, luckily, not everything is different. Difference is always challenging and problematic: one must either adapt to it or develop a method of ignoring it, and both these strategies are stressful, especially given the temporality of exposure to the particular set of differences. Similarity allows for the continuity of practices.

The previous chapters discussed briefly the issue of similarity: for example, the importance of similar practices (routines), and the role of the standardized networks of the IO and their supplements in sustaining the extensive mobility of the IO employees. Chapter Six considered the role of similarity in the constitution of home. It showed how similarity supports the constitution of home within networks. In this aspect, familiarity is a function of similarity and not of time, which the mobile individuals lack. Earlier in this chapter, I showed that not all differences are relevant to the individuals. The same is true of similarities: not every not-different element is similar. There are two aspects of similarity to be discussed: similarity that the individuals seek, and similarity that the individuals find, often where they least expect it. The first type of similarity relates primarily to infrastructure, which enables the mobile individuals to lead their lives without great change, no matter where they are:

» [...] you could, as most people do, you can live in these western compounds and you can actually spend, except for work, you can actually spend the rest of your time exclusively in one of those compounds and then you may as well be anywhere else in the world, except for the temperature perhaps, there is perhaps a little bit hotter than elsewhere. But with all these expatriates you can be eating beef and you do all these other things, you can talk to Australians and Danes, and Swedes and so on so actually you are not a part of the Arabian world, you can actually never in your life come across an Arabian.« (110: 48)

The existence of an infrastructure – housing, schools, shops, cinemas, etc. – that is similar to the one the interviewees know, in their home country and their place of residence, allows for continuity in their everyday practices. No matter the location, their lives remain similar over the years. Long work days, drive home, dinner, gym or swimming, sometimes a movie – the same activities are possible everywhere (14: 23). However, the usual expectation of the mobile individuals is that things are more different than similar in a different location. Discovering similarities between places strikes them and, as with differences, brings on the »wow« reaction:

» [...] especially Guyana is like I found it I mean Africa, not like in Caribbean, not like Latin America – so poor so poor Guyana you would not believe that it is so close to America, like Africa and also the mixture of the races like Indian and hmm...like Africa.« (15: 33)

The two levels of difference – the individual and the collective level – apply to similarity as well. However, unlike difference, where generalization applies at a collective level, in the case of similarities a kind of generalization applies at an individual level, in the form of a certain human universalism.

Interestingly, the discourse of equality is absent from the interviews, as a strategy to blur or alleviate differences and to justify similarities. The individuals do not call on any universal values, but rather recognize and confirm the existing differences. However, they use certain equalizing strategies towards their own friends who are culturally different. The experience that the interviewees have is that every person may become your friend, no matter his or her nationality, religion, or place of residence.

At this very individual level of personal contact, all people are similar: there are always similar interests and problems that people can share. Interests and problems are those attributes that people must have to be equal despite racial or cultural difference. However, at the collective level, problems and interest seem completely different, and someone who grew up in Europe does not have much in common with Americans (I11) or Africans (I13).

7.2. Managing the difference

A part of discovering the differences is discovering the people, how they think, what they do, and how they do it. Both recognitions – that somewhere else people think and act similarly to us, or differently from us– constitute the sense of mobility, according to the interviewees:

»Actually, I was very interested to discover the world, I was really curious of different place and people especially to meet different people, what moves them, what got them excited, what were how they lived, what influenced them, what moved them.« (I8: 65)

However, as already mentioned, the confrontation with others' differences is stressful. It seems that the interviewed individuals work out a strategy of coping with the »otherness« of the people they meet, and they categorize the experience at two levels: personal contact with particular people, and generalization of the Otherness.

When traveling, all the interviewees have contact with the local population, and they get to know it by observing the behavior of people in hotels, shops, on the streets, etc. or by talking to certain individuals: their business partners, local office staff, taxi drivers, hotel personnel, and sometimes also their own friends who are local inhabitants. However, especially when they come to a country on regular business trips, they have little time to interact with people from outside the working environment. Despite this deficiency, they work out their own opinion of the local population rather quickly. Such opinions are usually neutral and contain statements about things that the interviewees find unusual or different. For example, Rodrigo thinks that people in Africa mistrust their governments (I13: 46), Ann thinks that people in Poland in the early nineties were sad and tired (I11: 34), Diego believes that Saudis are afraid of losing the homogeneity of their society (I10: 50), and Ludmila considers all people in Ukraine to be tall and handsome (I7: 121). The scope of factors that are considered in such statements is very broad – from appearance to attitudes. Although these observations were made during short stays in a country, and usually only in the capital city, somewhere between breakfast in a hotel, a meeting in the ministry, and a business dinner with the IO colleagues, they are projected on to the population of the country: the Ukrainians are handsome, the African mistrust the government, the Polish were sad, etc.

It would be, however, unjust to claim that the interviewees code differences into nationalities by the simple ascription of certain qualities to certain nationalities. No Africans distrust the government because they are Africans. The interviewees always try to justify the behavior of the group, by citing current circumstances, and the political and historical background, or economic situation. By providing a structural explanation of the difference (in social and economic status), they de-naturalize these differences. In this way, they offer a powerful counter-argument to the notion that the »others« are fundamentally different. [44] Therefore, the Africans mistrust their governments because the authorities have often betrayed their trust, and the Poles were sad because their hopes relating to the political change did not improve their personal economic situation.

All the interviewees had personal contact with some of the local inhabitants, and most of them had positive experiences. They tend to project these positive experiences on to the whole group. The individual they meet becomes a representative of the whole group. For example, in Kenya, Reiner met predominantly friendly people, and he says that the Africans are friendly. Such generalization relates, of course, not only to local inhabitants, as Rodrigo gathers from his experience with the IO staff in three African countries:

»[…] the people who work on Africa have the more strong commitment I would not say that somewhere else they don't have the commitment but it is just a sense everything needs to be done there is more sharing and more of teamwork.« (I13: 58)

---

44 Lamont and Aksartova (2002: 12) associated this strategy with white European individuals. In my sample, this strategy was employed by all interviewees, not only those of European origin. This suggests that it is related to a broadly understood European culture, or to education.

The comparison he made put him in a difficult situation. In stating his opinion about his IO colleagues in Africa, he simultaneously expressed a negative judgment about »all the others«. The interviewees try to avoid such statements as much as possible. Even if they have had negative experiences in a country, they try to justify and excuse them, by stressing that such experiences related only to a particular person, and they believe that otherwise people in this place are very nice.[45] They distinguish two levels: that of individuals, and that of a collective. For example, as a group, the IO employees are mistrusted, yet »when you establish« contact at the individual level, »you don't feel this mistrust« (I13: 48).

On the other hand, it may happen that, partly owing to one's own observation, and partly owing to the shared knowledge and observation of others (newspapers, TV, talking to colleagues, etc.), the interviewees arrive at a rather negative estimation of the local inhabitants. In such cases, they also try to distinguish the two levels, and to temper their opinions about the group by expressing the hope or suspicion that there are surely individuals who think and act differently from the whole group. For example, according to Diego, society in Saudi Arabia is very closed, and people there are in general threatened by the idea of American and Western influence in their country. Yet this situation does not exclude the possibility of finding very good friends among the Saudis, or meeting people who are able to accept that there are some »good things about the USA« (I10: 52).

At the collective level, differences tend to be coded into nationality, but at the individual level nationality plays no role. The issue of generalization into nationality is thus a problem of the »first and only« contact made in a place. As friendship develops, qualities other than nationality gain in importance, whereas, during the »first and only« contact, the individual becomes a representative of a whole group, his or her qualities lose their individual character, and are ascribed to the whole group.

The following matrix gives an overview of the possible situations.

---

45 Avoiding negative generalization is not only a strategy used by highly qualified mobile individuals who are frequently exposed to culturally different groups. Lamont and Aksartova (2002) showed how non-college educated workers in France and in the USA deal in everyday life with racial and cultural prejudices, by relating to universal human values and differentiating individual experience from generalizations.

Table 9. Projection of experience

		Own experience		No own experience	
Opinion	Level	Positive	Negative	Hearing	Observing
Positive	Individuals	x		x	x
	Group	x	x		x
Negative	Individuals		X		
	Group			x	X

Both types of generalization – those based on experience with individuals, and on one's own or others' observations – result in two processes: homogenizing and abstracting. In the first process, a whole group is seen as homogeneous: the individual differences between its members are irrelevant, as the relevant differences are categorized only at the level of personal experience. In the second process, experiences and observations are changed into the abstract category of »culture«. Such statements as »it is also cultural thing« how people perform their work, »everywhere it is different« (15: 87), or »in terms of culture I prefer to work in Europe« (13: 142), are typical of this process:

»It is fascinating how different people are in these countries. Despite that this is a Slavic culture in each of these countries, well perhaps except from Latvia, but in each of these countries people are completely different, different reactions [...] Latvians are completely different, I mean in Riga, because I know only Riga, the Latvians are very different there, perhaps because there are so many Russians there as well, many Russians so the culture, I mean it is difficult to catch this Latvian culture, it is so mixed with the Russian, so...« (17: 121)

The following process occurs: during observation and experience, the mobile individuals notice differences between themselves (and other people familiar to them) and the people they meet. The existence of such differences is desired because it constitutes a sense of their mobility. The more unusual and exotic these differences, the more they are stressed. Depending on the combination of personal experience and observation, and the quality of both, two levels are distinguished, that of an individual and that of a group. The interviewees use this strategy to deal with the problem of negative experiences and opinions. The principle of tolerance and openness drives their mobility and is strengthened by it, and their job requires them to be objective and neutral in their judgments. Any positive or negative generalizations are abstracted into a category of »culture«.[46] Abstracting has a clear function: what is abstract can easily be neutralized. What is abstract no longer bothers one. What is abstract is not dangerous. When abstracted, all differences can be ignored. On the other hand, due to a positive experience with the difference of the »Others«, both a group and an individual tend to represent all the other individuals. However, this relation does not take place when the experience with a group or an individual is negative: in this case, the interviewees rather abstract the qualities into a general category of culture.

Elisabeth Beck-Gernsheim writes about a very similar process in relation to immigrants in Germany, who are perceived as a homogenous group and, as such, are excluded from the majority of the society (2004: 11, 13). However, the mobile individuals interviewed are not »at home« in their countries of residence or work. They are guests there, and have no means of excluding the local population. They can, however, make an abstraction of it, and in practice they do so. Beck-Gernsheim speaks about the folklore of »half-knowing« (2004: 13), when the differences are stressed and only the exotic and unusual characteristics of a group are selected, instead of the complete and complex picture. »Half-knowing« is indeed a real problem for the IO's employees. If, as private people, they can enjoy the »privilege of not knowing« (Beck-Gernsheim 2004: 165), as IO employees they are obliged to have more than the »not-exact-image« (Beck-Gernsheim 2004: 164) of the place and its population.

7.3. Comparison patterns

To determine whether two things are similar or different means to compare them. As noted before, not all differences and not all similarities are relevant to the interviewees. This is because they compare only certain aspects of things, and their references for comparison are also limited. The interviewees do not compare everything with everything. The interviewees

---

46 The term »culture« used in the present work is an empirical term and cannot be compared to any definition adopted in social sciences (for the changes in the understanding of the term in ethnology, anthropology, and sociology, see Wimmer 1996).

compare those factors that are, for them, decisive about the quality of living:

- People: especially how open, friendly, and cooperative they are, whether it is easy to make friendships with them; all these determine a general climate in a place – a friendly or hostile atmosphere of living;
- Infrastructure: whether it is present, and its quality: spare time facilities (cinemas, theatres, and landscapes), living facilities (housing, schooling), general infrastructure (roads), security, etc., and
- Weather.

In addition, the interviewees compare structural aspects, like the level of economic development, measured both in economic indicators and in the availability and quality of infrastructure, political regimes, and relationships between authorities and population. All these factors relate to their job, and are, with some small exceptions, related to the whole country and not to the particular place of residence.

The reference units of comparison are

- place of origin; places of residence; places of business destination, and
- family; friends; other people.

Two perspectives result from this selection of reference units: »me (we) and here« and »they and there« perspectives. The first relates to the judgment of all the above listed aspects, through the lenses of one's own experience – comparison to me and to my closest reference people – my family and my friends; and comparison with »my« and »our« place of residence – the country of origin and the countries of residence. The second relates to the resemblance to and contrast between two non-familiar aspects – between two unfamiliar groups and countries, between »they« and »they«, and »there« and »there«.

The first type of comparison is usually decisive in the choice of place of residence. For example, Martin would not like to live in a place where the infrastructure is not sufficient, or where there are no cinemas or theatres, to which he is used in his country of origin and current place of residence. So there exists always a common unit of comparison that is external to all the compared things (Foucault 1994: 53). The choice of a unit – a place, people with whom one has been closely related, the person himself or herself – implies that this type of comparison contains emotional elements: it expresses preferences and a lack of sympathy towards certain aspects that are different or similar. The second, in contrast, gives the impression of being more neutral or objective, because the interviewees do not have any emotional relation to the objects of the comparison. In the second comparison, the units that are compared with each other vary: one contrasts A with B, then B with C, then D and X, and then perhaps D with A, and so on. Any two elements can be compared and arranged according to their measured qualities: for example, from the least to the most developed, from the nicest to the ugliest, from the least complicated to the most complicated. A relationship is established between the elements compared. In this way, an arbitrary order of things is passed (Foucault 1994: 54).

By comparison, elements can be clustered together. So, for example, Reiner compared Kenya to Switzerland as »the moon and the planet Earth«, then Kenya and Nigeria »there was not really a difference«, and all these countries to the USA, when he could assign Kenya and Nigeria to one category, and Switzerland and the USA to a second. Similarly, Martin assigned the USA and Austria to one category, and distinguished it from the category of countries with insufficient infrastructure. Most interviewees combined Poland, Croatia, Latvia, Hungary, and Slovenia into one category of country, which are »almost as developed as the Western countries«, and also contrasted them with Africa.

It may seem that there are an indefinite number of categories that the interviewees can employ in comparisons. However, as already mentioned, they tend to use only a few of them: in the first type of comparison, they apply those factors that relate to the functionality and quality of life; and, in the second, they classify by structural aspects. In the above-mentioned comparison, existence of infrastructure was selected: all the countries that have, for example, electricity in houses and asphalt roads, are in one category, no matter what other elements may differ between them. In this way, in one class, differences between elements are suppressed.

At this point, another division becomes visible. All differences and similarities are classified at two levels: social and structural. At the level of social differences, the mobile individuals employ various strategies to deal with it: reduce it to two categories (individual and collective), then generalize, homogenize, and finally abstract it into culture. Another strategy consists of justifying and explaining the social differences between people by reference to the structural conditions to which they are exposed, for example, poverty. Similarly, strategies of equalizing are used, by referring to universal values and attributes common to all humans. As a result, any differences between people are neutralized, and can be explained, accepted, or ignored. Although direct contact with other people is one of the main motivations for mobility, in the end, the differences between people do not play any important role in the mobile individuals' decisions to travel to or settle in a place.

The opposite can be said of structural differences. Not only do they take on importance as an explanation for social differences, but they also play a key role in the choices of the mobile individuals. Structural differences between places – infrastructure and political and economic conditions that influence their development – may induce change in the mundane practices of the individuals. This factor strongly influences their decision about mobility and settlement.

Thus far, various aspects of the differences and principles of comparison have been identified, and the strategies for dealing with these differences have been analyzed. This made it possible to identify which differences are relevant for the mobile individuals. It turned out that structural differences are especially important; however, little has been said about how these differences are spatially fixed to particular territories (Figure 3).

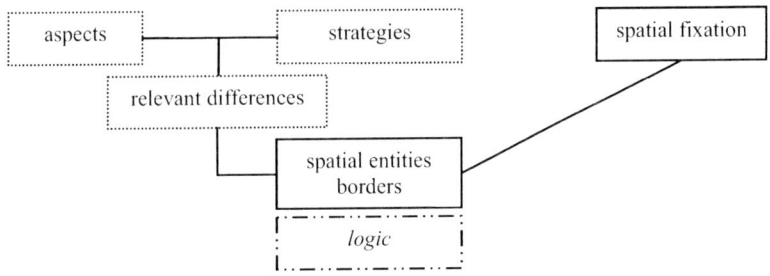

Figure 3. Fixation of difference

The following sections look more closely at the spatial fix of the relevant differences. They ask what kind of spatial entities are constructed, how they are constructed, and how the borders between them are drawn. The logic of spatial fixation should thus become clear.

7.4. Topologies

Social theory is well acquainted with two types of formations that are based on the categories of similarity and difference: regions and networks. The first relates, for instance, to the familiar world of nation-states[47]; the second has successfully entered social theory in recent decades, together with network analysis.[48] In the first, similarity and difference are marked by boundaries. In the second, similarity and difference are a matter of relations. The two processes and their coexistence have been discussed in the literature: the Actor-Network Theory drew attention to how networks constitute regions, and how both the processes of clustering and networking produce relative stabilities. Recent globalization studies have pointed to the opposite processes of the de-construction of regions (in particular nation-states), due to the growing prominence of technical, social, and financial networks. The latter called into question the solidity of such regions (comp. Beck 1993; 1997b; 2002b; 2004; Elkins 1995; Albrow 1998; Creveld 1998; Zürn 1998; Grande 2001).

In regions, objects are clustered together and boundaries are drawn around each cluster. This definition can be derived from Plato, for whom regions were primal zones in which elementary qualities cling to each other in momentary assemblages, thanks to the cosmological rule that like seeks like (Casey 1998: 34). Although a region later became nothing more than a mere unit of space, the rule of regionalization has not changed: when a region is defined, the differences inside it are suppressed. They are minimized or marginalized. It is the effect of averaging (Mol/Law 1994: 646). Any population is defined by suppressing individual differences between its members, and drawing the median, the mean, and the lowest values that characterize the whole group. Inclusion in population is a matter of comparison to the median value and the measurement of deviation.

---

47 Regional thinking is broadly practiced in social theory. For example, an extreme version of regional social thought would be that of Habermas (1992), who seeks to separate life world from system, and to sort out all the concomitant subdivisions (for instance, power versus money, or morality versus ethics), or Goffman (1971).

48 Since the seminal work of Barnes (1954) and Bott (1971), sociological studies have frequently utilized network analysis in various fields of research and theorizing on social structure. Its practitioners include Breiger, Granovetter, Knoke, Marsden, Wellman, White. Compare also Emirbayer/Goodwin 1994, and Castells 2001.

Regions and networks can be understood as two complementary and competing logics of space construction. Spaces based on a regional logic enclose similar elements (where similarity is achieved by suppression of differences) within fixed boundaries. Within such spaces, what is similar is close, what is different is far. Social or individual characteristics can be territorialized, and associated with a particular geographic entity. A population, for instance, that of a nation, may map on to a geographic region: for example, a territory of a nation-state or a population with primary education can map on to the continent Africa.[49]

Certain problems result from the production of regions. First, there is the problem of overlapping regions, and sorting out smaller units within each region. Though clustering is by definition border setting, it takes an effort to build and maintain boundaries. The further from the center, the more fluid and fuzzy these boundaries are. Mobility and flows between the centers of regions allow the comparison of regional peripheries and the setting of borders. However, the role of mobility is ambivalent: linkages and networks across the divisions create relative stabilities, but at the same time they may lead to liquefaction of the regional divisions. Second, regionalism produces local norms that may lead to a problem of derivative incomparability between regions. The recent discussion of social inequality and European statistics provides a good example of this.

Third, regionalism enforces easy associations, for example, between poor and uneducated, Africa and disease. Such associations may be mobilized to depict the population: for example, Africans (the population of people who live in Africa) as unruly, decaying, chaotic, and hopeless (Comaroff 1993). Such associations can be powerful tools of exclusion and discrimination. Within the »national order of things« (Malkki), they take the form of stereotypes, for example, that of »a normal German« (Beck-Gernsheim 2004: 171). Another effect of regionalism is the confusion of geographical and social regions. The practice of mapping social regions on

---

49 In these processes, official statistics play an important role. They describe the group-internal and specific conditions and facts that otherwise would not be accessible and understandable to someone outside the group (comp. Scott 1998). Statistical description is a standardized description, which reduces the complex social reality to a common denominator and makes it measurable and comparable. The key of the statistic is its perspective on a group from outside, which Hagendijk (1999) calls »distance-technology«. Since the end of the 20th century statistics have been the powerful tool of a nation-state (Koren 1970; Grohmann 1989; Johansson 1992; comp. Garonna/Sofia 1996; Maarseveen/Gricour 1999).

to geographical regions results in methodological nationalism (Beck 2004a: 47). The national geographic follows the exclusive logic of either-or (Beck 2002b), as in Gellner's comparison of maps drawn under the principle of nationalism to the paintings of Modigliani: »neat flat surfaces are clearly separated from each other, it is generally plain where one begins and another ends, and there is little if any ambiguity or overlap« (Gellner 1983: 140).[50]

Another difficulty arises here: the stabilization and institutionalization of regions and their borders. Beck (2004b: 78ff) enumerates five strategies for dealing with the »Otherness of the Others« that are included in the ideologies of universalism, relativism, nationalism, ethnicism, and cosmopolitanism. Each of these ideologies institutionalizes regions of similarities that are based on different principles: universalism equalizes all human forms within a single civilizational order (supreme principle), and thus the difference becomes either irrelevant (is subordinated), or has to be excluded. Diverse relativisms (local, national, cultural), on the contrary, stress the differences, and grow from the incomparability of perspectives and positions. A combination of both these strategies can be found in nationalism and ethnicism. Nationalism reinforces them by a territorial fix of the difference. The »Other« is either spatially excluded, or spatially included and at the same time subordinated to the nation. In contrast, cosmopolitanism accepts the »Other« and the »Otherness«. Within the national scheme, simple questions – who is different, who belongs to us, and who does not - are highly tense socially. It is characteristic of modern nation-states to constantly order according to nationality, meaning the assignment of people to a single nationality. The question of nationality accompanies an individual throughout his or her life, and a state requires a simple answer that can be institutionally confirmed and determines inclusion or exclusion from the state (Beck-Gernsheim 1998: 127).

The legal and political exclusion of the »Other« is reinforced and made durable by the reference to space (Simmel 1958: 693). Spatial fixation of

---

50 The image of the world divided into nation-states is so powerful that it is projected also on to times when the world was not represented through maps: for example, our historical atlases show medieval Christendom divided into demarcated and homogeneous territories – they differ from the modern representation of the world only in that their configuration is different; however, such a representation would have been utterly unknown to the people of the time, who rarely used maps to represent geographical information, and did not imagine states (or rather, realms) as enclosed spaces demarcated by linear boundaries (Biggs 1999: 374).

difference stabilizes it, either by exclusion from a territory, or by a political and legal definition of the difference of those who are physically present within the territory. In the first case, regionalism is confirmed; in the second, diverse minorities are defined in such a way that a region does not have to be split into smaller territorial units. Although the territorial principle is less exclusive than one that relates to genetic or qualitative attributes, a combination of both is a forceful tool. All these strategies are strategies of power over the »Other«.

In the case of nation-states, nationality becomes a relevant difference: anybody who is German (by the definition adopted by the German state) enjoys particular rights, and has certain obligations towards Germany and its citizens. Other attributes of a person, such as gender, are at first irrelevant for the national question. Regional mapping is thus not about any difference, but about establishing the relevant difference, or, in other words, defining the principle of ordering and bordering. In the national order of things, the situation is simple: individuals living within the territory of a particular nation-state are either of this nationality, or are qualified as a minority (individuals of different nationality who are present on the territory of another state). In the national framework, the difference is coded primarily into nationality. Someone who has a different nationality is different. A »Stranger« is someone who comes from outside the state. The »Others« are those who live somewhere else. As nationality is composed of other attributes described as »culture« (language, habits, cuisine, etc.), the »Others« are also culturally different: they speak a different language, eat different food, etc.

Beyond the context of nation-states, the principles of spatial ordering are not so obvious in the case of extensive mobility, and temporary but frequent and continual migration. Certainly, the national order of things is still present and powerful[51]; however, geographical mobility may explode the territorial reference of qualitative attributes. When political, economic, and technical access to places is assured, due to the existence of effective networks, there may be a need to establish a commonly agreed norm to describe the spaces on both sides of the previous border. It is a contingent

---

51 Several authors stress that the territorial claims of nation-states and the national ordering of difference has not decreased – the newest empirical examples discuss especially non-Western spaces (Rodriguez 1999; comp. Spaan et al. 2002). Compare also Sassen 1996; Hiebert 2002; Knippenberg 2002.

matter which name or characteristics will be assigned to these spaces. A national discourse may re-appear, or be replaced by another discourse.

7.4.1. Regions

In all the interviews, three regions were most frequently contrasted, the regions which the interviewees call »Africa«, »Europe«, and »the USA«. It was expected that, thanks to such a clear contrast, it would be possible to define the decisive factors that constitute these clusters of »here« and »there«, and the boundaries between them. However, it seems that the boundaries between these entities are rather undetermined and fluid. How are these regions drawn? What logic governs the clustering of differences and similarities into the geo-political units of Africa, the USA, and Europe?

Almost all the interviewees have worked at some time in one of the African countries. They traveled there frequently; and some lived there for a certain period of time. They are all familiar with a number of studies of the African economy and society, they are all familiar with the economic indicators produced by specialists, and they have all had a certain work program and tasks to fulfill. Although each interviewee had a chance to get to know a different African country, their stories and their impressions are very similar: Africa is poverty, Africa is poor infrastructure, Africa needs foreign assistance, Africa has beautiful nature, Africa has very friendly inhabitants, and Africa is full of contrasts. For the interviewees, these conditions are clearly a challenge. They have an impression that »Africa is always beginning its way«, there is always »something that needs to be done«, and what needs to be done »is very important« (I13: 58):

»[…] in African countries I think the satisfaction comes from the fact that there is a real need and the fact that a lot can be done you feel actually compelled to try to accomplish as much as you can in the least amount of time […] you had a sense of the need, that it was urgent, that made a difference […] in African countries […] it is a matter of survival what is happening, the rate of mortality, infant mortality, it is the situation like that.« (I13: 48)

Africa does not progress. Africa always starts from the very beginning, and development has a very different meaning there, as the first step is only to survive, not to improve. Development does not mean restructuring, as in other countries, development is about having a more or less functioning system, like agriculture, or a water supply (I6: 111). In Africa, it all fits together: its image, and the real situation the interviewees experience while there. »Africa«'s image is poor hungry people, and that's what you see most of the time« (I5: 39). And although the Africans are very friendly and always have time to talk to you (I13), although they like children (I2), Africa is not really a place you look forward to — unless you are able to find a piece of »Europe« there (I5).

Unlike Africa, Europe has a decent infrastructure: safe roads, comfortable hotels; unlike in Africa, one does not have to be afraid of food poisoning and can eat all fruits, even those that you cannot peel. In Europe, the countries have a certain structure, and they are already organized (I13: 47). Perhaps some things need to be improved in Central and Eastern Europe: the tax system may need to be reformed, and some governments need advice on how to make their health systems more effective, but otherwise there is not really a great difference between Europe and Central Europe. Unlike Africa, Europe is not dangerous and »no real adventure can happen there« (I1: 13). This means that travel and work in Europe are easy to manage (I6: 22), and that things always go their »normal way« (I1: 13). And Europe is small: any travel within Europe takes no longer than a week.

But where are the borders of Europe? There is nothing definite about its borders. During the interview, Sabah refers to the IO assigning some Asian post-Soviet republics to the European department. However, in some other passages, she says that Uzbekistan is in Central Asia (I8: 55-57). Sabah worked there for a couple of years. However, in an earlier passage, she clearly stated that she had never worked in Asia (I8: 53). Finally, it turns out that it does not matter where all the »stans« (Uzbekistan, Azerbaijan, Kazakhstan, and Turkmenistan) are geographically: they are either Russian, like Russia itself, or like Latvia, or Arabian, Persian, or Turkish, but definitely not Asian, because, in her description, Asia and Central Asia do not belong to the same category.

One thing is clear: Europe is not the USA. Unlike the USA, Europe has a past. Unlike the USA, the quality of life is high: one works fewer hours and life after work is richer. Unlike in the USA, the clothes are of good quality. European products have style (I6: 146). European society is not a consumption society, whereas the Americans »buy things to throw them away«; European textiles keep longer, the Europeans »take care of things«, they have them for years (I6: 146). Unlike the USA, Europe is noble. However, the USA wins the technological race and attracts more young ambitious people (I10: 56). Unlike in the USA, people in Europe are open-minded.

For some of the European interviewees, the USA shows many unexpected sides. There are provincial places »more conservative« than one might expect, where married women are not expected to work at all, but to stay at home with the children:

»It is worse than anything that I could have expected. The culture shock of the American Midwest, the American Midwest has the narrowest attitude, you can see it now when you see the television debates, Iowa, we were just North of Iowa, my God this place was like living, I might as well have living in the worst rural part of Ireland, the most backwards, the most narrow minded, I thought I would go crazy...« (I11: 126)

However, the USA also has its »European stains«, big cities which are more Europe-like (I5: 113). It is a melting pot, and in this pot there is a »crazy society«. Again, from the point of view of the interviewees, this is rather ambiguous, and many claim that »it is not exactly where you would like to grow up your children...« (I11: 136). The Americans are different from the Europeans, they are »more open« toward other people, and the first contact with them is easy »no matter of race or origin« (I12: 50). Even if many contacts in the USA remain at the surface, the first impression of the people is usually positive. They are friendly, exactly like the environment: kind and helpful, good at service (I6: 66). Friendly and easy does not mean of high quality. What makes this »quality of life«? In comparison to Europe, one is required to work longer, and therefore has less private time: one loses the evenings and the weekends. On the other hand, social security is worse than in Europe: someone who loses his or her job loses everything, and this increases the pressure on the individuals to behave like workaholics (I6: 127). If you lose your steady income, you have no medical insurance, and you are not able to pay for your house: being poor in the USA is not easy, »so these are the dark sides of it« (I6: 66). The interviews were dominated by negative opinions about the USA and its society. Materialism, arrogance, superficiality, ignorance, and intolerance draw the borders of the USA, and distinguish it from Europe and Africa. These negative characteristics seem to be more powerful in setting the borders of the region.

However, a clear and fixed definition of borders is of secondary importance to the interviewees. This is a result of the process of creating such regions. The individuals have not been to every corner and every area of the region. They have perhaps been to the capital city and two sites of their projects, perhaps two towns or villages, sometimes to another region or some tourist attractions. They project the average image of these sites on to the whole region. They »use« the already set political and administrative borders to limit this region, and they use the already existing name for this limited region: Poland, Ukraine, Latvia, Congo, Europe, Africa, etc. However, for the interviewee, this name is just a name: it is itself irrelevant, exactly as the political-administrative borders are. It becomes clear that these borders become irrelevant as soon as the interviewees are able to cross them. In their case, border crossing does not induce any immediate change, supposedly because, when moving, they relocate within networks.

7.4.2. Networks

Regions do not exist in the order of things but are an effect that depends on networks. To define a region of, for example, GDP per person lower than x, a network of measurement is needed: a network of specialists who regulate the knowledge of economic indicators, statistical offices that gather the data, statistical documents in which a record of indicators is kept, etc.[52]

Regional thinking implies that any change of location between regions (border crossing) means a change of practices. This is closely related to spatial determinism, which implies that a change of location within a geographical space leads to a change within social space. The opponents of this view stress the effects of the standardization of networks, which allows for routine practices independent of geographical location (comp. Castells 2001). Here are meant networks, in the sense of Urry's »scapes«. »Scapes« are the networks that connect machines, technologies, organizations, and documents together. Urry speaks of the following global »scapes«: the system of transportation of people by air, sea, rail,

---

52 An interesting example is the attempt to »translate« cultural difference into measurable values (attitudes towards religion, democracy, and participation in civil society organizations), which are projected on to the nation-state of Turkey and the European Union, while, within the latter, sub-regions (old EU members, new EU members, candidate countries) are determined (comp. Gerhards 2004). In this example, social science and scientists play a role in such a network defining a region.

motorways, and other roads; the transportation of objects via postal and other systems; diverse cables that carry telephone messages, television pictures, and computer information; microwave channels and satellites (Urry 1998: 2). Such networks overcome the friction of (regional) space. This definition assumes the commonality of identity of the elements constituting a network (Strathern 1996: 255). Another definition has been adapted by Actor-Network-Theory: a network is a series of elements with well-defined relations between them. Networks may contain all sorts of elements – they are heterogeneous. In a network, those elements that are similar and that are connected by similar relations are close (Mol/Law 1994: 649). In this sense, it is possible to distinguish a network that supports a certain function: Mol and Law give the example of a laboratory, which is just such a heterogeneous network of specialists, measurement equipment, and technology. All these elements make it possible to measure the hemoglobin level in blood.

In the first sense, a hotel chain is a network: each of its elements is similar to all the others, whatever its geographical location. For a mobile individual, this means that she or he is able to perform routine practices in each hotel in a particular chain, because every one of these hotels is similar. In the second sense, a practice stays in the foreground: a routine behavior is possible, not necessarily because of the common attributes of such hotels (standards), but rather because of a successfully functioning network of technologies, people, and material components. The length and the boundaries of such a network are seemingly unlimited (Strathern 1996: 524), and they contribute to (unintended) global inter-connectedness (Beck 1997a, Urry 2003).

The role of some of these successful (successfully functioning) networks was described in the previous chapters. These networks temper the (negative) effects of change of location, and they enable a smooth transition from one location to another. They permit the transmission of information, by both technical and human media of communication (tools of distance communication and mobile individuals), and they enable continuity. Successful networks are very complex: even in the case of travel, the individuals report how many different elements play a role before and after the physical movement from location A to location B takes place. For that trip to take place and its aim to be fulfilled, diverse factors must function: from travel agents who arrange for necessary hotel and plane bookings, to the Health Department that provides a traveler with the necessary medications, and the local partners who enable the communication with a client. How complex such a network is becomes apparent only when one or more of its elements do not fulfill their function.

Communication networks are one example of successful networks in which diverse elements co-work. They consist not only of technical means of distant communication, like e-mails, cables, satellite receivers, videoconference equipment, telephones, etc. but also of humans: translators and interpreters. To ensure communication, it is often not enough that the technical equipment works:

»[…] I make a conference call. I have the interpreter on the line and the person I would like to talk to. So the interpreter interprets it as in a real meeting […] e-mail …Hmm…but then you can only communicate with these people who write understand English. And sometimes also we have for bigger things we have videoconferences, again with or without interpretation.« (I2: 61-63)

This example also shows that successful networks are those that have »self-repairing« mechanisms: one component of a network is replaced by its functional equivalent, and so the whole network functions undisrupted. The above example points to another successful network: the English language. If you speak it, and you find some people who also speak it, you can communicate, no matter the geographical location, their culture, or their origin (I3: 132). As in the first example, those people who do not speak English can be »extended« by those who do so, and can become an intermediate element in the network, so that communication between the partners is assured. If such an extension is not possible, the practices (in the second example, the travel or change of place of residence) must be abandoned or adapted. The above examples show that successful networks do not depend primarily on their coherence, but on their incoherence and ambivalences (compare also Singleton/Michael 1993 and Strathern 1996), and less on similarity and continuity and more on difference and discontinuities (compare Latour 1996).

Networks make possible individuals' routine practices, independently of their physical location. When practices remain the same in every location, one can assume that they take place within well-functioning networks. However, in the previous chapter, a situation was identified in which practices and infrastructure simply do not fit together. This discrepancy suggests that sometimes networks fail. The interviewees give many examples of situations in which networks reach the limits of their functionality. For example, one may stay overnight in a four-star chain hotel and eat in its luxurious restaurant, but that does not prevent the food from being poisoned. Most interviewees complain that staying in expensive and good hotels, in every place, does not protect them from water or food diseases. One must then call a doctor, but, depending on location, doctors may be helpless, or proper medications cannot be found (I5: 37). It may happen that, although one can perform everyday practices in such a hotel, normal life is nevertheless not possible, because, as soon as one leaves the hotel, one faces extreme poverty and many material shortages. Similarly, transportation networks quite often fail: the usual practice of taking a taxi from the airport to a hotel, which works well in the USA, can turn out to be dangerous in Africa or Albania, as the roads there are in very bad condition; and even if the roads are secure, taxi drivers cannot be trusted (I6: 40). It may also, of course, be that transportation networks are limited: there are no roads, and even good imported cars cannot make the trip (I12: 78). Sometimes it seems that a network can be extended, for example, the educational system in Africa. One can transport books and hire teachers from Europe, but such networks have other limitations, and often parents have to teach their children at home (I2: 107), or children have to attend a boarding school elsewhere (I2: 114). Mobile individuals may take not only books to Africa, but also other belongings, like kitchen equipment. Yet even the best mixer cannot work without electricity, and even in good condition it is absolutely useless (I2: 107). A transportation network, which normally ensures smooth transfer of people and goods, can be interrupted by other systems, for example, political regulations:

»I remember I used to work in Senegal and every time I traveled to Senegal from Paris and the plane was arriving at three in the morning I used to spend the whole night, they used to have a little like a jail room there at the airport and I spent many nights in that jail room because they wouldn't let me in.« (I8: 85)

Although the plane was on time, the traveler hardly ever arrived punctually at the destination. The transportation network functioned well, but it was interrupted by the political and legal regulations of the host country, whose government suspected all travelers of a certain nationality of smuggling weapons and supporting the local revolutionary groupings. Each time, an additional effort had to be made. In this case, a high official had to confirm that this person was allowed to enter the country (I8: 87). These problems now belong to the past – a more efficient solution was found – and this »problematic traveler« has changed citizenship to one that is accepted worldwide and recognized as »secure«. An alternative would be for the regulations of this host country to change, or for one either to resign from traveling or change organization, to one that guarantees more protection, thanks, for example, to diplomatic passes.

When a network fails, the following solutions are hypothetically possible:

- Practices are mutated and adapted to the circumstances;
- New practices are developed when the existing network fails and cannot be replaced by a new or alternative network;
- The network is restructured to enable it to perform the same practices (arrangements are made that can remain stable in a wider range of circumstances);
- New networks are created to enable the performance of the same practices;
- Both new networks and new practices come into effect;
- Both the network and the practices are abandoned.

In theory, poor food hygiene and frequent poisoning can be »repaired« by a supplementary network of doctors. In practice, this option is also very limited:

»Every time I was going for a trip I knew I was going to be poisoned and sometimes it would knock me down for three days that you would not be able to eat or drink anything […] I was always carrying with me some medications for diarrhea or nausea and I was trying to take care of it myself. I am not quite sure that local facilities were any helpful and I would not risk. Sometimes it is better not to deal with it in a hotel. It is not extremely serious, you just have fever, and you for three days you can't move much, you stay in bed and you try to support yourself among the walls 'cause you are so weak […] there are many other countries where there is malaria and you never know how you will catch it and other diseases like jaundice, it makes you lactose intolerant, intolerant for a longer time and you can have it for years you don't know how to deal with it even the doctors here don't know how to deal with some of the tropical diseases there is no cure for it.« (16: 38-40)

In this particular case, practices are adapted to failing networks: one always carries medications or avoids eating certain foods (19: 98). Unlike in the USA, one does not trust local doctors and, instead of relying on the health care system, one deals with the sickness alone. When there is no school for expatriate children, the parents take over the teaching themselves. When there is no electricity, one uses gas lamps and perhaps goes to bed earlier, one reads books instead of watching TV, etc. In many situations, however, practices cannot be mutated: they must either be abandoned (one does not travel to countries where every drive from the airport to the hotel is a risk to life), or continued (one takes a taxi and hopes that no accident happens). The individuals have rather limited chances of expanding or changing existing networks, or constituting new networks that would allow them to continue customary practices, at least in the short term. For example, many interviewees limited contacts with their friends drastically, because of inadequate telecommunication networks. Phoning used to be very expensive and, depending on the location, the quality of the connection might be too poor. At that time, there were no alternative methods of regular communication: e-mail and the Internet either did not exist, or were not available to all their friends; postal services took too long, or post would be lost, and frequent private trips to meet friends were also not possible. However, this situation has changed: telephone costs have been reduced, and the quality of connections improved, thanks to the IO's satellite network. In the long term, the change in telecommunication networks was achieved by the enlargement of the institutional network of the IO. The social networks of the IO's members are no longer interrupted, although they may change over time for other reasons.

Another example illustrates the situation in which one insufficient network is replaced by another, to ensure the continuity of practices. The interviewees often experience problems with collecting data and information remotely for their projects, reviews, studies, or reports:

»[...] unless you have someone there to do it for you...again it requires a lot of good coordination and cooperation with the people in this country. It causes a bit delay as well. Even if these people are extremely good, it causes delay because if one day you realize you need this kind of information you ask him to get it however in the meantime you realize that it would be helpful that you would have also something else as a data to work with so there are delays...So I think travel is important and it is essential.« (16: 26)

In this example, a distance communication network has to be replaced by a travel network. Also, the social networks of the individuals prove to be more vulnerable than is suggested by their (unrestricted) access to technical means of communication and travel. Mobility negatively influences many friendships and business contacts. Although the mobile individuals have a large number of business contacts, their partners and clients do not know each other. When the mobile individual »quits« the network, there is no longer any connection between his or her partners and clients.

Thus far, three situations have been discussed: when practices are changed, when a network fails or is replaced by another, and when a network must be extended in order to ensure the continuity of practices. The mutation of practices is a result of failing networks. The will to sustain practices in their current form is a reason for network extension. This picture is far from a simple »network optimism«, of the sort that dominates globalization studies. However, it is also hypothetically possible that networks may adapt to new circumstances. This would mean that networks are not robust, that they do not hold their shape as they pass through geographical space. Are networks fragile?

The most obvious example that comes to mind, when talking about fragile networks, is the one that links friends and relatives over distances. Not only do many links break down due to a change of place of residence, but most of them also continue in an altered form. People change their interests and perspectives, and after a number of years the relationship also changes. In proximity or at a distance, different issues are discussed, different feelings transmitted (I2: 81-83). An effort must be made for the exchange of information to be possible at all. Work needs to be done to maintain technical links, like telephone connections, cables, devices, etc. and to continue using these technical possibilities over time. Such networks are in constant danger of breaking down. They never stay constant over time. They fluctuate.

These fragile, »fluctuating«, »trembling« networks influence the relations of proximity and distance. The interviewees described the following situation: persons A and B are close friends. They met at university: they attended the same lectures, prepared together for exams, went regularly to a pub, and chatted about intimate problems. They finish studying: A gets a job at this university, and B in another country. The physical proximity between them is interrupted but the relationship continues. They exchange professional information by e-mail, chat on the Internet, and phone at least once a week to talk about their problems. Physical distance does not influence the type of relationship they have, but the time that they can dedicate to maintaining this relationship shortens dramatically, as soon as their job demands more attention, and they stay long hours at work, marry and have children, build a house, and get to know other people. Despite the availability of communication networks, their relationship changes: they write short e-mails to agree when to meet when B, as he does once a year, visits his parents in the town where A lives. They phone rarely, and exchange only the most important news. Their relationship has changed. The network they constitute, together with all other materialities that circulated between them (photos, letters, e-mails), and which they use to maintain the relationship (phone cables, computers, planes, pens, paper, etc.), has also transformed.[53]

7.5. Bordering

Within the regional logic of spatial differentiation, the problem of maintaining borders and their durability is central. Mol and Law (1994), and later Beck (2004b: 124), notice that neither boundaries nor relations mark the difference between one place and another. At first glance, the empirical findings seem to confirm this thesis. The interviewees themselves claim that there are no borders:

»We live in the world practically without any borders…at least I do not have such the impression in my work that borders exist. One day I am at this continent, the other day at the other continent, especially our children do not have the awareness of spatial limitations, they cannot imagine at all that it is not possible to travel somewhere, when there is a place on a map then you can get there and get into contact with someone there and spend time together.« (112: 52)

For Atanas, no clear rigid boundaries can be identified, and relations are not restricted by geographical distance. The analysis of all the interviews shows that, in relation to regions and borders, the national discourse seems to be replaced by the discourse of accessibility. The above example from the interview with Atanas also confirms this recognition. When access to places is assured, thanks to the networks – political, economic and technical – there may appear a need to establish a commonly agreed-upon norm in public and private discourse to describe the spaces on each side of the (former) border between two places (Galasinska/Meinhof/Rollo

---

53 Depending on the constituents of a network, distance is created. Distance in a network is a matter of time – longer distance is a longer period of time needed for a transfer. For example, a telephone network dramatically reduces the time needed to transfer a message, in comparison to a postal service, for example. Proximity however, is no longer about physical distance, but about the content of the message.

2002). This is contingent upon which name or characteristics these spaces will be assigned. A national discourse may re-appear or, due to everyday practices, another discourse, the discourse of accessibility or, as Galasinska calls it, of »popping down the road«, may appear instead. The above analysis points to the second option, to the discourse of accessibility. Spaces on both sides of a (regional, nation-state) border are equally easily accessible for the mobile individuals.[54] This regional (in this case a nation-state) border thus neither regulates the flow of people, nor makes a difference to their day-to-day activities. Instead, the infrastructure in place is the relevant factor in defining the regions in which practices are similar or different. Change is brought about by inclusion in a system of different structural conditions. This may take place when crossing a border that is defined according to a different, non-regional logic.

The empirical material discussed earlier shows that the individuals experience these places as different or similar: they possess or lack the infrastructure that enables or disables certain practices. From the point of view of mobile individuals, as long as they move within a certain infrastructure, their geographical location does not play a role: they stay in the same place and remain embedded in a network. This is a double process: on the one hand, space is defined by a network – one space is a network space. On the other hand, this infrastructure creates regions, and as long as one is in the same region, no change will occur. More than one region covers another but they do not overlap completely. Within one region, infrastructure and practices fit together. A shift to another region is marked by dissonance between infrastructure and practices: in this case, one or the other has to be changed and made compatible. The mobile individuals' only choice is to adapt their practices, and in this way they confirm the region.

There are thus regions of bad and insufficient infrastructure and regions of good and sufficient infrastructure. However, this is not entirely true: even in Africa, there are skyscrapers and luxurious hotels, and in the USA there are areas of poverty, and roads in a very bad condition. In the city center of Cape Town, one can lead exactly the same life as in New York or Paris. If one loses one's job in the USA, one ends up on the street

---

54 What constitutes a gateway to some is a border to others. Borders are not experienced in the same way by all people (Yuval-Davis 2004). Personal circumstances may well decide on what we perceive as a border. Further, borders may arise where access to a network is denied (Rumford 2006: 156).

and suffers from insufficient medical care. There is therefore no clear border at which one variant stops and other begins. There are variations within these regions. Can we thus speak of regions in this case? Do we have to deal with regions, if either the borders or the areas of such spatial entities cannot be clearly defined and maintained?

Mol and Law (1994) claim that the spatial does not exist as a single type, because the processes of construction of space may follow different principles. In their research, they focus on a mobile element: they show how networks co-constitute regions, and how two different complementary and exclusive spatial topologies are constructed. Moreover, they claim that sometimes neither networks nor regions can be identified, and they point to the third alternative: the fluid spaces in which the principle of liquid continuity is decisive.[55] Fluid spaces come into being only under the condition that regions and networks have failed: when the regions are not able to sustain their borders, and when mobile elements that are transported through a network are transformed. However, a network perspective »generates« a point of view within which three situations occur: first, successful networks produce regions; second, failing networks struggle to maintain the identity of their elements, and the links between them; and third, failing networks generate fluid spaces. Fluid spaces are thus an effect of failing networks. In such spaces, the mobile not only moves, but it is also mutable. Fluid spaces are defined by liquid continuity: there are no boundaries, but rather variations and transformations. This perspective neglects regional logic and its effects, and therefore it undervalues the problem of borders. Moreover, it seems to lump together all those situations in which neither regional nor network logic can be identified, and assigns them to the third generalizing category of liquid continuity. The following question seems justified: if no clear fixed borders can be identified, does this mean that there are no borders at all?

The interviews provided many examples of how the mobile individuals establish the difference between one place and another, by referring to the

---

55 In their more recent paper, Mol and Law (2000) distinguish a fourth type of space, fire space. Unlike fluid space, fire space is about abrupt and discontinuous movements. Continuity in such space is an effect of discontinuity. For continuity, absence is as important as presence. Stable shapes in such fire topology are created in patterns of relations of conjoined alterity (Mol/Law 2000: 8). However, from the point of view of the analysis presented here, especially the interest in how distinctions, divisions, and borders are constituted, fire spaces are less relevant.

infrastructure. For example, when he moved to Africa, Reiner was forced to change his behavior as a parent: there were no adequate school facilities and he, along with other parents, organized teaching for his children outside any formal schooling system. For him and his family, one of the main differences of living in Africa was how their family life became constructed around self-organized activities to a much greater extent than elsewhere.

It would, however, be wrong to talk about regions of infrastructure; rather, the discontinuity of mundane practices makes a difference.[56] It is not the regions and their borders that can be identified, but thresholds. A threshold means a point of entering or beginning something, or a limit of reaction; it seems more appropriate then the term border, which has a clear territorial connotation, or boundary, which points to the symbolic character of the division. Threshold is more appropriate to describe the points of passage from one spatial entity to another. I consciously do not use the term entity, rather than region, to stress the impossibility of drawing fixed borders between them, as in the case of regions. Such entities can co-exist with regions: they do not exclude each other.

Thresholds can be identified in those places where the discontinuity of practices appears. The interviews provided many examples of such discontinuities. Somewhere between Europe and Asia, there is a threshold, before which the mobile individuals do not have to carry any medications, can eat any fruit, and need not bother about being food poisoned. However, beyond it their daily practices have to change drastically: they must avoid certain food and hope that the medications they have brought from Europe are helping, so that they do not have to rely on local doctors. However, it is not possible to pin down this threshold precisely to a

---

56 Barry (2006) claims the existence of »technological zones«, understood as spaces within which differences between technical practices, procedures, and forms have been reduced, or common standards have been established. He enumerates three forms of such spaces: metrological zones (common forms of measurement), infrastructural zones (common connection standards), and zones of qualification (common assessment standards). Such zones can have more or less clear borders, which increasingly do not correspond to the borders of nation-states. Berker's (2003) analysis revealed a far-reaching de-territorialization of the practices of mobile researchers, as a result of which the temporal and spatial structures of everyday life change. Nevertheless, Berker identified »residual« boundaries in space, for example cultural differences or language struggles. The migrants' own attitudes and their definition of the problem create a residual boundary, although some residual boundaries depend on the qualities of the place.

particular point in space. Moreover, no institution marks this threshold: there are no political or administrative rules to confirm that, by passing this threshold, an individual comes under a different rule; yet such thresholds are more relevant for the mobile individuals than any state border.

I suggest the use of the term (b)ordering[57] in relation to non-state processes of ordering in space, and when asking how borders are constructed in the process of ordering the difference and reducing the ambivalence. Putting the (b) in brackets symbolizes how the territorial fixing of constructed borders is increasingly problematic territorially. Within this spatial order, an asymmetry appears: the differences and otherness cannot be simply and directly territorially excluded, and no purification and homogenization of spaces (on either side of a border) can take place. Rather, differences and otherness can be related to structural conditions, which, when linked to territorially organized political systems (which follow the territorial principle of fixation: for example, nation-states), indirectly bound the difference territorially. However, not all differences are managed in the same way: certain differences are abstracted and neutralized, some are graded as banal, and some gain in importance, because they lead to discontinuity of practices. Though it may still be possible to exclude homogenized groups territorially, it seems impossible to do the same with the individualized »other«. The existence of the latter is a fact with which the mobile individuals have to deal. The strategy of abstraction into culture makes it possible to exclude the »other« socially rather than territorially.

The three topologies – regional, network, and fluid – can thus be extended by another type, in which the difference between places is marked by thresholds of discontinuity of practices. The immediate

---

57 The term was proposed by Houtum, who used it to describe those processes of ordering that lead to spatial fixation of the differentiation of »us« and »them« (Houtum/Naerssen 2002; Houtum et al. 2005). It was based on the recognition that bordering processes do not begin or stop at demarcation lines in space, and that borders do not represent a fixed point in space or time, but rather symbolize a social practice of spatial differentiation. According to Houtum, territorial strategies of (b)ordering often take place at the spatial scale of states. In such a case, practices of inclusion and exclusion are framed by nation-building and nation-confirming projects. The making of nation-state regions – the process of purification of space – is supported in the process of (b)ordering. (B)ordering rejects as well as erects othering – borders are erected to erase territorial ambiguity and ambivalent identities, in order to shape a unique and cohesive order, but they thereby create new, or reproduce latently existing, differences in space and identity (Houtum/Naerssen 2002: 126).

question appears to be whether, and how, such spaces and thresholds stabilize. This study captures only a short period of time and adopts the individuals' perspective, and therefore it does not allow us to observe and articulate statements on long-term changes. It may be that thresholds can be projected on to existing political-territorial borders and symbolic boundaries. The second question relates to the relationship between the four different logics of spatial topology. Both problems are reflected in the current debate on the prospective accession of Turkey to the European Union. Opponents of the Turkish accession often stress cultural differences, while their adversaries, who are also against the accession, tend to neutralize the cultural difference and stress structural incompatibility.[58] At this point two arguments appear: the first claims that the Turkish cities have already achieved the EU's development level, and that they alone could join it; however, the countryside, with the exception of (tourist infrastructure in) the coastal region, is backward and would be a significant burden on the EU. This argument points to the impossibility of setting clear borders within the regional logic. Rather, there are variations within regions. These variations may be marked by thresholds of discontinuous practices: while the (European) tourists enjoy the comfort of well-developed infrastructure in the coastal resorts, and the (European) businessmen transact, without disruptions, a deal in a modern building in Ankara or Istanbul, the IO employees, when visiting a site far from these (European) centers, struggle with difficulties similar to those experienced in Tajikistan. The networks have successfully struggled to overcome such thresholds and enable continuity of practices in tourist resorts and large cities, but the rest of the country has remained (culturally, structurally) different.

Besides the political and economic significance of such bordering processes, there is a question as to what it means for the mobile individuals to move between spaces marked by thresholds. The possibility of trespassing thresholds, and the compulsion to do so, mean that they move between multiple normalities. This requires a competency in changing practices, a competency that can partly be eased by networks. Without the IO's Health Department, with its system of monitoring dangers, issuing warnings, and providing medications, the mobile individual would be at risk of serious disease. Where one network fails and contributes to the

---

58 Compare Hans-Ulrich Wehler, »Fass ohne Boden«, *Hamburger Abendblatt*, 08.01.2005.

constitution of a threshold, another helps to overcome it successfully and thus prevents abrupt changes. Here again the ambivalent role of networks appears.

The spaces marked by thresholds are much more transparent and porous than those of regions, but they do not support the impression of the »one-world« society. The interviewees related this impression to the political borders of nation-states, which, to them, are increasingly losing their relevance in their world organized around mobility. From the perspective of the mobile individuals, networks, which may well create restrictions on access and border out some groups, erase regional divisions.[59] Thresholds seem to complement regions and networks, but the possibility that they harden the regional spaces, rather than compete with them, cannot be excluded. Certainly, the individuals' increasing consciousness of the changing character of borders and their plurality has far-reaching implications. The fact that nation-state borders are now considered as one among several types of borders, and the nation-state logic of regional divisions is only one of many possibilities, decides on the de-naturalization of nation-states and their homogenizing mechanisms. Territories, political systems, cultures, and populations are no longer perceived as closed within single borders. Social theory has thus far addressed this possibility and termed it globalization, transnationalization, or cosmopolitanization from below (Balibar 1998; Bauman 2002; Beck 2004b). It has been argued that there is a need to revise the general theoretical framework for understanding borders and their relation to social, communal, and economic boundaries (Anderson 2001); under the premise that, throughout history, periods of the relative openness and closure of nation-state borders can be identified (Anderson/O'Dowd 1999). The future research agenda is to identify the mutual influences of such multiple spaces and their borders, and to theorize the effects of their dynamics on social processes.

---

59 Bærenholdt (2004) has shown how networking strategies can lead to new divisions between those included and excluded. He distinguishes two forms of networks: bridging and bonding. The first builds connections between different social groups or fields; the second characterizes the practices of binding one social group or field, as opposed to others. Bonding defends and intensifies already-established social groupings. There are two types of bonding, territorial and mobile: the first is often used to defend particular territories, the second to link within functional fields, for example professions, business, or hobbies. The first confirms regional divisions, whereas the second establishes new ones.

8. Conclusions

Chapter Three described how the understanding of space has been changing in recent decades, and how this has resulted in a methodological change. A shift from considering space to investigating spatialities can be observed. This has consequences not only for the design of the empirical study, but also for the interpretation of its findings.

First, at present space is seen as being in construction: the authors speak about the multiplicity of spaces. This heterogeneity is not restricted to the present: space has always been re-produced in social practices, but earlier scientific and public discourse did not see it this way. Although the dominant interpretation was that space is absolute and infinite, this does not mean that space was then more absolute or more infinite than in those times when it was interpreted as relational. Thus, space has not changed from then to now, but societies and their spatialities may have changed. Those who have been expecting the conclusion that in modernity space was like »a« and in post-modernity space is like »b« will thus be disappointed. Such answers would be possible only if we assume that space is like a material object that can change its form: for example, be separated into units, or reunified into a single, common thing.

Second, this also means that there is no single space. The empirical study presented here is incomplete, in the sense that it is restricted to one particular group and its practice. It is an attempt to understand the processes of spatialization in mobility, and it must be recognized that its results, although pointing to some possible general developments, cannot be generalized to other groups and practices. However, empirical research has no alternative but to deliver such incomplete pictures, extracts of complex processes of spatialization at multiple levels. The multiplicity of spatial relations can barely be grasped in a single study, but certain processes can be made visible.

Further, the question should not be »what is space now«? It is, rather, »what has changed in socio-spatial structuration since then«? Thus the new or modified practices constituting space should be taken into account, as postulated in the section on cosmopolitan sociology in Chapter Three. In the newest approaches to space, practices and the interpretation of space cannot be investigated separately, because they are two sides of the process of spatialization. In applying the theses of the theory of reflexive modernization, Chapter Three proved how they hang together. However, and this is the point made by this theory, this does not mean that there are no tensions between the practice and its interpretation. Both the theoretical considerations and the empirical findings point to the necessity of investigating spatializations at different levels: practice, scientific interpretation, and public discourse.

Accordingly, this chapter addresses all the above concerns. The first part returns to the main themes in the recent literature, to ask about the change in spatial relations and social structuration. It focuses on certain dualisms and dichotomies, for several reasons. First, the dissolution of such dichotomies as presence-absence or near-far was said to be the sign of a shift from modernity to post-modernity. Second, the blurring of the distinction between each of the elements of a pair in such a dualism was understood as a sign of a shift towards the second modernity. Third, the dualisms best illustrate the thesis of categorial dissonances, proposed by the theory of reflexive modernization, and can therefore help to assess the periodization imposed by this theory. Further, the chapter attempts to answer the question of periodization, which, in the light of the theoretical considerations and the empirical findings, seems problematic.

8.1. Beyond the modern dichotomies?

The question driving the empirical research was whether and how geographical mobility challenges the spatial frames to which the individuals are accustomed, whether they are wrenched out of them, and what consequences this has: how, if at all, these frames become transformed, and which new frames are being constituted in the practices of these individuals. Further, if the answer is positive, we may ask if the thesis of a shift towards a new stage in modernity (or to a post-modern period) can be maintained, and which model best applies; or whether the empirical results suggest a new mode of explanation.

In this section, I confront selected results from the empirical study with some of the main theses discussed in Chapters Two and Three, regarding the theory of mobility and space. I focus on the dualisms that have had a prominent place in the discussion of the changing nature of space and social structuration. When we look at the catalogue of dualisms, which bothered such observers of modernity as Simmel, we see that presence and absence motivated a set of metaphors of inclusion and exclusion (Shields 1992: 191). The spatial dualism of near and far, and its temporal counterpart presence and absence, were combined with further dualisms (Sayer 1991). The problem – and the source of change – lies in their constellation. Modernity was characterized by linking categories into dichotomy pairs: inclusion-exclusion, presence-absence, space-place, local-global, immobility-mobility, and attachment-disembeddedness. Some of these have a long tradition. More important, inclusion was linked with presence, proximity, attachment, place, and locality, while exclusion was associated with absence, distance, disembeddedness, mobility, space, and globality. Such constellations have their political meaning, and they can be employed, for example, to exclude certain groups (on the political consequences of particular imaginings of space see also Massey 2005, multiple pages). Often, mobile individuals are considered uprooted or disconnected (Malkki 1997), and local communities are believed to be disadvantaged because they are disconnected from each other, and from the 'spaces of flow' constituted by mobile elites (Castells 1996).

I examined in detail whether these dualisms are relevant for the mobile individuals, whether and how they relate them to each other, or construct other pairs. I focus below on two dualisms that have been broadly discussed in the postmodern literature, have a prominent role in the liquid models, and were employed by the theory of reflexive modernization, which claims that such dualisms cannot be understood as dichotomies (mutually exclusive aspects), because the differences between each element of a pair are increasingly blurred. First, there is the problem of inclusion and exclusion, and, second, the issue of embeddedness and disembeddedness, both of which relate to the question of proximity and distance. The postmodern discourse has increasingly focused on the dualism of presence and absence in relation to the development of communications technology and globalization (Beck 1986; Giddens 1990;

Berger 1999). It has pointed to the continuously high relevance of this duality in each personal relationship, but also to increasing mutual interdependency with distant people, events, and decisions in the globalized world (Giddens 1990; Robertson 1992; 1998). Globalization is also considered a factor that disembeds mobile people, goods, and information from particular places. These (qualitatively new and powerful) flows are opposed to locally embedded, territorially fixed cultures (Berking 1998: 383). All these developments are said to cause a change of spatial relations that marks the transition to light or post-modernity. In contrast, the theory of reflexive modernization claims that such binary schematizations and clear-cut boundaries were a feature of the first modernity. Under conditions of extensive mobility, such demarcations become artificial, or even impossible to maintain (Beck/Giddens/Lau 1994; Beck/Bonß 2001; Beck/Bonß/Lau 2003).

Two examples are especially interesting, because they not only show the relevance of such dichotomies in daily practices, but they also tend to confirm the thesis of dissonance, and at the same time address the differentiation between the stages in modernity. The first demonstrates the dissonance between individual practices and collective observers, and the second the dissonance between individual practices and their scientific interpretation, although only analytically can these dimensions be so sharply distinguished. Indeed, they confirm and extend the results of such anthropologists as Ferguson and Gupta (1997) and Oaekes (1993), who contest the opposition between locality and the space of flows, and challenge the neat periodization schematized by Giddens and others.

8.1.1. Inclusion – exclusion

Chapter Four discussed in detail how long-term and short-term mobility is mediated by the individuals between the exogenous and endogenous factors: the requirements of the business, availability of distance communication tools, private obligations and family events, general life opportunities, own desires, dreams, goals, and aspirations. All these factors decide whether or not the individuals are present or absent, and the duration of their presence. In other words, they influence the relationship between presence and absence, and their spatial equivalents – proximity and distance. The research revealed that presence and absence are of key importance to the interviewed individuals: however, not as absolute categories that are mutually exclusive, but as gradual change in the quality of interaction. My informants are frequent travelers and migrants. This means that they are away much of the time: from their parental home, their immediate family, friends and relatives, and from their work colleagues (either in their main office when they travel; or in any other offices in their destinations, when they are present in their main location). On the other hand, those who are usually away – people of a different culture, for example – are often in direct proximity. For mobile individuals, the dualism of presence and absence is a part of normality, and an intrinsic ingredient of daily activities. Presence and absence are dealt with, mediated, and coordinated daily. For these people, distance communication tools are often the only way of remaining connected with those whom they leave behind, and they rely on these tools frequently. The first impression from the interviews is that remote communication wipes away any physical or political borders between people, and tends to annihilate distance. However, I then looked more closely at how mobile individuals manage their absence, communicate at a distance, experience the difference between being physically present and absent in place, and how they develop and sustain their social networks.

My informants confirmed that the instruments of distance communication cannot in any way replace face-to-face interaction. Personal contact in physical proximity remains the most important form of communication. There are several reasons for this, the interviewees say. First, most people are used to communicating face-to-face and avoid mediated communication, which they either do not trust, or consider difficult. More important, one can benefit more from the »personal touch« that face-to-face meetings have, especially when the issues discussed are complex or problematic, and require detailed examination. Body language is necessary to understand the motivations and decisions of the partners. Personal encounters also have another aspect: one not only meets people, one meets places. Distance communication disconnects people from their environments. When communicating by phone or the Internet, the partners do not receive any impression of how the other lives, of how she or he fits into the surroundings, or how the location may influence this person. Being physically present in place provides a much better understanding of the situation of a particular person. When in place, one can talk to many people, see the streets, get an idea of people's living conditions, etc. This knowledge gives my informants greater satisfaction from communication, performing the tasks in the job, and personal relationships. One can participate in the stories of others better when in spatial proximity. Otherwise, the others are experienced as being »caught in the moment«, immobilized, and atemporalized, as extracted from spatial and temporal contexts. In turn, spatial distance increases emotional distance. Therefore, the forms of communication are, in the informants' opinion, not interchangeable. The form of communication influences its content. Complex and difficult business issues that require the imparting of trust and empathy, and in which any misunderstandings would have serious consequences, are better discussed face-to-face. Similarly, personal conversations with the use of media are limited to regular updates and exchange of the most urgent information. One does not talk about emotions on the phone, and not about »really important things«. Relationships to the nearest and dearest therefore suffer under the physical distance. Although ties between children and parents cannot be disturbed by spatial separations, friendships are often in danger, and only true friends can tolerate the difficulties of my informants' mobile life-style.

Relationships in proximity and at a distance are qualitatively distinct and inconvertible, even when interaction over distance becomes a banal part of everyday life. Within the networks that span beyond traditional boundaries, proximity ceases to be metric, and becomes about the content of the message, the things being discussed or agreed upon: distance transforms into a matter of the time, money, access, or effort needed for the transfer of information. Distant places and people are those who are difficult to reach – to contact them is time-consuming and money-consuming.

The research revealed, in particular, that the temporal aspects of distance and proximity are of key importance to the individuals interviewed. It is not simultaneity of events that bother the individuals, but rather time delays, temporal shifts, and gaps between action and reaction. This influences the content and the form of messages and, in turn, the relationships between partners at a physical distance.

More important, presence itself is more ambivalent than remoteness. This becomes apparent when analyzing the mobile individuals' relations to places. The mobile individuals sustain their relationships to more than one distant locality, and remain a part of »elsewhere«. For a certain time they are an integral part of a place, but their physical presence in a place does not mean a simple and durable attachment to it, understood as participation in the local community. The temporality, and the choice of the form and the extent of the attachment and involvement, which is to a large degree mediated also with the non-local inhabitants and over local networks, all stress the ambivalence of proximity, especially in relation to inclusion, participation, and attachment.

In their places of residence, the mobile individuals easily escape the category of insiders, as they also do when they return to their home countries. The very specific experience of migration, attachment to multiple groups and locations, makes them into »strangers at home«. Most of their friends do not understand their way of life and the problems related to extensive mobility, claim the informants. They complain that their frequent absences render them unable to participate in any group activities or associations. They even have problems attending language courses, because any activity requiring regularity is often interrupted by periods of travel. Their friends are tired of scheduling meetings or organizing parties only when their mobile colleagues happen to be in town. Slowly, they detach from the communities in which they live.

In their destinations, they are an invisible group and, as such, are not clearly excluded from the society, which hardly ever notices their presence. This is amplified by the possibilities, which transnational networks offer them, of regulating their own exposure to places, cultures, and communities. These networks of foreigners and expatriates, English-speaking television, cinemas and bookstores, etc. but also the »local« infrastructure, such as supermarkets, translations, translators and interpreters, and fitness studios, which support the individualized, de-localized practices (by making direct contacts with the inhabitants and the language unnecessary), enable any foreigner to decide whether or not to encounter the »unknown«, and the specifics of the place. If they do, they act as experts and as tourists, each role appearing in a different context. For example, they may have a more or less direct influence on political and economic developments in the country where they conduct their projects, although they themselves are never affected by these decisions. They play the role of experts when they passively encounter a place: they read about a country, are interested in its history, go to exhibitions of native artists, read the books of local authors, even though they always run the risk of repeating stereotypes transmitted by these media. They discover the connections between their country of origin and the place of settlement, although they do not establish connections that will endure. At the same time, they are tourists in a country. They choose the kind of leisure activities that are typical of tourists. They travel a lot, are interested in architecture, famous monuments, and art. Although they are convinced that they are more than tourists, because they extend their knowledge and do not stay on the surface of things, their practices do not differ significantly from those of tourists.

Presence and proximity, absence and distance, are no longer indicators of insider status, of citizenship, or of cultural membership. Presence and absence first become uncoupled from inclusion and exclusion, and are then connected with them in a new pattern. For mobile individuals, what should be present – the immediate family, best friends, relatives – is often absent. The contrary is also true: what should be absent, according to the old regime, as institutionalized in modernity, – the »strangers«, the cultural others – is often physically present. At the same time, the quality of relationships blurs the distinction between physical and mental proximity in a new way.

8.1.2. Embeddedness and disembeddedness

The ambivalences of presence point to the dichotomy of embeddedness and disembeddedness. In the researched sample, this dichotomy was doubly relevant: not only are the individuals highly mobile and change their places of residence regularly, but they are also functionally excluded from nation-states and included in the institutional networks of the international organization, which follows the non-territorial principle of fixation. The organization has its own retirement plan, offers medical services to its employees, and provides resettlement benefits and support networks, including advice on housing or schooling, and job search for spouses. Its employees do not pay income taxes and they enjoy immunities from immigration restrictions. They are not subject to any national social system. Furthermore, they are embedded in networks of offices and communication technologies that span the globe, and their social networks and way of life are internationalized. Many of them are bilingual or trilingual, and mixed nationality marriages are common. The individuals' choices of location of home are driven by factors related predominantly to job and educational opportunities, not to a particular geographical location.

Often, the informants' preferred or dream future place of residence is anywhere where they can have interesting leisure opportunities, and can socialize easily. For them, a place called home is wherever their family is, where they are surrounded by objects they own, and where they feel well in the surroundings of people, landscape, architecture, and infrastructure. They are attached to homes that are mobile. Many informants cannot geographically locate their home, and laugh as they say that it is in the middle of the Atlantic; or they point to multiple localities.

However, their immersion in transnational networks, and the flexibility and temporality of the individual decision on location, should not be mistaken for either territorial disembeddedness or uprootedness. Rather, it is an indication of a breakup with territorial dictates and the sign of individual spatial freedom. Although many aspects of life are not permanently fixed to a particular individual place, certain aspects remain localized in a social sense. The interplay of »attachment« and »disembeddedness« is about participation in stories that happen through the time in a place. One informant said that he may visit his parents across the Atlantic only once every couple of years; but, when he is there for a month, he eats only local specialties, reads local newspapers, vividly discusses local problems with the neighbors, and participates with his mom in the meetings of a local association. Then he lives elsewhere for another couple of years, and he does not miss any of these experiences; nor does the local community notice his absence, and life there goes on smoothly without him. Being physically present in another place means to miss part of the story of this place.

The moral claims of attachment to place are of greater relevance to the mobile individuals than being present. This is the claim of continuity, the expectation that physical presence guarantees continuing participation in the life of a place, its development, and its trajectories. They are confronted with this claim every day, and they experience it as a pressure, a postulate which they cannot fulfill, to their own disappointment and that of the local inhabitants. Further, they (usually unreflectively) redefine what it means to be local: local is to be in a particular place at a particular time, to be affected by events happening in this time in this place, and to react to them. The second and third components of this definition often do not apply to my mobile informants. In their destinations, their work influences the politics and economy of a place, but they are not affected by these changes. In any location, they are functionally disembedded by their inclusion in the structures of the organization in which they work.

In place, two competing logics meet – national (regional) and cosmopolitan (network) – as do two complementary discourses – that of national affiliation and that of access (Galasinska et al. 2002). Both discourses are supported by mobile individuals and long-term settlers, and they relate to the same place. The first, national, logic attempts to set clear boundaries between individuals and groups, by assigning them to particular spaces that are labeled as national. This is the regional, container logic, that employs the existing categories, like nation, race, etc. and makes them durable by relating them to particular, exclusive units of space. Within this logic, the individual qualities (of humans and of places) are subordinate, and any differences between them are suppressed (Mol/Law 1994). Within this logic, the categories of uprootedness (Malkki 1997; Ahmed 2003), homelessness, and disembeddedness make sense. Someone who is mobile and frequently away, or someone who left due to migration, no longer belongs to this place. This person is no longer simply »local«. Someone who is a newcomer in a place, and is »different« from its inhabitants (has a different race or nationality, or is a member of another cultural group) also does not belong.

The accessibility discourse is a discourse of everyday practices, and it stresses the openness of groups and spaces. At the same time, it denaturalizes national labels. It is based on universal values connecting all humans, on the one hand, and on well-functioning transnational networks, on the other hand. This discourse recognizes that it is increasingly difficult to assign people to concrete territories. Accessibility, however, does not decide on inclusiveness, on a common living space. It rather questions the territorial borders between groups, cultures, languages, and nations, but without making other boundaries irrelevant. It appears as the most relevant and socially tense issue. It questions the status of insiders and outsiders in the »figuration of the nation-state« (Rundell 2004: 92), and calls for new differentiation strategies between »us« and »them« (Beck-Gernsheim 2004). In turn, such differentiation is not secondary to existing territorial borders: rather, the territorial demarcation appears in the process of redefining who belongs and who does not, who is the insider and who is the outsider, who is a member and who not, a foreigner or a local, and setting such boundaries anew.

The accessibility of places and people does not decide on their inclusiveness. There is no attempt to create a common space for living. Each travel, each encounter with a place links it to the previously visited locations, but these linkages are temporary. Under this condition, it becomes almost impossible to pin down territorially the boundary between »us« and »them«, those who belong and who do not, to assign places to particular regions, and people to these particular places. On no account does this mean that such boundaries disappear and that the world becomes singular. On the contrary, certain places and people remain remote, not necessarily in metric geographical distance, but emotionally. They can be »dropped off« from the common story: when their stories stop forming a part of someone else's story, they no longer belong to the common space.

The tensions between the two discourses discussed – mobile individuals and settled host communities, regional and network logics of spatial fixation, individual practices, their collective judgments, and scientific interpretations – constitute the contemporary spatialities, before our very eyes. The question of interest is whether they correspond to the diagnoses of the liquid and postmodern models, and to the thesis of dissonances proposed by the theory of reflexive modernization.

The liquid models tend to overestimate the scope of change in human spatialization, and they also fail to describe the nuances of time-spatial relations. The postmodern authors claim that the dissolution of the dichotomy of presence and absence certifies the shift from modernity to post-modernity (Shields 1992). They assert the collapse of the far-off into the nearby, which challenges the sense of control and mastery over the local realm, and entails a decline in the authority of ordering discourses that set out the ideal division, enacted as social spatialization. If we give credence to the postmodernists who focus on distance communication tools and global media events, the world becomes one, understood as a single space and as a single global present – instantaneity. The findings from the interviews clearly disagree with these claims, because the postmodern view has been blind to how time-space really matters. Spatial distance matters for the individuals because of the temporal dimension. Being »here« is always being »now« and linking to a particular past and future. Postmodern authors would claim a common single past and future for the whole global space, and refuse heterogeneity to both. This heterogeneity and its growing consciousness is assigned to people alone: to their cultures, religions, behaviors, and their constant exchange, due to the acceleration of mobility, and global flows. Jameson (1991) speaks here of constant confrontation, and Harvey (1990) of worlds falling together.[60] However, the heterogeneity of time-space-social is the only basis of the ambivalence of the dualism of presence-absence, and its linkage with involvement, attachment, commitment, etc., and not the mosaic of diverse cultures.

The theory of reflexive modernization, in contrast, underestimates, if it does not neglect, the importance of space as a premise of modernity. Territorial borders matter to it primarily as nation-state borders, and the boundaries are of symbolic character and relate to the »purely« social. Its thesis of sharp distinctions between elements (terms) of a pair in each dualism derives from the assumption that both terms become ambivalent, unclear, and impossible to distinguish from each other. The terms blur, and the boundary between them is no longer sharp. The dissolution of the »either/or« principle is central to the theory of reflexive modernization (Beck/Lau 2005: 527). However, this principle, derived from the observation and conceptualization of the purely »social«, and the thesis of its dissolution, can hardly be applied to the dualisms of presence and absence, or distance and proximity. To the interviewees, these experiences are qualitatively distinct. Only when combined with further dualisms, for instance of attachment and disembeddedness, do their commonly assumed definitions, as conveyed in the public discourse, become vague. Being present does not mean being involved; being absent does not mean being detached, and so on. This recognition corresponds to the second claim made by the theory of reflexive modernization, that the shift towards these dualities relates to the emergence of a new structural logic. However, this new structural principle co-exists with the old one. Thus, in many cases, but not in all, the structural principle of exclusive distinctions no longer seems sustainable (Beck/Lau 2005: 541). Plurality of boundaries is therefore claimed. Considering the spatio-temporal dualism, this plurality

---

60 Such a »post-modern« impression, however, was discussed by the modernists like Simmel, who wrote about the experience of near and far being disturbed by the Stranger or the Wanderer, who bring otherwise distant and separate worlds close together, and by the second-modernist Beck (2004b: 13), who speaks of cosmopolitan empathy or the globalization of emotions. Not only does the physically distant influence and perforate the physically close local, but distant events induce an emotional relation in the locality. The Stranger no longer remains psychologically distant but calls for an ethical relationship, for responsibility, like those in proximity (comp. Levinas 1982: 95-101; Manderson 2006).

results from the shift in linkages between dualisms, and not from the ambiguity alone of each term, and it leads to the denaturalization of a particular spatial order based on them.

Certainly, the theory of reflexive modernization offers an interesting approach, in which spatial relations can be researched as a dynamic process full of contradictions and repetitions. The short overview of the development of thought on space, in Chapter Three, illustrates this thesis best. In this approach, space cannot be understood as a simple determinant of social change, and it cannot be separated from it. According to the theory, there is no simple causality, as the liquid models would like to see. The old, the changed, and the new forms appear at the same time, influencing one another, and at all levels: scientific notions of space, discourse on space, and practices in space. For example, the expansion of networks, or the acceleration of transfer alone, cannot be mistaken for the beginning of a completely different new era; although the effects of this expansion of networks on regional logic, and the fact that is questions old boundaries, can be considered as signs of a new period within modernity, in which container space, regional logic, and national discourse are present and relevant to individuals and institutions, life policy makers, and global system politics. Similarly, as perfectly shown by Doreen Massey (2005), the discourse on space is being influenced by such processes as scientific discoveries, globalization, the spread of networks, and the acceleration of mobility. For example, mobility, and the related ambivalences of inclusion, disembeddedness, and access, have not only become normality to concerned individuals and to groups, but have also been increasingly included in the recent literature (e.g., Albrow et al. 1994; Hannerz 1996; Gupta/Ferguson 1997; Berking 1998; Favell 2003; Kennedy 2004). Anthropology, the discipline that traditionally focused on particular territorially fixed communities, moves towards »mobile fields« in its expertise. However, there is no consensus on the interpretation of these phenomena: many authors stress the negative role of mobility on personal social networks and identity, whereas others see its possibilities for enlarging individuals' life-space.

To prove the change at one level alone seems a dubious task. To grasp the change means necessarily to grasp the mutual influences at all levels at the same time. At the level of human spatialization, new and old patterns of fixation of socio-spatial processes appear together. More than one logic of spatial constitution competes: the regional logic represented, for example, by nation-states, the network logic of transnational organizations, or the fluid logic (Mol/Law 1994) of indifferently transforming processes. At the same time, it is necessary to remember that the scientific comprehension of space is an integral part of the processes of spatialization, and that the observers' (social scientists') imagination and interpretation of spatial relations and their production are interrelated.

8.2. Second modern spatialization and beyond

»Space matters« might be one conclusion of the empirical research. It matters to the individuals not only because it enables them to move. It reconstitutes how they socialize with others: their families who are in proximity, their friends who are at a distance, the way they experience difference« and similarity, the way they make use of differences to »locate« them in space and »immobilize«. Space matters, because in space their practices change. Importantly, it matters because of the temporal dimension of social praxis. Movement also matters, as it challenges their spatial imaginations: the way they used to imagine the world from the perspective of their location, the way they believed that what is far is different, and the way they accepted borders between states, cultures, and people. When moving, they notice that certain divisions are artificial, that some borders do not have any effect, that cultures cannot be defined as homogenous entities. They are surprised that distance is not always metric, that someone who does not have a telephone is much more remote than someone who does; but, at the same time, that physical proximity does not guarantee belonging to the same group, being included, or feeling attached. Mobility through space challenges their spatial order and demonstrates to them that public discourse on space, which is often associated with a single interconnected globality, does not find its confirmation in reality. They are often surprised that, despite their mobility and their problems with locating their homes geographically, their identity is not in danger, and they do not feel homeless. Yet they suffer from the pressure to be attached to one single place, and experience it as a burden that they cannot share their experiences with their immobile friends.

Space also challenges the social scientists, as it neglects the complexity of the social as the outcome of interrelatedness through space, its multiplicity and heterogeneity, and constantly changing character. This multiplicity has certainly not been sufficiently grasped by the present study. However, the empirical findings and the theoretical analysis do prove the borders of the discussed theories. In this last section of the book, I return to the problem of the periodization of social structuration in relation to space-time.

The findings clearly contradict many of the claims of the post-modern literature. Space is not annihilated by time, space does not compress, distance and proximity matter for social relations, the dualisms do not blur, we cannot give evidence of de-territorialization, and there is no space of flows that could contradict a space of places. However, the processes of bordering, temporality of arrangements, the diminishing role of nation-state borders and their relative structuring power, unclear or shifting definitions and division between elements of pairs in dualisms, dissonances between the public discourse and the scientific comprehension of space, or between public discourse and individual practices, all suggest that the theory of reflexive modernization provides a mode of interpretation that reflects the current spatialization. Yet the empirical findings cast some doubts and point to the limits of this theory. Paradoxically, these limits become visible when following the thesis of the categorial dissonances. This thesis turned out to be a useful tool in investigating spatial relations, and its merits or correctness cannot easily be called into question. However, when the complete theory is related to spatial relations, the theory becomes problematic. Its assumptions can be empirically proved, with greater or lesser difficulty, as long as the focus is on the »purely social«, when it excludes space as an integral part of social structuration. Then its periodization also seems to be plausible. However, when space is consciously included in the research, this periodization becomes problematic. For the theory of reflexive modernization, time is the ordering principle of social structuration. Societies change in time: some have already achieved the stage of the second modernity, while for others it is a future project. They are still behind the others, but sooner or later they will become reflexive-modern, because this is the logic of modernization. Modernization is a steering force of the transformation. How can this be reconciled with the idea of the heterogeneity of time-space, and the co-temporal multiplicity of socialization, which is necessarily spatial and temporal? When assuming, in accordance with the theory of reflexive modernization, that in modernity previous forms of socialization cumulate, can we still insist that epochs can be distinguished in which categorial consonances indeed dominated, and that such periods can be clearly differentiated from any other period? Any such attempt at periodization necessarily underestimates the role of space in socialization. Any attempt to distinguish spatial relations typical of a particular time, or dominant in a particular epoch only, has until now ended by distinguishing »purely« social relations without considering their spatial constitution. On the other hand, any such attempt produces temporal containers: despite the explicit claim of a new cosmopolitan methodology, in which such container thinking must necessarily be abandoned, the theory of reflexive modernization understands time as linear and divisible into epochs, each of them characterized by different qualities. A more radical reading of the theory of reflexive modernization and cosmopolitan methodology would be unable to make such distinctions, and open up for space as well. Only as long as time and space are placed on a temporal axis, does multiplicity of space mean the co-existence of kaleidoscopic spaces within simultaneity, or between the past and the present.

The empirical findings have proved the importance of the temporal dimension in the study of spatialization processes. Time matters as the dynamics of processes (change in time), the multiplicity of spaces in time (simultaneity), and the plurality of trajectories (multiple times) in space. Certainly, one aspect that must be researched is how certain imaginations of space institutionalize, and are made durable. It seems most important, however, that the social science of time-space should not reproduce distinctions that daily mobility has already blurred, and that the studies of the social should involve reflection on time-space, and on the intrinsic role of spatialization in socialization, at all scales. Without the sufficient involvement of space in the analysis, the postulate of a conscious, cosmopolitan sociology cannot be completely fulfilled, nor can the role of mobility in contemporary sociation be understood.

Bibliography

Adam, Barbara (2003), »Reflexive Modenization Temporalized«, *Theory, Culture & Society*, Vol. 20, pp. 59-78

Agnew, John (1987), *Place and Politics: The Geographical Mediation of State and Society*, Boston: Allen & Ulwin

— (1989), »The devaluation of place in social science«, in: Agnew, John/Duncan, James (eds), *The Power of Place: Bringing Together Geographical and Sociological Imaginations*, Boston: Unwin Hyman, pp. 9-30

— /Duncan, James (1989) (eds), *The Power of Place: Bringing Together Geographical and Sociological Imaginations*, Boston: Unwin Hyman

Ahmed, Sara (2003) (ed.), *Uprootings/Regroundings. Questions of Home and Migration*, Oxford/New York: Berg

Albrow, Martin (1997), »Auf Reisen jenseits der Heimat. Soziale Landschaften in einer globalen Stadt«, in: Beck, Ulrich (ed.), *Kinder der Freiheit*, Frankfurt a.M.: Suhrkamp, pp. 288-314

— (1998) *Abschied vom Nationalstaat*, Frankfurt a.M.: Suhrkamp

— /Eade, John/Fennell, Graham/O'Byrne, Darren (1994), *Global/Local Relations in a London Borough: Shifting Boundaries and Localities*, Roehampton Institute, Department of Sociology and Social Policy, London

Allen, John (2000), »On Georg Simmel. Proximity, distance and movement«, in: Crang, Michael/Thrift, Nigel (eds), *Thinking space*, London, New York: Routledge, pp. 54-70

— /Massey, Doreen/Pryke, Michael (1999), *Unsettling Cities: Movement and Settlement*, London: Routledge

Altman, Irvin/Low, Setha M. (1992) (eds), *Place attachment*, New York: Plenum

Anderson, James (2001), *Therizing State Borders: 'Politics/Economics' and Democracy in Capitalism*, CIBR Working Papers in Border Studies, CIBR/WP01-1

— /O'Dowd, Liam (1999), »Contested borders: globalization and ethno-national conflict in Ireland«, *Regional Studies*, Vol. 33(7), pp. 681-696

Appadurai, Arjun (1988), »Putting hierarchy in place«, *Cultural Anthropology*, Vol. 3(1), pp. 36-49

— (1990) »Disjuncture and Difference in the Global Cultural Economy«, *Theory, Culture & Society*, Vol. 7, pp. 295-310

— (1996) *Modernity at Large*, University of Minnesota Press

— (1998) »Globale Ethnische Räume. Bemerkungen und Fragen zur Entwicklung einer transnationalen Anthropologie«, in: Beck, Ulrich (ed.), *Perspektiven der Weltgesellschaft*, Frankfurt a.M.: Suhrkamp, pp.11-40

Ardrey, Robert (1967), *The Territorial Impretive*, London: Collins

Arensberg, Conrad/Kimball, Solon T. (1940), *Family and Community in Ireland*, Cambridge, MA: Harvard University Press

Ariew, Roger (1985), *Medieval Cosmology: Theories of Infinity, Place, Time, Void and the Plurality of Worlds*, Chicago: University of Chicago Press

Augé, Marc (1994), *Orte und Nicht-Orte*, Frankfurt a.M.: S.Fischer

Axhausen, Kay W. (2001), *Social networks and travel behaviour*, ESRC Workshop »Mobile network seminar series - Seminar 2: New communication technologies and transportation systems«, February 2002, Lucy Cavendish College, Cambridge UK

Azaraya, Victor (2004),»Globalization and International Tourism in Developing Countries: Marginality as a Commercial Commodity«, *Current Sociology*, Vol. 52(6), pp. 949-967

Balibar, Etienne (1998),»The Borders of Europe«, in: Cheah, Pheng/Robbins, Bruce (eds), *Cosmopolitics: Thinking and Feeling Beyond the Nation*, Minneapolis: University of Minnesota Press, pp. 216-229

Basch, Lina/Glick Schiller, Nina/Szanton Blanc, Cristina (1994), *Nations unbound: transnational projects, postcolonial predicaments and deterritorialized nation-states*, New York: Gordon & Breach

Barnes, John A. (1954),»Class and committees in a Norwegian island parish«, *Human Relations* 7, pp. 39-58

Barry, Andrew (2006),»Technological Zones«, *European Journal of Social Theory*, Vol. 9(2), pp. 239-253

Bartles, Dietrich (1974),»Schwierigkeiten mit dem Raumbegriff in der Geographie«, *Geographica Helvetica* Vol. 2/3, pp. 7-21

— /Hard, Gerhard (1975), *Lotsenbuch für das Studium der Geographie*, Bonn/Kiel

Bærenholdt, Jørgen Ole (2004),»Territoriality and Mobility – Coping in Nordic Peripheries«, in: Bærenholdt, Jørgen Ole/Simonsen, Kristian (eds), *Space Odysseys. Spatiality and Social Relations in the 21st Century*, Aldershot: Ashgate, pp. 119-135

Bauman, Zygmunt (1997), *Postmodernity and Its Discontents,* Cambridge: Polity Press

— (2000a), *Liquid Modernity*, Cambridge: Polity Press

— (2000b),»Time and Space Reunited«, *Time and Society*, Vol. 9(2/3), pp.171-185

— (2002), *Society under Siege*, Cambridge: Polity Press

Beaverstock, Jonathan (2005),»Transnational Elites in the City: British Highly-Skilled Inter-Company Transferees in New York City's Financial District«, *Journal of Ethnic and Migration Studies*, Vol. 31(2), pp. 245-268

Beck, Ulrich (1986), *Risikogesellschaft –Auf dem Weg in eine andere Moderne*, Frankfurt a.M.: Suhrkamp

— (1993), *Die Erfindung des Politischen. Zu einer Theorie reflexiver Modernisierung*, Frankfurt a.M.: Suhrkamp

— (1994), *Reflexive Modernization*, Cambridge: Polity Press
— (1997a), *Was ist Globalisierung?*, Frankfurt a.M.: Suhrkamp
— (1997b), *The Reinvention of Politics: rethinking modernity in the global social order*, Cambridge: Polity Press
— (1999), *World Risk Society*, Cambridge: Polity Press
— (2002a), »The Cosmopolitan Society and its Enemies«, *Theory, Culture & Society*, Vol. 19(1-2), pp. 17-44
— (2002b), *Macht und Gegenmacht im globalen Zeitalter. Neue Weltpolitische Ökonomie*, Frankfurt a.M.: Suhrkamp
— (2004a), »Cosmopolitical realism: on the distinction between cosmopolitanism in philosophy and the social sciences«, *Global Networks*, Vol. 4(2), pp. 131-156
— (2004b), *Der kosmopolitische Blick oder: Krieg ist Frieden*, Frankfurt a.M.: Suhrkamp
— /Bonß, Wolfgang (2001) (eds), *Die Modernisierung der Moderne*, Frankfurt a.M.: Suhrkamp
— /—/Lau, Christoph (2003) »The Theory of Reflexive Modernization: Problematic, Hypotheses and Research Programme«, *Theory, Culture & Society*, Vol. 20 (2), pp. 1-35
— /Lau, Christoph (2004) (eds), *Entgrenzung und Entscheidung*, Frankfurt a.M.: Suhrkamp
— (2005), »Second modernity as a research agenda: theoretical and empirical explorations in the ›meta-change‹ of modern society«, in: Beck, Ulrich/Lau, Christoph (eds), *Entgrenzung und Entscheidung*, Frankfurt a.M.: Suhrkamp, pp. 13-64
— /Giddens, Anthony/ Lash, Scott (1994), *Reflexive Modernization: Politics, Tradition and Aesthetics in the Modern Social Order*, Stanford: Stanford University Press
Beck-Gernsheim, Elisabeth (1998), »Schwarze Juden und griechische Deutsche«, in: Beck, Ulrich (ed.), *Perspektiven der Weltgesellschaft*, Frankfurt a.M.: Suhrkamp, pp. 125-168
— (2004), *Wir und die Anderen*, Frankfurt a.M.: Suhrkamp
Berger, John (1984), *And our Faces, My Heart, Brief as Photos*, London: Writes and Readers
Berger, Peter A. (1995), »Anwesenheit und Abwesenheit. Raumbezüge sozialen Handelns«, *Berliner Journal für Soziologie*, Vol. 5(1), pp. 99-111
— (1999) »Kommunikation ohne Anwesenheit. Ambivalenzen der postindustriellen Wissensgesellschaft«, in: Rademacher, Claudia (ed.), *Spiel ohne Grenzen? Ambivalenzen der Globalisierung*, Opladen: Westdeutscher Verlag, pp. 145-168
Berghe van den, Pierre L. (1974), *Class and Ethnicity in Peru*, Leiden: Brill
Berker, Thomas (2003), *Boundaries in a Space of Flows. The Case of Migrant Researchers' Use of ICTs*, a report within the European Media and Technology in Everyday Life Network II 2000-2003, NTNU, Department of Interdisciplinary Studies of Culture, Trondheim
Berking, Helmut (1998), »Global Flows and Local Cultures: Über die Rekonfiguration sozialer Räume im Globalisierungsprozeß«, *Berliner Zeitschrift für Soziologie* Vol. 3, pp. 381-392

Beteille, Andre (1965), *Caste, Class and Power,* Berkley, CA: University of California Press

Bhabha, Homi B. (2000), *Die Verortung der Kultur,* Tübingen: Stauffenburg Verlag

Biggs, Michael (1999), »Putting the State on the Map: Cartography, Territory and European State Formation«, *Comparative Studies in Society and History,* Vol. 41, pp. 374-405

Bilden, Helga (1997), »Das Individuum – ein dynamisches System vielfältiger Teil-Selbst. Zur Pluralität in Individuum und Gesellschaft«, in: Keupp, Heiner/Höfer, Renate (eds), *Identitätsarbeit heute. Klassische und aktuelle Perspektiven der Identitätsforschung,* Frankfurt a.M.: Suhrkamp, pp. 227-250

Billig, Michael (1995), *Banal nationalism,* London: Sage

Blau, Peter M./Duncan, Otis D. (1967), *The American Occupational Structure,* New York: John Wiley and Sons Inc.

Blotevogel, Hans H. (1995), *Handwörterbuch der Raumordnung,* Hannover: ARL

Boden, Deirdre/Molotch, Harvey L. (1994), »The Compulsion to Proximity«, in: Friedland, Roger/Boden, Deirdre (eds), *NowHere: Space, Time and Modernity,* Berkeley: University of California Press, pp. 257-286

Body-Gendrot, Sophie/Martiniello, Marco (2000) (eds), *Minorities in European Cities: The Dynamics of Social Integration and Social Exclusion at the Neighborhood Level,* London: Macmillan

Bohnsack, Ralf (2000), *Rekonstruktive Sozialforschung,* Opladen: Leske+Budrich

Bommes, Michael (2003), »Der Mythos des transnationalen Raums. Oder: Worin besteht die Herausforderung des Transnationalismus für die Migrationsforschung?«, in: Thränhardt, Dietrich /Hunger, Uwe (eds), *Migration im Spannungsfeld von Globalisierung und Nationalstaat,* Wiesbaden: Westdeutscher Verlag, pp. 90-116

Bonß, Wolfgang/Kesselring, Sven (2001), »Mobilität am Übergang von der Ersten zur Zweiten Moderne«, in: Beck, Ulrich/Bonß, Wolfgang (eds), *Die Modernisierung der Moderne,* Frankfurt a.M.: Suhrkamp, pp. 177-191

— /Kesselring, Sven/Weiß, Anja (2004), »›Society on the Move‹. Mobilitätspioniere in der Zweiten Moderne«, in: Beck, Ulrich/Lau, Christoph (eds), *Entgrenzung und Entscheidung,* Frankfurt a.M.: Suhrkamp, pp. 258-280

Bott, Elizabeth (1971), *Family and social network,* London: Tavistock

Boyd, Monica (1989), »Family and Personal Networks in International Migration: Recent Developments and New Agendas«, *International Migration Review,* Vol. 23(3), pp. 638-670

Brown, Barbara B./Perkins Douglas D. (1992), »Disruptions in place attachment«, in: Altman, Irvin/Low, Setha M. (eds), *Place Attachment,* New York: Plenum Press, pp. 63-86

Brubaker, Robers (1994), *Citizenship and Nationhood in France and Germany,* Cambridge/London: Harvard University Press

Cairncross, Frances (1998), *The Death of Distance,* London: Orion

Calhoun, Craig J. (1980), »Community: towards a variable conceptualization for comparative research«, *Social History,* Vol. 5(1), pp. 105-129

— (1991), »Indirect relationships and imagined communities: Large-scale social integration and the transformation of everyday life«, in: Bourdieu, Pierre/Coleman John S. (eds), *Social theory for a changing society*, Bourlder, CO: Westview, pp. 95-121

Callon, Michael (1980), »Struggles and Negotiations to define what is Problematic and what is not: the Sociology of Translation«, in Knorr, Karin/Krohn Roger/ Whitley Richard (eds) *The Social Process of Scientific Investigation: Sociology of the Sciences Yearbook*, Boston: Reidel, pp. 197-219

Canter, David (1977), *The psychology of Place*, London: Architectural Press

— (1997), »The facets of place«, in: Moore, Gary T./Marans, Robert W. (eds), *Advances in environment, behavior, and design: Vol. 4. Towards the integration of theory, method, research and utilization*, New York: Plenum, pp. 109-147

Carter, Paul (1992), *The Sound In Between. Voice, Space, Performance*, Sydney: New South Wales University Press

Casey, Edward (1993), *Getting back into place. Towards a renewed understanding of the place-world*, Bloomington: Indiana University Press

— (1998) *The Fate of Place. A Philosophical History*, Berkley/Los Angeles/London: University of California Press

Castells, Manuel (2000) *The Rise of the Network Society*, Oxford: Blackwell

— (2001), *Das Informationszeitalter. Der Aufstieg der Netzgesellschaft*, Opladen: Leske+Budrich

Castles, Stephen/Davidson, Alastair (2000), *Citizenship and Migration: Globalization and the Politics of Belonging*, London: Macmillan

— /Kosack, Godula (1973), *Immigrant Workers and Class Structure in Western Europe*, Oxford: Oxford University Press

— /Miller, Mark (1997), »Die Formung der modernen Welt durch globale Migration. Eine Geschichte der Wanderungsbewegungen bis 1945«, in: Pries, Ludger (ed.) *Transnationale Migration*, Soziale Welt Sonderband 12, Baden-Baden: Nomos, pp. 47-63

Chan, Bun Kwok (1997), »A family affair: migration, dispersal and the emergent identity of the Chinese cosmopolitan«, *Diaspora*, Vol. 6, pp. 195-213

Chaney, Elsa M. (1985) *Migration from the Caribbean Region: Determinants and Effects of Current Movements*, Hemispheric Migration Project, Intergovernmental Committee for Migration and Georgetown University, Center for Immigration Policy and Refugee Assistance

Claesges, Ulrich (1963), *Edmund Husserls Theorie der Raumkonsitution*, Köln: Universität Köln

Clarke, Nick (2005), »Detailing Transnational Lives of the Middle: British Working Holiday Makers in Australia«, *Journal of Ethnic and Migration Studies*, Vol. 31(2), pp. 307-322

Clifford, James (1988), *The predicament of culture*, Cambridge, MA: Harvard University Press

— (1997) *Routes*, Cambridge, MA: Harvard University Press

Cohen, Robin (1997), *Global disaporas: and introduction*, London: Universtity Collage London Press

Colic-Peisker, Val (2002), »Migrant communities and class: Croatians in Western· Australia«, in: Kennedy, Paul/Roudometof, Victor (eds), *Communities across borders: new immigrants and transnational cultures*, London: Routledge, pp. 29-40

Comaroff, John (1993), »The Diseased Heart of Africa«, in: Lindenbaum, Shirley/Lock, Margret (eds), *Knowledge, Power and Practice: The Anthropology of Medicine and Everyday Life*, Berkeley, CA: University of California Press, pp. 305-329

Cox, Kevin R. (1997) (ed.), *Spaces of globalization: reasserting the power of the local*, New York: Guilford

Crang, Michael/Thrift, Nigel (2000) (eds), *Thinking space*, London/New York: Routledge

Creveld, van Martin L. (1998), *Aufstieg und Untergang des Staates*, München: Gerling Akademischer Verlag

Cwerner, Salou B. (2000), »The Chronopolitan Ideal: time, belonging and globalization«, *Time and Society*, Vol. 9(2/3), pp. 331-345

Daniels, P, Lever, W. (eds) (1996), *The global economy in transition*, Harlow: Longman

Deleuze, Gilles/Guattari, Felix (1976), »Rhizome«, *Internationale marxistische Diskussion* 67

— (1986), *Nomadology*, New York: Semiotext(e)

Dezalay, Yves (1990), »The big bang and the law: the internationalization and restructuration of the legal field«, in: Featherstone, Michael (ed.), *Global culture: nationalism, globalization and modernity*, London: Sage, pp. 279-294

Doel, Marcus A. (1996), »A hundred thousand lines of flight: a machnic introduction to the nomad thought and scrumpled geography of Gilles Deleuze and Félix Guattari«, *Environment and Planning D: Society and Space,* Vol. 14, pp. 421-439

Douglas, Mary (1991), »The Idea of Home: A kind of Space«, *Social Research,* Vol. 58(1), pp. 287-307

Doyle, Judith/Nathan, Max (2001) *Wherever Next? Work in a Mobile World*, London: The Industrial Society

Döring, Nicola/Dietmar, Christine (2004), »Mediated Communication in Couple Relationships: Approaches for Theoretical Modeling and Initial Qualitative Findings«, in: *Forum: Qualitative Social Research,* Vol. 4(3) 17.03.2005 http://www.qualitative-research.net/fqs-texte/3-03/3-03doeringdietmar-e.htm

Duck, Steve (1998), *Relating to others*, Chicago Il: Dorsey

Duncan, Nancy (1996) (ed.), *Body-space: destabilizing geographies of gender and sexuality*, London and New York: Routledge

Durand, Jorge/Massey Douglas S. (1992), »Mexican Migration to the USA«, *Latin American Research Review,* Vol. 27(2), pp. 3-42

Earman, John (1970), »Who's afraid of absolute space?«, *Australasian Journal of Philosophy,* Vol. 48, pp. 287-319

— (1989), *World Enough and Space-Time. Absolute versus Relational Theories of Space and Time*, Cambridge, MA: The MIT Press

Ecarius, Jutta/Löw, Martina (1997) (eds), *Raumbildung Bildungsräume. Über die Verräumlichung sozialer Prozesse*, Opladen: Leske+Budrich

Eisel, Ulrich (1980), »Die Entwicklung der Anthropogeographie von einer Raumwissenschaft zur Gesellschaftwissenschaft«, *Urbs et regio Kasseler Schriften zur Geographie und Planung*, Vol. 17

Elkins, David J. (1995) *Beyond Sovereignty. Territory and Political Economy in the Twenty-first Century*, Toronto: University of Toronto Press

Emirbayer, Mustafa/Goodwin, Jeff (1994) »Network Analysis, Culture, and the Problem of Agency«, *American Journal of Sociology*, Vol. 99(6), pp. 1411-1454

Entrikin, Nicholas J. (1991), *The Betweeness of Place: Towards a Geography of Modernity*, Baltmimore: John Hopkins University Press

— (1999), »Political Community, Identity and Cosmpolitan Place«, *International Sociology*, Vol. 14(3), pp. 269-282

Espinosa, Kristin/Massey Douglas S. (1997), »Undocumented Migration and the Quantity of Social Capital«, *Transnationale Migration*, Sonderband 12 der Zeitschrift *Soziale Welt*, pp. 141-162

Faist, Thomas (2000), »Transnationalism in international migration: implications for the study of citizenship and culture«, *Racial and Ethnic Studies*, Vol. 23, pp. 189-222

Favell, Adrian (2003), *Eurostars and Eurocities: Towards a Sociology of Free Moving Professionals in Western Europe*, The Center for Comparative Immigration Studies Working Paper No. 71, La Jolla, CA: University of California-San Diego

Fawcett, James T. (1989), »Networks, Linkages, and Migration Systems«, *International Migration Review*, Vol. 23(3), pp. 671-680

Feldman, Roberta M. (1990), »Settlement-identity: Psychological bonds with hime places in a mobile society«, *Environment and Behavior*, Vol. 22, pp. 183-229

Ferguson, James (1997) (ed.), *Culture, Power, Place: Explorations in Critical Anthropology*, Durham: Duke University Press

— /Gupta, Akhil (1997), »Beyond ›Culture‹: Space, Identity, and the Politics of Difference«, in: Ferguson, James (ed.), *Culture, Power, Place: Explorations in Critical Anthropology*, Durham: Duke University Press, pp. 33-51

Fortier, Anne-Marie (2003), »Making Home: Queer Migrations and Motions of Attachment«, in: Ahmed, Sara (ed.), *Uprootings/Regroundings. Questions of Home and Migration*, Oxford/New York: Berg, pp. 115-136

Foucault, Michel (1973), *The Birth of the Clinic: An Archaeology of Medical Perception*, New York: Pantheon

— (1977), *Discipline and Punish: The Birth of the Prison*, New York: Pantheon

— (1991), »Andere Räume«, in: Wentz, Martin (ed.), *Stadträume*, Frankfurt a.M.: Campus, pp. 65-72

— (1994), *The Order of Things. An Archaeology of the Human Sciences*, New York: Vintage Books

Franklin, Sarah/Lury, Celia/Stacey, Jackie (2000), *Global Nature, Global Culture*, London: Sage

Fried, Marc (2000), »Continuities and discontinuities of place«, *Journal of Environmental Psychology*, Vol. 20, pp. 193-205

Friedman, Jonathan (1994), *Cultural Identity and Global Process*, London/Thousand Oaks/New Dehli: Sage

Frisby, David (1984), *Georg Simmel*, London: Tavistock

— (1986), *Fragments of Modernity. Theories of Modernity in the Work of Simmel, Kracauer and Benjamin*, Cambridge, MA: The MIT Press

— (1992), *Simmel and Since*, London/New York: Routledge

Galasinska, Aleksandra/Meinhof Ulrike/Rollo, Craig (2002), »Urban Space and the Construction of Identity on the German-Polish Border«, in: Meinhof, Ulrike (ed.), *Living (with) Borders. Identity discourses on East-West Borders in Europe*, Aldershot: Ashgate, pp. 119-140

Gane, Nicholas (2001), »Zygmunt Bauman: Liquid Modernity and Beyond«, *Acta Sociologica*, Vol. 44, pp. 267-275

Garonna, Paolo/Sofia, Francesca (1996), *Statistics and Nation-Building in European History*, in: *Seminar on Official Statistics – Past and Future*, Lissabon: United Nations Statistical Commision, United Nations Economic Commission for Europe

Geertz, Clifford (1988), *Works and Lives*, Stanford: Stanford University Press

Gellner, Ernest (1983), *Nations and nationalism*, Ithaca: Cornel University Press

Gerhards, Jürgen (2004), »Europäische Werte – Passt die Türkei kulturell zur EU?«, *Aus Politik und Zeitgeschichte*, Vol. B38, pp. 14-20

Gerson, Kathleen/Stueve, Anne/Fischer, Claude (1977), »Attachment to Place«, in: Fischer, Claude/Jackson Robert Max/Stueve, Anne/Gerson, Kathleen/ Jones Lynn/Baldassare Mark, *Networks and Places. Social Relations in the Urban Setting*, New York: The Free Press, pp. 139-161

Giddens, Anthony (1977), *Studies in Social and Political Theory*, London: Hutchinson

— (1984), *The Constitution of Society*, Berkley, LA: University of California Press

— (1990), *The Consequences of Modernity*, Stanford: Stanford University Press

— (1991), *Modernity and Self-Identity. Self and Society in the Late Modern Age*, Stanford, CA: Stanford University Press

— (1997), *Die Konstitution der Gesellschaft*, Frankfurt a.M.: Campus

— /Stanworth, Philip (1974) (eds), *Elites and Power in British Society*, London/New York: Cambridge University Press

Giuliani, Vittoria/Ferrera, Fiorenza/Barabotti, Silvia (2003), »One Attachment or More?«, in: Moser, Gabriel/Pol, Enric/Bernard, Yvonne/Bonnes, Mirilia/ Corraliza, Jose/Giuliani, Vittoria, *People, Places, and Sustainability*, Seattle/ Toronto/Bern/Göttingen: Hogrefe&Huber, pp. 111-122

Glick Schiller, Nina/Basch, Linda/Blanc-Szanton, Cristina (1992) (eds), *Towards a Transnational Perspective on Migration. Race, Class, Ethinicity, and Nationalism Reconsidered*, New York: New York Academy of Science

— (1997) »Transnationalismus: Ein neuer analytischer Rahmen zum Verständnis von Migration«, in: Kleger, Heiz (ed.) Transnationale Staatsbürgerschaft, New York: Campus, pp. 81-107

Glaser, Barney G. (1978), *Theoretical Sensibility*, Mill Valley, CA: Sociology Press

Goffman, Erwin (1971), *Presentation of the Self in Everyday Life*, Harmondsworth: Penguin

Goldberg, Barry (1992), »Historical Reflections on Transnationalism, Race, and the American Immigrant Saga«, in: Glick Schiller, Nina/ Basch, Linda/Blanc-Szanton, Cristina (eds), *Towards a Transnational Perspective on Migration. Race, Class, Ethnicity, and Nationalism Reconsidered*, New York: New York Academy of Science, pp. 201-217

Grande, Edgar (2001,) »Globalisierung und die Zukunft des Nationalstaats«, in: Beck, Ulrich/Bonß, Wolfgang (eds), *Die Modernisierung der Moderne*, Frankfurt a.M.: Suhrkamp, pp. 261-275

Grasmuck, Sherri/Pessar, Patricia B. (1991), *Between Two Islands: Dominican International Migration*, Berkely, CA.: University of California Press

Gregory, Derek (1989), »Presences and absences: time-space relations and structuration theory«, in: Held, David/Thompson, J.B. (eds), *Social theory of modern societies: Anthony Giddens and his critics*, Cambridge: Cambridge University Press, pp. 185-215

— (1994), *Geographical Imaginations*, Oxford: Blackwell Publishers

Gregory, Derek/Johnston, R. (2000) (eds), *Dictionary of human geography*, Oxford: Blackwell Publishers

— /Urry, John (1985) (eds), *Social Relations and Spatial Structures*, London: Macmillan Publishers

Grieco, Margret (1987), »Family networks and the closure of employment«, in: Lee, Gloria/Loveridge, Ray (eds), *The manufacture of disadvantage: stigma and social closure*, Milton Keynes: Open University Press, pp. 701-707

Grier, Michelle (2004), *Kant's Critique of Metaphisics*, in: Zalta, E.N. (ed.), *The Stanford Eycyclopedia of Philosophy* (Spring 2004 Edition), 24.07.2004, http://plato.stanford.edu/archives/spr2004/entries/kant-metaphysics

Groat, Linda (1995) (ed.), *Giving places meaning*, London: Academic Press

Grohmann, Heinz (1989), »Von der Kabinettstatistik zur Statistischen Infrastruktur«, *Allgemeines Statistisches Archiv*, Vol. 73, pp. 1-15

Gupta, Akhil (1997) (ed.), *Anthropological Locations: boundaries and grounds of a field science*, Berkley: University of California Press

— /Ferguson, John (1992), »Beyond Culture: Space, Identity and the Politics of Difference«, *Cultural Anthropology*, Vol. 7(1), pp. 6-23

Gustafson, Per (2001a), »Roots and Routs. Exploring the Relationship Between Place Attachment and Mobility«, *Environment and Behavior*, Vol. 33(5), pp. 667-686

— (2001b), »Meaning of place: everyday experience and theoretical conceptualizations«, *Journal of Environmental Psychology*, Vol. 21, pp. 5-16

Habermas, Jürgen (1992,) *Fakzitität und Geltung. Beiträge zur Diskurstheorie des Rechts und des demokratischen Rechtsstaates*, Frankfurt a.M.: Suhrkamp

Hage, Ghassan (1997), »At home in the entrails of the West«, in: Grace, Helen et. al, *Home/World: Space, Community and Marginality in Sydney's West*, Sydney: Pluto, pp. 99-153

Hagendijk, Rob (1999), »An Agenda for STS: Porter on Trust and Quantification in Science, Politics and Society«, *Social Studies of Science*, Vol. 29, pp. 629-637

Hannerz, Ulf (1996), *Transnational Connections, Culture, Power, Place*, London/New York: Sage

— (2003) *Foreign News*, Chicago: The University of Chicago Press

Hard, Gerhard (1970), »Die ›Landschaft‹ der Sprache und die ›Landschaft‹ der Geographen. Semantische und forschungslogische Studien zu einigen zentralen Denkfiguren in der deutschen geographischen Literatur«, *Colloquium Geographicum*, Vol. 11

Harré, Rom (1970), *The principles of Scientific Thinking*, Chicago: University of Chicago Press

Harvey, David (1982), *The Limits to Capital*, Oxford: Blackwell

— (1990), *The Condition of Postmodernity*, Cambridge/Oxford: Blackwell

— (1994), »Die Postmoderne und die Verdichtung von Raum und Zeit«, in: Kuhlmann, Andreas (ed.), *Philosophische Ansichten der Kultur der Moderne*, Frankfurt a.M.: Fischer Taschenbuch Verlag, pp. 48-78

— (1996), *Justice, nature and the geography of difference*, Oxford and Cambridge, MA: Blackwell

— (2001a), *Spaces of Capital: Towards a critical geography*, New York: Routledge

— (2001b), »Globalization and the ›Spatial fix‹«, *Geographische Revue*, No. 2, pp. 23-30

— (2003), *The New Imperialism*, Oxford: Oxford University Press

Hay, Robert (1998), »Sense of place in developmental context«, *Journal of Environmental Psychology*, Vol. 18, pp. 5-29

Health, Anthony (1981), *Social Mobility*, Cambridge: Fontana

Heller, Agnes (1995), »Where are we at home?«, *Thesis Eleven*, No. 41, pp.1-18

Helvacioglu, Banu (2000), »Globalization in the Neighborhood: From the Nation-State to Bilkent Center«, *International Sociology*, Vol. 15(2), pp. 326–342

Herbert, Ulrich (2005), *Europa in der Hochmoderne – ein historisches Periodisierungskonzept*, München: Beck Verlag

Herod, Andrew/O'Tuathail, Gearoid/Roberts, Susan (1998) (eds), *Unruly world? Globalization, governance and geography*, London: Routledge

Hetherington, Kevin (1997), »In place of geometry: the materiality of place«, in: Hetherington, Kevin (ed.), *Ideas of difference*, Oxford: Blackwell, pp. 183-199

Hiebert, Daniel (2002), »The spatial limits to enterpreneurship: Immigrant enterpreneurs in Canada«, *Tijdschrift voor Economische en Social Geografie*, Vol. 93(2), pp. 173-190

Hinchliffe, Steve (1997), »Home-made space and the will to disconnect«, in: Hetherington, Kevin (ed.), *Ideas of difference*, Oxford: Blackwell, pp. 200-219

Hoffmann-Riem, Christa (1980), »Die Sozialforschung einer interpretativen Soziologie - Der Datengewinn«, *Kölner Zeitschrift für Soziologie und Sozialpsychologie*, Vol. 32, pp. 339-372

Hopf, Christel (1995), »Qualitative Interviews in der Sozialforschung«, Flick, Uwe et.al, in: *Handbuch Qualitative Sozialforschung*, Weinheim: Beltz Psychologie Verlags Union, pp. 177-182

Houtum van, Henk/Naerssen van, Ton (2002), »Bordering, Ordering and Othering«, *Tijdschrift voor Economische en Sociale Geografie*, Vol. 93(2), pp. 125-136

— /Kramsch, Olivier/Zierhofer, Wolfgang (2005) (eds), *B/ordering space*, Aldershot: Ashgate

Hunter, Albert (1975), »The Loss of Community: An Empirical Test Through Replication«, *American Sociological Review*, Vol. 40(5), pp. 537-551

Hyndman, Jennifer (2000), *Managing Displacement: Refugees and the Politics of Humanitarianism*, Minneapolis: University of Minnesota Press

Immerfall, Stefan (1998) (ed.), *Territoriality in the Globalizing Society. One Place or None?*, Berlin-Heidelberg: Springer Verlag

Inglis, David/Bone, John (2006), »Boundary Maintenance, Border Crossing and the Nature/Culture Divide«, *European Journal of Social Theory*, Vol. 9(2), pp. 272-287

Jaffe J. Michael/Aidman Amy (1998), »Families, Geographical Separation, and the Internet. A Theoretical Prospectus«, in: Robertson, Ann S. (ed.) *Proceedings of the Families, Technology and Education Conference in Chicago, Illinois, USA, October 1997*, Champaign, Il: ERIC Clearinghouse, pp. 177-187

Jameson, Frederic (1984), »Postmodernism, or the cultural logic of late capitalism«, *New Left Review*, No. 146, pp. 53-92

— (1991) *Postmodernism. Or the cultural logic of late capitalism*, London: Verso

Jessop, Bob (2004), *Spatial Fixes, Temporal Fixes, and Spatio-Temporal Fixes*, Department of Sociology, Lancaster University, 02.10.2004, http://www.comp.lancs.ac.uk/sociology/papers/jessop-spatio-temporal-fixes.pdf

Johansson, Sten (1992), »Statistics in the Epistempology of the Democratic Process«, in : Hölder, Egon, Malaguerra Carlo, Vukowich, Gyorgy (eds), *Statistics in the Democratic Process at the End of the 20th Century*, Wiesbaden: Federal Statistical Office

Kaplan, Caren (1996), *Questions of travel*, Durham, NC: Duke University Press

Kaeble, Hartmut (1977), *Historical Research on Social Mobility*, Cambridge: Fontana

Kaufmann, Vincent (2002), *Re-thinking Mobility. Contemporary Sociology*, Aldershot: Ashgate

— /Bergman, Manfred M./Joye, Dominique (2004), »Motility: Mobility as Capital«, *International Journal of Urban and Regional Studies*, Vol. 28(4), pp. 745-756

Kearney, Michael (1995), »The local and the global: The anthropology of globalization and transnationalism«, *Annual Review of Anthropology*, No. 24, pp. 547-565

Kennedy, Paul (2002), *Everyday life under globalizing conditions – community, culture and place*, paper given at the GSA Conference *Globalization and Social Justice*, May 2002, Chicago

— (2004), »Making global society: frienship networks among transnational professionals in the building design industry«, *Global Networks*, Vol. 4(2), pp. 157-179

Kern, Stephen (1983), *The Culture of Time and Space, 1880-1914*, London: Weidenfeld&Nicolson

Kesselring, Sven (2001a), *Mobile Politik. Ein soziologischer Blick auf Verkehrspolitik in München*, Berlin: Edition Sigma

— (2001b), »Beweglichkeit ohne Bewegung«, *Die Mitbestimmung*, Vol. 9, pp. 10-14

— (2003), »Eine Frage der Logistik – Karrieren im Spannungsfeld von Mobilität und Flexibilität«, in: Hitzler, R., Pfadenhauer, M. (eds), *Karrierepolitik*, Opladen: Leske + Budrich, pp. 327-342

— /Vogl, Gerlinde (2004), *Mobility Pioneers. Networks, scapes and flows between first and second modernity*, Discussion paper presented to the Alternative Mobilities Futures Conference, 9-11 January 2004, Lancaster University, Lancaster, UK

Keupp, Heiner (2003), »Beheimatung als Identitätsarbeit in einer entgrenzten Welt«, *Politische Studien*, Sonderheft 2 *Heimat Bayern – Identität mit Tradition und Zukunft*, pp. 23-35

King, Anthony (1990), »Architecture, capital and the globalization of culture«, in: Featherstone, Mike (ed.), *Global culture: nationalism, globalization and modernity*, London: Sage, pp. 397-411

Kirby, Andrew (1998), »Wider die Ortslosigkeit«, in: Beck, Ulrich (ed.), *Perspektiven der Weltgesellschaft*, Frankfurt a.M.: Suhrkamp, pp. 168-175

Knippenberg, Hans (2002), »Assimilating Jews in Dutch nation-building: the missing ›pillar‹«, *Tijdschrift voor Economische en Sociale Geografie*, Vol. 93(2), pp. 191-207

Knorr-Cetina, Karin (2003), *Micro-Globalization: Towards a Theory of Social Globalization*, paper presented at the annual meetings of the Eastern Sociological Society, 28 February – 1 March, Philadelphia

Konau, Elisabeth (1977), *Raum und soziales Handeln*. Sttutgart: Enke

Konstan, David (2005), »Epicurus«, in: Zalta, E. (ed.) *Stanford Encyclopedia of Philosophy*, Spring 2005 Edition, 02.05.2005,http://plato.stanford.edu/archives/spr2005/entries/epicurus

Koren, John (1970) (ed.), *The History of Statistics. Their Development and Progress in Many Countries,* New York: Burt Franklin

Koyré, Alexandre (1957), *From the Closed World to the Infinite Universe*, Baltimore: John Hopkins University Press

König, René (1979), »Gesellschaftliches Bewußtsein und Soziologie«, *Kölner Zeitschrift für Soziologie und Sozialpsychologie*, Sonderausgabe »Deutsche Soziologie seit 1945«, pp. 358-370

Kuhn, Norbert (1994), *Sozialwissenschaftliche Raumkonzeptionen*, Saarbrücken: Universität Saarbrücken

Lamont, Michele/Aksartova, Sada (2002), »Ordinary Cosmopolitanism. Strategies for Bridging Racial Boundaries among Working-Class Men«, *Theory, Culture & Society*, Vol. 19(4), pp.1-25

Lash, Scott (2003), »Reflexivity as Non-linearity«, *Theory. Culture & Society*, Vol. 20 (2), pp. 79-57

— /Urry, John (1994), *Economies of Signs and Space*, London/Thousand Oaks/New Delhi: Sage

Latour, Bruno (1990), »Drawing things together«, in: Lynch, Michael/Woolgar, Steve (eds), *Representation in Scientific Practice*, Cambridge, MA: MIT Press, pp. 19-68

— (1991), »Technology is society made durable«, in: Law, John (ed.), *A sociology of monsters: Essays on Power, Technology and Domination*, London/New York: Routledge, pp.103-132

— (1995), *Wir sind nie modern gewesen,* Berlin: Akademie-Verlag

— (1996), »Social theory and the study of computerized work sites«, in: Orlikowski, Wanda J./Walsham, Geoff/Jones, Matthew R./DeGros, Janice I. (eds), *Information Technology and Changes in Organizational Work*, London: Chapman&Hall, pp. 295-307

— (2003), »Is Re-modernization Occuring – And If So, How to Prove It? A Commentary on Ulrich Beck«, *Theory, Culture & Society*, Vol. 20 (2), pp. 35-48

Law, John (1986), »On the methods of long-distance control: vessels, navigation and the Portuguese route to India«, in: Law, John (ed.), *Power, Action and Belief*, London/Boston/Henley: Routledge & Kegan Paul, pp. 234-263

— (1992), »Notes on the Theory of the Actor-Network: Ordering, Strategy, and Heterogeneity«, *Systems Practice*, Vol. 5(4), pp. 379-393

— (1997) *Traduction/Trahison: Notes on ANT.* 02.06.2002, http://www.comp.lancs.ac.uk/sociology/stslaw2.html, Department of Sociology, Lancaster University

— (2000a), »Tansitivities«, *Environment and Planning D: Society and Space,* Vol. 8, pp. 133-148

— (2000b),*Objects, Spaces, Others,* draft manuscript, Centre for Science Studies, Department of Sociology, University of Lancaster, 10.03.2003, http://www/comp.lancs.ac.uk/sociology/soc027jl.html

Läpple, Dieter (1991), »Gesellschaftszentriertes Raumkonzept. Zur Überwindung von Physikalisch-Mathematischen Raumauffassungen in der Gesellschafts-analyse«, in: Wentz, Martin (ed.), *Stadt-Räume*, Frankfurt a.M.: Campus Verlag, pp. 35-46

Leeds, Anthony (1973), »Locality Power in Relation to Supralocal Power Institutions«, in: Southall, Aidan (ed.), *Urban Anthropology. Cross-Cultural Studies of Urbanization*, New York: Oxford University Press, pp. 15-41

Lefebvre, Henri (1970 [2003]), *The urban revolution*, Minneapolis, MN: University of Minnesota Press

— (1991) *The production of space*, Oxford/Cambridge, MA: Blackwell

— (1996) *Writings on Cities*, Oxford: Blackwell

Levinas, Emmanuel (1982 [1991]), »Wholly Otherwise«, in: Bernasconi, Robert/Critchey, Simon (eds), *Re-Reading Levinas,* Bloomington, IA: Indiana University Press, p. 3-10

Löw, Martina (1995) *Geschlecht, Körper und Raum. Neuere Diskussion in der Frauenforschung,* in: *Frei-Räume,* No. 8, pp. 172-181

— (2001) *Raumsoziologie,* Frankfurt a.M.: Suhrkamp

Maarseveen van, Jacques/Gircour, MBG (1999) *A Century of Statistics. Counting, accounting and recounting in the Nertherlands,* Amsterdam: Stichting beheer IISG

Mackensen, Reiner (1975) *Probleme regionaler Mobilität,* Berlin: Schwartz (Kommission für wirtschaftlichen und sozialen Wandel 19)

Malkki, Liisa .H. (1997) *National Geographic: The Rooting of Peoples and the Territorialization of National Identity among Scholars and Refugees,* in: Ferguson, John (ed.), *Culture, Power, Place: Explorations in Critical Anthropology,* Durham: Duke University Press, pp. 52-74

Manderson, Desmond (2006), *Proximity, Levinas and the Soul of Law,* Kingston, ON: McGill Queens University Press

Marshall, Gordon (1998) (ed.), *Oxford Dictionary of Sociology,* Oxford/New York: Oxford University Press

Martins, Herminio (1974), »Time and Theory in Sociology«, in: Rex, John A. (ed.) *Approaches to sociology: an introduction to major trends in British sociology,* London/Boston: Routledge & Kegan Paul, pp. 246-294

Martins, Mario Ru (1982), »The Theory of Social Space in the Work of Henri Lefebvre«, in: Forrest, Ray/Henderson, Jeff/Willaims, Peter W., *Urban Political Economy and Social Theory. Critical Essays in Urban Studies,* Aldershot: Gower, pp. 160-183

Marx, Karl (1973) *Grundrisse. Foundations of the Critique of Political Economy,* Harmondsworth: Penguin Books

Massey, Doreen (1994), *Space, Place and Gender,* Cambridge: Polity

— (1995), »The conceptualization of place«, in: Massey, Doreen/Jess, Pat (eds), *A Place in the World? Places, Cultures and Globalization,* Oxford: Open University/Oxford University Press, pp. 45-77

— (2005), *For Space,* London: Spage

— /Allen, John/Sarre, Philip (1999), *Human geography today,* Cambridge: Polity Press

Michalski, Krzysztof (1978), *Heidegger i filozofia współczesna,* Warszawa: PIW

Mol, Annemarie/Law, John (1994), »Regions, Networks and Fluids: Anaemia and Social Topology«, *Social Studies of Science,* Vol. 24, pp. 641-671

— (2000), *Situating Technoscience: an Inquiry into Spatialities,* published by the Centre for Science Studies, Lancaster University, Lancaster UK, 23.01.2004, http://www.comp.lancs.ac.uk/sociology/papers/Law-Mol-Situating-Technoscience.pdf

Moulaert, F. (2003) (ed.), *The globalized city. Economic restructuring and social polarization in European cities,* Oxford: Oxford University Press

Neuberger, Oswald (1995), *Mikropolitik. Der alltägliche Aufbau und Einsatz von Macht in Organisationen*, Stuttgart: Enke

Nkosi, Lewis (1994), »Ironies of Exile: Post-colonial Homelessness and the Anticlimax of Return«, *Times Literary Supplement* 4748, p. 5

Oakes, Tim S. (1993), »Ethnic tourism and place identity in China«, *Environment and Planning D: Society and Space*, Vol. 11, pp. 47-66

Oevermann, Ulrich (1983) »Zur Sache. Die Bedeutung von Adornos methodologischem Selbsverständnis für die Begründung einer materialen soziologischen Strukturanalyse«, in: Habermas, Jürgen/Friedeburg, von Ludwig (eds), *Adorno-Konferenz 1983*, Frankfurt a.M.: Suhrkamp, pp. 234-289

Ohmae, Keinichi (1992) *The Borderless World*, London: Fontana

Ong, Aihwa/Nonini, Donald (1997) (eds), *The Cultural Politics of Modern Chinese Transnationalism*, New York: Routledge

Papastergiadis, Nikos (2000), *The turbulence of Migration. Globalization, Deterritorialization and Hybridity*, Malden, MA, Cambridge: Polity Press

Paulu, Constanze (2001), *Mobilität und Karriere*, Wiesbaden: Deutscher Universitäts-Verlag

Pelizäus-Hoffmeister, Helga (2001), *Mobilität: Chance oder Risiko? Der Einfluss beruflicher Mobilität auf soziale Netzwerke - das Beispiel freie JournalistInnen*, Opladen: Leske + Budrich

Pohl, Jürgen (1993), »Kann es eine Geographie ohne Raum geben? Zum Verhältnis von Theoriediskussion und Disziplinpolitik«, *Erdkunde*, No. 47, pp. 255-267

Polanyi, Karl (1973), *The Great Transformation*, New York: Octagon Books

Portes, Alejandor/Sensenbrenner, Julia (1993), »Embeddedness and Immigration: Notes on the Social Determinants of Economic Action«, *American Journal of Sociology*, No. 98, pp. 1320-1350

Pott, Andreas (2002) *Ethnizität und Raum im Aufstigsprozeß*, Opladen: Leske+Budrich

Pries, Ludger (1997), *Transnationale Migration*, Sonderband 12 der Zeitschrift *Soziale Welt*, Baden-Baden: Nomos

— (1998) »Transnationale Soziale Räume. Theoretisch-empirische Skizze am Beispiel der Arbeitswanderungen Mexiko-USA«, in: Beck, Ulrich (ed.) *Perspektiven der Weltgesellschaft*, Frankfurt a.M.: Suhrkamp, pp.55-87

— (2000) (ed.), *New Transnational Social Spaces. International Migration and Transnational Companies*, London: Routledge

— (2001), *Internationale Migration*, Bielefeld: transcript Verlag

Putnam, Robert D. (2000), *Bowling Alone: The Collapse and Revival of American Community*, New York: Simon and Schuster

Rapport, Nigel (1994), »»Busted for Hush«: Common Catchwords and Individual Identities in a Canadian City«, in: Amit-Talai, Vered/Lustiger-Thaler, Henri (eds), *Urban Lives. Fragmentation and Resistance*, Toronto: McClelland & Stewart

— /Dawson, Andrew (1998), »Home and Movement: A Polemic«, in: Rapport, Nigel/Dawson, Andrew (eds), *Migrants of Identity. Perceptions of Home in a World of Movement*, Oxford: Berg, pp. 19-38

Rawlins, William K. (1992), *Friendship Matters: Communication, dialectics, and the life course*, New York: Aldine de Gruyter

— (1994), »Being There and Growing Apart. Sustaining Friendships during Adulthood«, in: Canary, Daniel J./Stafford, Laura (eds), *Communication and Relational Maintenance*, San Diego: Academic Press, pp. 275-294

Relph, Edward (1976), *Place and placelessness*, London: Pion

Ritter, Joachim (1982) (ed.), *Historisches Wörterbuch der Philosophie*. Basel: Schwabe & Co Ag Verlag

Ritzer, George/Murphy, James (2002), »Festes in einer Welt des Flusses: Die Beständigkeit der Moderne in einer zunehmend postmodernen Welt«, in: Junge Matthias/Kron, Thomas (eds), *Zygmunt Bauman. Soziologie zwischen Postmoderne und Ethik*, Opladen: Leske + Budrich, pp. 51-80

Robertson, Roland (1992), *Globalization: Social Theory and Global Culture*, London: Sage

— (1998), *Glokalisierung: Homogenität und Heterogenität in Raum und Zeit*, in: *Perspektiven der Weltgesellschaft*, Beck, Ulrich (ed.), Frankfurt a.M.: Suhrkamp, pp. 192-220

Rodriguez, Nestor (1999), »The Battle for the Border: Notes on Autonomous Migration, Transnational Communities, and the State«, in: Jonas, Susanne/Dod Thomas, Suzie (eds), *Immigration: A Civil Rights Issue for the Americas*, Wilmington, DE: Scholarly Resources, pp. 27-43

Rojek, Chris/Urry, John (1997), *Touring cultures: Transformations of travel and theory*, London: Routledge

Roudometof, Victor (2003), »Glocalization, Space and Modernity«, *The European Legacy*, Vol. 8(1), pp. 37–60

Rouse, Roger (1991), »Mexican Migration and the Social Space of Postmodernism«, *Diaspora*, No. 1, pp.8-23

Rumford, Chris (2006), »Introduction. Theorizing Borders«, *European Journal of Social Theory*, Vol. 9(2), pp. 155-169

Rundell, John (2004), »Strangers, Citizens and Outsiders: Otherness, Multiculturalism and the Cosmopolitan Imaginary in Mobile Societies«, *Thesis Eleven*, No. 78, pp.85-101

Rushdie, Salman (1983), *Shame*, London: Jonathan Cape

Rynasiewicz, Robert (1995) »By Their Properties, Causes and Effects: Newton's Scholium on Time, Space, Place and Motion«, in: *Studies in History and Philosophy of Science 26, Part I: The Text*, pp. 133-153, and "*Part II: The Context*, pp. 295-321

Sack, Robert David (1980), *Conceptions of Space in Social Thought: A Geographic Perspective*, London: Macmillan

— (1986), *Human Terrritoriality. Its theory and history*, Cambridge: Cambridge University Press

Said, Edward (1979 [2000]),»Zionism from the standpoint of its victims«, in: Said, Edward, *Edward Said Reader*, New York: Vintage, pp. 114-168

Salamandra, Christa (2002),»Globalization and Cultural Mediation: The Construction of Arabia in London«, *Global Networks*, Vol. 2(4), pp. 285-300

Salt, John (1997), *International Movements of the Highly-Skilled*, OECD International Migration Unit Occassional Paper No. 3

Sassen, Saskia (1991), *The Global City: New York, London, Tokyo*, Princeton: Princeton University Press

— (1994), *Cities in a World Economy*, Thousand Oaks: Pine Forge Press

— (1996), *De-facto transnationalizing of immigration policy*, Florence: Robert Schuman Center Papers

— (1998), *Globalization and its Discontents. Essays on the New Mobility of People and Money*, New York: The New York Press

Sayer, Andrew (1984), *Method in Social Science*, London: Hutchinson

— (1985),»The Difference that Space Makes«, in: Gregory, Derek/Urry, John (eds), *Social Relations and Spatial Structures*, London: Macmillan Publishers, pp. 49-66

— (1991),»Behind the locality debate: deconstructing geography's dualisms«, *Environment and Planning A*, No. 23, pp. 283-308

Schiedeck, Jürgen/Stahlmann, Martin (1999) *Heimatlos im Global Village*, in: *Brückenschlag*, Vol. 15, pp. 79-85

Schneider, Norbert/Limmer, Ruth/Ruckdeschel, Kerstin (2002) *Mobil, flexibel, gebunden. Beruf und Familie in der mobilen Gesellschaft*, Frankfurt a.M: Campus

Schuhmann, Karl (2004) *Selected papers on Renaissance philosophy and on Thomas Hobbes*, Heidelberg: Springer

Schwartzman, Helen (1989), *The Meeting*, New York/London: Plenum

Scott, James (1998), *Seeing like a State: How Certain Schemes to Improve the Human Condition Have Failed*, New Haven, London: Yale Universtity Press

Sennett, Richard (1994), *Flesh and Stone: The Body and the city in Western Civilization*, New York: St.Martin's Press

— (1995), *Fleisch und Stein. Der Körper und die Stadt in der westlichen Zivilisation*, Berlin: Berlin Verlag

— (1998), *Der flexible Mensch*, Berlin: Berlin Verlag

Sheller, Mimi (2003), *Consuming the Caribbean: from Arawaks to Zombies*, London and New York: Routledge

Shields, Robert (1991), *Places on the margin. Alternative geographies of modernity*, London and New York: Routledge

— (1992),»A truant proximity: presence and absence in the space of modernity«, *Environment and Planning D: Society and Space*, No. 10, pp. 181-198

— (1999) *Lefebvre, Love and Struggle. Spatial dialectics*, London/New York: Routledge

Short, John Rennie (1999)»Foreword«, in: *At home. Space, place and society*, Cieraad, Irene (ed.), Syracuse N.Y.: Syracuse University Press

Shove, Elisabeth (2002), *Rushing around: coordination, mobility and inequality*, ESRC Mobile Network Meeting October, draft paper

Simmel, Georg (1908), »Exkurs über den Fremde«,, in: Simmel, Georg, *Soziologie. Untersuchungen über die Formen der Vergesellschaftung.*, Berlin: Duncker & Humblot Verlag, pp. 509-512
— (1909), »Brücke und Tür«, in: *Der Tag. Moderne illustrerter Zeitung,* No. 683, Morgenblatt, Berlin 15 September 1909, Illustrierter Teil No. 216, pp. 1-3
— (1958), *Soziologie. Untersuchungen über die Formen der Vergesellschaftung,* Berlin: Duncker & Humblot
— (1983[1903]), »Soziologie des Raumes«, in: Dahme, Heinz-Jürgen/Rammstedt, Otthein (eds), *Georg Simmel. Schriften zur Soziologie. Eine Auswahl,* Frankfurt a.M.: Suhrkamp, pp. 221-242
Sigman, Stuart J. (1991), »Handling the discontinuous aspects of continuing social relationships: toward research on the persistence of social forms«, *Communication Theory,* No. 1, pp. 106-127
Singleton, Vicky/Michael, Mike (1993), »Actor-networks and Ambivalence: General Practitioners in the UK Cervical Screening Programme«, *Social Studies of Science,* No. 23, pp. 227-264
Smelser, Neil J. (2003), »Pressures for Continuity in the Context of Globalization«, *Current Sociology,* Vol. 51(2), pp. 101-112
Smith, Anthony D. (1983), »Nationalism and Social Theory«, *British Journal of Sociology,* No. 34, pp. 19-38
Smith, Neil (1984), U*neven development: nature, capital and the production of space,* Oxford and Cambridge, MA: Blackwell
Soja, Edward W. (1989), *Postmodern Geographies,* Cambridge MA:
— (1995), »Heteropologies: A remembrance of Other spaces in the Citadel-LA«, in: Gibson, Catherine/Watson, Sophie (eds.), *Postmodern Cities & Spaces,* Cambridge, MA: Blackwell Publishers, pp. 13-34
— (1996), *Thirdspace. Journeys to Los Angeles and other real and imagined spaces,* Malden MA, Oxford UK: Blackwell
Southerton, Dale/Shove, Elizabeth/Warde, Alan (2001), ›*Harried and Hurried‹: time shortage and the co-ordination of everyday life,* CRIC Discussion Paper No 47, University of Manchester, UK
Spaan, Ernst et al. (2002), »Re-imagining Borders: Malay Identity and Indonesian Migrants in Malaysia«, *Tijdschrift voor Economische en Sociale Geografie,* Vol. 93(2), pp. 160-172
Strathern, Marilyn (1992), *Reproducing the Future: Anthropology, Kinship and the New Reproductive Technologies,* Manchester: Manchester University Press
— (1996), »Cutting the Network«, *Journal of the Royal Anthropological Institute,* No. 2, pp. 517-535
Strauss, Anselm (1987), *Qualitative analysis for social scientists,* New York: Cambridge University Press
— /Corbin, Juliet (1996), *Grounded Theory: Grundlagen Qualitativer Sozialforschung,* Wienheim: Beltz Psychologie Verlags Union
Sturm, Gabriele (2000), *Wege zum Raum,* Opladen: Leske+Budrich

Thompson, John B. (1989),»The theory of structuration«, in: Held, David/Thompson, John B. (eds), *Social theory of modern societies: Anthony Giddens and his critics*, Cambridge: Cambridge University Press, pp. 56-76

Thrift, Nigel (1996), *Spatial Formations*, Thousand Oaks/New Dehli: Sage

— (1999),»The place of complexity«, *Theory, Culture & Society*, Vol. 16(3), pp. 31-69

— (2004), *Movement-Space: the development of new kinds of spatial awareness*, Paper presented to the Alternative Mobilites Conference, University of Lancaster, January 9-11, Lancaster, UK

Tickamyer, Ann R. (2000) »Space Matters! Spatial Inequality in Future Sociology«, *Contemporary Sociology*, Vol. 29(6), pp. 805-813

Tomlinson, John (1999) *Globalization and Culture*, Chicago: University of Chicago Press

Trusted, Jennifer (1991) *Physics and Metaphysics. Theories of Space and Time*, London and New York: Routledge

Urry, John (1987), »Survey 12: Society, Space and Locality«, *Environment and Planning D: Society and Space*, Vol. 5, pp. 436-444

— (2000a), *Sociology beyond Societies. Mobilities for the twenty-first century*, London and New York: Routledge

— (2000b),»Mobile Sociology«, *British Journal of Sociology*, Vol. 51(1), pp. 185-203

— (2002),»Mobility and Proximity«, *Sociology*, No. 36, pp. 255-274

— (2003), *Global Complexity*, Cambridge/ Malden MA: Polity Press

— (2004),»Small worlds and the new ›social physics‹«, *Global Networks*, Vol. 4(2), pp. 109-130

Velde van der, Martin (2000),»Shopping, Space and Borders«, in: Velde van der, Martin/Houtum van, Henk (eds), *Borders, Regions, and People*, London: Pion, pp. 166-181

Vertovec, Steven/Cohen, Robin (1999)(eds), *Migration, diasporas and transnationalism*, Cheltenham: Edward Elgar Publishing

Viehöver, Willy/Gugutzer, Robert/Keller, Reiner/Lau, Christoph (2004), »Vergesellschaftung der Natur – Naturalisierung der Gesellschaft«, in: Beck, Ulrich/Lau, Christoph (eds), *Entgrenzung und Entscheidung*, Frankfurt a.M.: Surhkamp, pp. 65-94

Virilio, Paul (1989), *Der negative Horizont*, München/Wien: Carl Hauser Verlag

— (1991), *La Vitesse*, Paris: Éditions Falmmarion

— (1992), *Rasender Stillstand*, München/Wien: Carl Hauser Verlag

— (1993), *Revolutionen der Geschwindigkeit*, Berlin: Merve Verlag

— (1995), *La Vitesse de libération*, Paris: Galilée

Warren, Daniel (1998),»Kant and the Aproprity of Space«, *The Philosophical Review*, No. 107, pp. 179-224

Weichhart, Peter (1993),»Mikroanalytische Ansätze der Sozialgeographie - Leitlinien und Perspektiven der Entwicklung«, in: Petermühler-Strobl,

Monika/Stötter, Johann (eds), *Der Geograph im Hochgebirge. Beiträge zur Theorie und Praxis geographischer Forschung*, Innsbrucker Geographische Studien 20, pp. 101-116

Werlen, Benno (1993), »Gibt es eine Geographie ohne Raum? Zum Verhältnis von traditioneller Geographie und zeitgenössischen Gesellschaften«, *Erdkunde*, Vol. 47(4), pp. 241-255

— (1995), »Landschaft, Raum und Gesellschaft. Entstehungs- und Entwicklungsgeschichte wissenschaftlicher Sozialgeographie«, *Geographische Rundschau*, No. 9, pp. 513-522

— (2004), »The Making of Globalized Everyday Geographies«, in: Bærenholdt, J.O., Simonsen, K. (eds) *Space Odysseys. Spatiality and Social Relations in the 21st century*, Aldershot: Ashgate, pp. 153-67

Westman, Bror (1991), »What does it mean to feel at home?«, in: GrØn, O./Engelstad, E./Lindblom, I., *Social space. Human Spatial Behaviour in Dwellings and Settlements*, Odense University Studies in History and Social Sciences Vol. 147, Odense: Odense University Press, pp. 17-20

Wilpert, Czarina (1992), »The Use of Social Networks in Tukish Migration to Germany«, in: Kritz, Mary M./Lim, Lin Lean/Zlotnik, Hania (eds), *International Migration Systems*, Oxford: Clarendon Press, pp. 177-189

Wimmer, Andreas (1996), »Kultur. Zur Reformulierung eines sozialanthropologischen Grundbegriffs«, *Kölner Zeitschrift für Soziologie und Sozialpsychologie*, Vol. 48(3), pp. 401-425

— /Glick Schiller, Nina (2002), »Methodological nationalism and beyond: nation-state building, migration and the social sciences«, *Global Networks*, Vol. 2(4), pp. 301-334

Witzel, Andreas (1982), *Verfahren der qualitativen Sozialforschung*, Frankfurt a.M.: Campus Verlag

— (1985), »Das Problemzentrierte Interview«, in: Jüttermann, Gerd (ed.), *Qualitative Forschung in der Psychologie. Grundfragen, Verfahrensweisen, Anwendungsfelder*, Weinheim: Beltz

— (2000), »The Problem-Centered Interviews«, *Forum: Qualitative Social Research*, Vol. 1(1), 14.01.2002, http://www.qualitative-research.net/fqs-texte/1-00/1-00witzel-e.htm

Yuval-Davis, Nira (2004), »Borders, Boundaries and the Politics of Belonging», in: May, Stephen/Madood, Tariq/Squires, Judith (eds), *Ethnicity, Nationalism and Minority Rights*, Cambridge: Cambridge University Press, pp. 214-230

Zalta, Edward N. (2004) Stanford Encyclopedia of Philosophy, Fall 2004 Edition, 22.11.2004, http://plato.stanford.edu/contents.html

Zapf, Wolfgang (1993), »Entwicklung und Sozialstruktur moderner Gesellschaften«, in: Korte, H., Schäfers, B. (eds), *Einführung in Hauptbegriffe der Soziologie*, Opladen: Leske u. Budrich, pp. 181-194

— (1998),»Modernisierung und Transformation«, in: Schäfers, B., Zapf, W. (eds), *Handwörterbuch zur Gesellschaft Deutschlands*, Opladen: Leske + Budrich, pp. 472-482

Zolberg, Aristide R./Smith, Robert C. (1996), *Migration Systems in Comparative Perspective. An Analysis of the Inter-American Migration System with Comparative Reference to the Mediteranean-European System*, New York: The New School for Social Reserach

Zorn, Wolfgang (1977) »Verdichtung und Beschleunigung des Verkehrs asl Beitrag zur Entwicklung der ›modernen Welt««, in: Koselleck, Reinhart. (ed.), *Studien zum Beginn der modernen Welt*, Stuttgart: Klett-Cotta, pp. 115-134

Zürn, Michael (1998), *Regieren jenseits des Nationalstaates. Globalisierung und Denationalisierung*, Frankfurt a.M.: Suhrkamp

Annex A. Interview Design

Before the interview, make a short statement about the project. Explain that the interview will be about 1.5 to 2 hours long, and that anonymity will be ensured. The material will be analyzed anonymously. The data will be coded: nobody will be able to learn the real name of the interviewee, nor the names of places/people mentioned by her/him. If he/she so wishes, the interviewee can obtain a transcript of the interview and the general results of the study.

For me, it is important to understand how you see things. So you can tell me anything you want to, whatever comes to mind on this topic. Do not hesitate to ask if you do not understand my questions, or if something is not clear. I will ask you additional questions if something is not clear to me, or if I want to know more. Do not be irritated if I do not say much. For me, the most interesting thing is what you have to say.

How to read the interview manual.

– Marked with a star: Questions which must be asked
– Marked with a double arrow: Additional questions that are important
– Marked with dots: Questions to be asked only if an interviewee has problems with speaking out, or gives unduly short answers or needs some context
– Underlined: Other important additional support questions
– Text in italics: For interviewer only
– Text in frame: General topics to be covered in the interview

Part I: Organization of work and business mobility

* For me, it is important to understand what your daily life looks like, and how you spend your time, both at work and after work. **Could you tell me how you come to be working for the IO?**

⇨ What did you do before the IO?
  • Did you particularly want to work for the IO?

⇨ What does your work concern?
  • Do you work alone?
  • Do you supervise the work of others?

* **Do you make business trips? If yes, can you tell me what they are like?**

⇨ Could you describe your current/latest/ trip?
  • How long did the journey take ?
  • Did you travel alone?
  • Which means of transportation means did you use?
  • Did someone back you up while you were away?
  • How did you organize your trip?
  • Did you prepare yourself in some way for the trip?
  • Were there any formalities that you had to take care of?
  • Where did you stay while abroad?
  • What did your stay abroad look like?

⇨ Have you ever experienced anything extraordinary or completely unexpected on your trips? / Did you experience anything extraordinary or completely unexpected on your trip?

⇨ How do you spend your time at airports or stations, or while stuck in a traffic jam?

⇨ Do you have any spare time while abroad?
  • What do you do then?

Depending on the course of the conversation, the next questions should relate to either family, private mobility or communication and contacts with friends.

Mobility in private life	Communication and social networks at work	Organization of family
Do you travel in your private life?	**During your business trips, do you contact friends?**	**When you are abroad, who cares for the house?**

Part II: Mobility in private life

* Do you also travel a lot in your private life, with family or friends?

⇨ Please tell me about your most recent holiday.
- What are your favourite destinations?
- What are your favourite activities while on holiday?
- Do you organize your trips yourself?
- How long do your holidays last?
- With whom do you spend your holidays?
- Do you like visiting new places?
- Do you make new friends while on holiday?

Possible passage to social networks in private life and communication:

⇨ When on holiday, do you stay in contact with your friends?

Part III: Communication and social networks in private life

* How do you maintain contact with your friends?
- Are you still in contact with your friends from school or university? If not, why not?
- Do you know your neighbours?
- When you move to another country/town, do you try to maintain contact with your friends?

- Do you update your friends regularly on new events in your life?
- Do you make many new friends?
- How do you get to know new friends?

Possible passage to communication and social networks in private life:

⇨ Do you make friends at work?

Part IV: Communication and social networks at work place

* Please tell me about your co-workers and your relations with them

- Who do you work with?
- Where are they located?
- How do you contact them?
- Do you meet these people outside work?
- How can your co-workers reach you outside the office?
- How well do you know your co-workers?

Part V: Organization of private/family life

* Can you tell me more about your family?
Perhaps you have photos of your nearest and dearest with you?
- Do you have children?
- Does your wife/husband work?
- Who cares for the children?
- Do you support your partner in housekeeping?

If the interviewee in single:
* How do you manage your housekeeping?
- Do you do all the shopping yourself?

* How do you spend your spare time?
- Do you like spending time at home?
- Do you go out?

- What kind of hobbies do you have?
- Do you like reading? If yes, what?
- Do you like watching TV? If yes, what programs do you watch?

Possible passage to technology use:

⇨   Do you use a computer at home?

Part IV: Technology use at home and at the work place

Questions in this section should be asked only when the interviewee has not provided enough information on technology use in the previous sections of the interview.

* Do you use a computer at home?

- What do you use it for?
- Do you have a private e-mail address?

⇨   What is your relation to the new media and technology?
- Do you try to keep up to date with the newest technologies?
- How do these technologies influence your daily life?
- Has anything changed for you personally as a result of technical progress?

⇨   Which new technologies do you use in the office?
- Do you find them useful?
- Do you any have experience with video conferencing?

Corrections, changes and additional questions:

Interviews 2-5
The new questions include those on IO support while settling in a new residence place or during travel. On the other hand, these interviews were conducted more openly, and the individuals were asked fewer questions from the list, so that the questions tended to follow the inner logic of their

story. Such questions as »Tell me about your most interesting trip« encourage the interviewees to talk about the unexpected experiences, problems and gratifications related to mobility.

Interviews 6-10
More specific questions were added:
Do your counterparts from different projects know each other?
Do you talk about your work at home?
Do you think your physical presence is necessary?

At the same time, certain questions were no longer relevant, or had already been fully explored. For example, most of the questions in Part IV, relating to the use of technology at office and at home, were dropped.

The interview thus focused more on the relationship with the destinations of mobility and the construction of private spaces. The questions focused on where the individuals feel at home, their favorite places, where they like to spend their leisure time, where they would like to live when retired, etc. but also where they shop, etc. In this phase, the interviews placed more emphasis on the temporal dimension of mobility practices: for example, they addressed the individuals' plans for the future, and retrospection.

Which place is most important to you, and why?
Is there one place that you always want to go to, a central/favourite place?
Where is your home?
Where do you usually do your shopping?
What are your plans for the future?
What are your dreams?

Interviews 10-13
The last two interviews were again more limited and focused on the individuals' experiences in different locations and, in particular, with different and familiar elements. The interviewees were asked to describe in detail their daily routines in two different places, for example, the current and previous places of residence, or place of residence and the destination of a business trip. They were also encouraged to talk about the most interesting and the most boring sides of traveling.

Tell me about your experience in a foreign country? What does your daily life there look like? What differences and similarities are there in comparison to your home country/other countries? How does it relate to your business life and private life?

Annex B. Questionnaire

Interview Nr. ....

Date ....

1. **How old are you?**

   ....

2. **Where were you born?**

   ....

3. **What is your sex?**
   Male   ○
   Female   ○

4. **What is your citizenship?**

   ....

Education and Job

5. **What is your current job position (title)?**

   ....

6. **For what occupation did you train?**

   ....

7. **What training or qualifications are/were needed for the job?**

   ....:....................

8.   **In your job, what kind of work do you do most of the time?**

     ....

9.   **To which of the following levels are you educated?**

     Not completed primary (compulsory) education   ○
     Primary education or first stage of basic education   ○
     Lower level secondary education or second stage
     of basic education   ○
     Upper secondary education (gymnasium, etc.)   ○
     Post-secondary, non-tertiary education   ○
     First stage of tertiary education (MA, MSc)   ○
     Second stage of tertiary education (Ph.D. or other)   ○
     Other   ....

10. **What level of education did your parents achieve?**

	Father	Mother
Primary (compulsory) education not completed	○	○
Primary education or first stage of basic education	○	○
Lower level secondary education or second stage of basic education	○	○
Upper secondary education (gymnasium, etc.)	○	○
Post-secondary, non-tertiary education	○	○
First stage of tertiary education (MA, MSc)	○	○
Second stage of tertiary education (Ph.D. or other)	○	○
Other	....	

Household

11. **How many times did you change your place of residence (town)?**

     Before your 18th birthday?   ....
     After your 18th birthday?   ....

12. **Which phrase best describes the area where you live?**

A big city　　　　　　　　　　　　　　　　　　　○
The suburbs or outskirts of a big city　　　　　○
A town or a small city　　　　　　　　　　　　　○
A country village　　　　　　　　　　　　　　　○
A farm or home in the countryside　　　　　　　○

13. **Do you have a...?**

　　　　　　　　　　　　　　　　　　　　　　Number

Flat　　　　　　　　　　○　　　　　　　........
House　　　　　　　　　　○　　　　　　　........
Holiday house　　　　　　○　　　　　　　........
other　　　　..

14. **Size of living place.**

How many m2 has your house/flat?　　　　　........
How many people live in it?　　　　　　　　　........

15. **How long have you lived in your present home?**

1 year or less　　　　　　　　　　　　　　○
From 1 year to 3 years　　　　　　　　　　○
From 3 years to 5 years　　　　　　　　　　○
From 5 years to 10 years　　　　　　　　　○
Over 10 years　　　　　　　　　　　　　　○ .

16. **Which of these descriptions applies to your current marital status?**

　　　　　　　　　　　　　　　　　Yes　　Since when
I am married　　　　　　　　　　　　○　　.....................
I have a steady life partner　　　　　○　　.....................
I am divorced　　　　　　　　　　　○　　.....................
I am a widower　　　　　　　　　　　○　　.....................
I have never been married　　　　　　○　　.....................

If you have no partner, go to question 21!

17. **What level of education did your spouse/partner achieve?**

Primary (compulsory) education not completed ○

Primary education or first stage of basic education ○

Lower level secondary education or second stage
of basic education ○

Upper secondary education (gymnasium, etc.) ○

Post-secondary, non-tertiary education ○

First stage of tertiary education (MA, MSc) ○

Second stage of tertiary education (Ph.D. or other) ○

Other ....

18. **What is the occupation of your spouse/partner?**

....

19. **Is your spouse/partner**

Employed full-time? ○

Employed part-time? ○

Working at home? ○

Unemployed? ○

Looking for a job? ○

Studying (also vocational)? ○

Permanently sick or disabled? ○

Retired? ○

Doing housework, looking after children? ○

Other? ....

20. **What is her/his main job?**

....

21. **Do you have children (including adopted and of your spouse only)?**

Yes ○

No ○

If you do not have children, go to question 25!

22. How old are your children?

	1. Child	2. Child	3. Child	4. Child
	....	....	....	....

23. Where do the children live?

	1. Child	2. Child	3. Child	4. Child
With me	○	○	○	○
With the other parent	○	○	○	○
Alone	○	○	○	○
Other	....	....	....	....

24. Who regularly has charge of the children?

	1. Child	2. Child	3. Child	4. Child
Children are already self-sufficient	○	○	○	○
Kindergarden (half day)	○	○	○	○
Kindergarden (full day)	○	○	○	○
School (half day)	○	○	○	○
School (full day)	○	○	○	○
Other institutions	○	○	○	○
Baby sitter	○	○	○	○
Family, cousins, friends	○	○	○	○
Only parents	○	○	○	○

Travel and technology

25. Which of these items do you use?

	private	business stationary in your office	when on a trip
Telephone	O	O	O
Mobile phone	O	O	O
PC	O	O	O
Laptop	O	O	O
Palmtop/Organizer	O	O	O
E-mail connection	O	O	O
TV	O	O	O
Radio	O	O	O
Car	O	O	O
Motorbike	O	O	O

Other:

private ....

in the office ....

on business trip ....

Thank you a lot for your help!

Annex C. Transcription rules

1. All names of interviewees, as well as the names of places and people mentioned in the interviews, are in general fictitious. The names used in the transcribed interviews are not the respondents' real names. However, as it was suspected that geographical location, for example, country of origin or destination, might play a role in how the interviewees perceived their mobility and re-settlement, geographical names were changed in such way that the region of the world of origin or destination corresponded to the real situation (for example, Africa).

2. (I2: 45) is to be read as Interview 2, passage 45. Passage numbers correspond to the numbers assigned by the Text Analysis System Maxqda 2001, which was employed for the analysis of the transcribed interviews.

3. Clearly audible sounds, for example laughter, are marked in brackets, thus (laughter).

4. Period (.) is used when a predicate is audibly finished, either by a stress or a pause, regardless of the rules of grammar.

5. A comma (,) is used when sentences, clauses or words are audibly separated by a stress or a pause. Otherwise, no comma is used, regardless of the rules of grammar.

6. A question mark (?) is used when it can be deduced from the sentence intonation that a question was used, regardless of the rules of grammar.

7. An exclamation mark (!) is used when it can be deduced from sentence intonation that anger, surprise or other strong emotion was expressed, regardless of the rules of grammar.

8. Dash (-) is used when a short pause within a predicate suggests extra information, a comment or an afterthought separated from the rest of the predicate, regardless of the rules of grammar.

9. Ellipsis (…) is used in case of hesitation.

10. Ellipsis in brackets ([…]) is used when a part of predicate is omitted in the quotation.
11. Stressed words or phrases are underlined: for example, <u>at all.</u>
12. Text in brackets in italics, followed by the initials MN, is used for comments by the author: for example, to indicate missing information that is necessary for the understanding of the quotation, and is provided before or after the quoted passage:

»Female colleagues do that (apply for a job within the IO which does not require traveling at all - MN) whenever they're pregnant or they have small children. It is also an option for us, male employees. Very few cases are there it is...Hmm....as far as possibilities are concerned.« (I2: 55)

A VALLEY TO DIE FOR

As the stagecoach approached Boonetown, the two passengers were surprised when the driver halted to greet a man called Taggart. The woman, Lizabeth FitzMaurice, noticed the cold, empty gaze of the man seated beside her – and knew he was in town to kill someone. Saul Jefferies, who wanted the T.T. valley, didn't care who died in the taking, but he hadn't reckoned on men like Billy Taggart; men who were proud and dangerous and fought to hold on to what was theirs. Taggart himself hadn't reckoned on Lizabeth, who came to Boonetown that summer for reasons of her own.